Texas
LAW OF
CONTRACTS

SECOND EDITION

President: Dr. Andrew Temte
Chief Learning Officer: Dr. Tim Smaby
Executive Director, Real Estate Education: Melissa Kleeman-Moy
Development Editor: Christopher Kugler

TEXAS LAW OF CONTRACTS SECOND EDITION
©2015 Kaplan, Inc.
Published by DF Institute, Inc., d/b/a Dearborn Real Estate Education
332 Front St. S., Suite 501
La Crosse, WI 54601

Printed in the United States of America

ISBN: 978-1-4754-2185-9 / 1-4754-2185-0
PPN: 3200-4393

Contents

Acknowledgements

We would like to thank Leonard Thomas, contributing editor, for his efforts in revising this new edition of *Texas Law of Contracts*. We would also like to thank Doris Barrell, contributing author, for her work on the first edition.

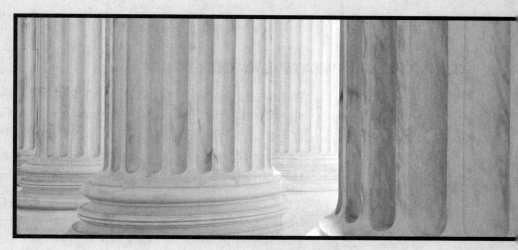

CHAPTER 1

Texas Contract Law

■ **LEARNING OBJECTIVES** *When you have completed this chapter, you will be able to*

■ **describe** the composition and duties of the Texas Real Estate Commission (TREC),

■ **describe** the unauthorized practice of law and how to avoid it,

■ **describe** the composition and duties of the Broker-Lawyer Committee,

■ **describe** TREC's rules regarding the use of promulgated forms,

■ **explain** and give examples of the exceptions to TREC's rules regarding the use of promulgated forms,

■ **describe** the requirement by Section 5.008 of the Texas Property Code for sellers to provide to buyers a written notice of a property's condition,

■ **identify** the exceptions to the seller's disclosure requirement,

■ **explain** when the seller has to provide the disclosure,

■ **describe** the buyer's rights based upon the receipt of the disclosure, and

■ **describe** how the Deceptive Trade Practices Act applies to real estate agents.

■ KEY TERMS

Broker-Lawyer Committee

Deceptive Trade Practices Act (DTPA)

promulgate

Texas Real Estate Commission (TREC)

Texas Real Estate License Act (TRELA)

1

■ TEXAS REAL ESTATE LICENSE ACT

Real estate agents in Texas were first licensed through the Securities Division of the Secretary of State's office, beginning in 1939 with passage of the Real Estate Dealers License Act (House Bill 17, 46th Legislature, Regular Session).

In 1949, the **Texas Real Estate Commission (TREC)** was created to administer the act (Senate Bill 28, 51st Legislature, Regular Session).

The act's name was changed to the **Texas Real Estate License Act (TRELA)** in 1955. The purpose of TRELA is to protect the public through regulation of licensed real estate brokerage practitioners, real estate inspectors, residential service companies, and entities offering timeshare interests.

The policy-making body of the Texas Real Estate Commission is a nine-member commission appointed by the governor with the advice and consent of the senate for overlapping six-year terms. Six members must be active in real estate as full-time brokers for five years immediately preceding appointment. Three members must not be licensed by the commission and have no financial interest in real estate, except as consumers.

The commission has rule-making authority, and the rules of the commission have the full force and effect of law. That authority is established in the part of TRELA that is reproduced in the following:

> *Sec. 1101.155. RULES RELATING TO CONTRACT FORMS.*
> *(a) The commission may adopt rules in the public's best interest that require license holders to use contract forms prepared by the Texas Real Estate Broker-Lawyer Committee and adopted by the commission.*
> *(b) The commission may not prohibit a license holder from using for the sale, exchange, option, or lease of an interest in real property a contract form that is:*
> > *(1) prepared by the property owner; or*
> > *(2) prepared by an attorney and required by the property owner.*
> *(c) A listing contract form adopted by the commission that relates to the contractual obligations between a seller of real estate and a license holder acting as an agent for the seller must include:*
> > *(1) a provision informing the parties to the contract that real estate commissions are negotiable; and*
> > *(2) a provision explaining the availability of Texas coastal natural hazards information important to coastal residents, if that information is appropriate.*

Before engaging in the business of completing any contract forms that bind the sale, lease, temporary lease, or rental of any real property, the licensee should become thoroughly familiar with what the rules do and do not permit.

■ UNAUTHORIZED PRACTICE OF LAW

TRELA specifically prohibits licensees from practicing law by giving opinions or counsel regarding the validity or legal sufficiency of an instrument that addresses real property rights or as to the status of title to real estate. Throughout the act, it is clearly established that, prior to signing a purchase contract, the licensee must give a buyer written advice to have the abstract covering the property examined by an attorney of the buyer's selection or to obtain an owner's title insurance policy prior to closing. Failure to do so may result in disciplinary action by TREC.

Licensees who choose to become REALTORS® subscribe to a REALTOR® Code of Ethics that demands a very high level of professional conduct. The National Association of REALTORS® Code of Ethics advises against the unauthorized practice of law. Again, licensees are to advise their clients/customers to seek an attorney's advice for matters that require it.

TRELA clearly establishes that it is illegal for the licensee to draw a deed, note, deed of trust, will, or other written instrument that transfers or may transfer an interest in or title to real property. However, the act goes on to give permission for a licensee to complete a contract form that may bind the sale, exchange, option, lease, or rental of any interest in real property as long as the forms used have been prepared by or are required by the property owner or have been provided by the real estate commission, prepared by an attorney licensed by the State of Texas, and approved by that attorney for a particular type of transaction. The applicable law is as follows:

> *Sec. 1101.654. SUSPENSION OR REVOCATION OF LICENSE OR CERTIFICATE FOR UNAUTHORIZED PRACTICE OF LAW.*
>
> *(a) The commission shall suspend or revoke the license or certificate of registration of a license or certificate holder who is not a licensed attorney in this state and who, for consideration, a reward, or in a pecuniary benefit, present or anticipated, direct or indirect, or in connection with the person's employment, agency, or fiduciary relationship as a license or certificate holder:*
>
> > *(1) drafts an instrument, other than a form described by Section 1101.155, that transfers or otherwise affects an interest in real property; or*
> > *(2) advises a person regarding the validity or legal sufficiency of an instrument or the validity of title to real property.*
>
> *(b) Notwithstanding any other law, a license or certificate holder who completes a contract form for the sale, exchange, option, or lease of an interest in real property incidental to acting as a broker is not engaged in the unauthorized or illegal practice of law in this state if the form was:*
>
> > *(1) adopted by the commission for the type of transaction for which the form is used;*
> > *(2) prepared by an attorney licensed in this state and approved by the attorney for the type of transaction for which the form is used; or*
> > *(3) prepared by the property owner or by an attorney and required by the property owner.*

The licensee is free to explain to the principals the meaning of the factual statements or business details contained in the contracts as long as no legal advice is offered or given.

■ THE BROKER-LAWYER COMMITTEE

One of the advisory committees that exists under the statutes of TRELA is the **Broker-Lawyer Committee.**

The committee is composed of six Real Estate Commission appointees (who are licensed real estate brokers), six lawyers appointed by the president of the State

Bar of Texas, and one public member, appointed by the governor. They serve staggered six-year terms.

The Broker-Lawyer Committee drafts and revises contract forms for use by real estate licensees. The purpose is to expedite real estate transactions and reduce controversies while protecting the interests of the parties involved.

This Broker-Lawyer Committee does not **promulgate**, or publish, forms for mandatory use by licensees; only TREC has been given rule-making authority. The Broker-Lawyer Committee develops forms and recommends their adoption, but it is TREC that promulgates the forms for mandatory use. The act clearly establishes the membership in and responsibilities of the committee. Carefully review the following text of the act:

> SUBCHAPTER F
> TEXAS REAL ESTATE BROKER-LAWYER COMMITTEE
>
> Sec. 1101.251. DEFINITION OF COMMITTEE. In this subchapter, "committee" means the Texas Real Estate Broker-Lawyer Committee.
>
> Sec. 1101.252. COMMITTEE MEMBERSHIP.
> (a) The Texas Real Estate Broker-Lawyer Committee consists of 13 members appointed as follows:
> (1) six members appointed by the commission;
> (2) six members of the State Bar of Texas appointed by the president of the state bar; and
> (3) one public member appointed by the governor.
> (b) Appointments to the committee shall be made without regard to the race, creed, sex, religion, or national origin of the appointee.
>
> Sec. 1101.254. POWERS AND DUTIES.
> (a) In addition to other delegated powers and duties, the committee shall draft and revise contract forms that are capable of being standardized to expedite real estate transactions and minimize controversy.
> (b) The contract forms must contain safeguards adequate to protect the principals in the transaction.

■ USE OF PROMULGATED FORMS

TREC rule 537.11 addresses the use of standardized forms and lists the forms that are currently promulgated (published), for mandatory use by a licensee when the form fits a particular transaction.

The promulgated forms available through TREC are listed below. The forms change regularly; visit TREC's website (click the "Forms, Laws & Contracts" tab) for information about current forms, including the date the form was promulgated and the current version number of the form. Earlier versions of forms may not be used; to do so could be considered the unauthorized practice of law, an illegal act. The version number (form number) of the form is included in the bottom-right corner of each page of the form (see Figure 1.1). Pay attention to the form numbers. In addition to providing version control, it's possible you might hear a form called by its number instead of its name (e.g., 20-12 instead of One to Four Family Residential Contract).

F I G U R E   1.1

One to Four Family Residential Contract Version Number

Initialed for identification by Buyer_____ _____ and Seller _____ _____   TREC NO. 20-12

Remember that you must use promulgated forms unless one of the four exceptions (see "537.11. Use of Standard Contract Forms" later in this chapter) comes into play.

Texas Real Estate Commission Forms

■ **Promulgated contracts**
  — Unimproved Property Contract
  — One to Four Family Residential Contract (Resale)
  — New Home Contract (Incomplete Construction)
  — New Home Contract (Completed Construction)
  — Farm and Ranch Contract
  — Residential Condominium Contract (Resale)
■ **Promulgated addenda**
  — Addendum for Sale of Other Property by Buyer
  — Addendum for Back-up Contract
  — Addendum for Release of Liability on Assumed Loan and/or Restoration of Seller's VA Entitlement
  — Seller's Temporary Residential Lease
  — Buyer's Temporary Residential Lease
  — Seller Financing Addendum
  — Environmental Assessment, Threatened or Endangered Species, and Wetlands Addendum
  — Addendum for Coastal Area Property
  — Addendum for Property Located Seaward of the Gulf Intracoastal Waterway
  — Addendum for Property Subject to Mandatory Membership in an Owners' Association
  — Third Party Financing Addendum for Credit Approval
  — Loan Assumption Addendum
  — Addendum for Reservation of Oil, Gas and Other Minerals
  — Short Sale Addendum
  — Addendum for Property in a Propose Gas System Service Area
■ **Promulgated amendment**
  — Amendment to Contract
■ **Promulgated resale certificates**
  — Condominium Resale Certificate
  — Subdivision Information, Including Resale Certificate for Property Subject to Membership in a Property Owners' Association
■ **Promulgated notice**
  — Notice of Buyer's Termination of Contract
■ **Promulgated consumer disclosures**
  — Disclosure of Relationship with Residential Service Company

■ **Approved optional/voluntary use forms**
— Notice to Prospective Buyer
— Seller's Disclosure of Property Condition
— Texas Real Estate Consumer Notice Concerning Hazards or Deficiencies
— Information About Brokerage Services
— Lead-Based Paint Addendum
— Non-Realty Items Addendum
— Reverse Mortgage Financing Addendum

In addition to itemizing the current inventory of available forms, the commission establishes the dos and don'ts for the completion of those forms. A careful reading of the rules tells licensees all they need to know:

537.11. Use of Standard Contract Forms
(a) When negotiating contracts binding the sale, exchange, option, lease or rental of any interest in real property, a real estate licensee shall use only those contract forms promulgated by the Texas Real Estate Commission (the commission) for that kind of transaction with the following exceptions:
(1) transactions in which the licensee is functioning solely as a principal, not as an agent;
(2) transactions in which an agency of the United States government requires a different form to be used;
(3) transactions for which a contract form has been prepared by a principal to the transaction or prepared by an attorney and required by a principal to the transaction; or
(4) transactions for which no standard contract form has been promulgated by the commission, and the licensee uses a form prepared by an attorney at law licensed by this state and approved by the attorney for the particular kind of transactions involved or prepared by the Texas Real Estate Broker-Lawyer Committee (the committee) and made available for trial use by licensees with the consent of the commission.
(b) A licensee may not:
(1) practice law,
(2) offer, give or attempt to give legal advice, directly or indirectly;
(3) give advice or opinions as to the legal effect of any contracts or other such instruments which may affect the title to real estate;
(4) give opinions concerning the status or validity of title to real estate; or
(5) attempt to prevent or in any manner whatsoever discourage any principal to a real estate transaction from employing a lawyer.
(c) Nothing in this section shall be deemed to limit the licensee's fiduciary obligation to disclose to the licensee's principals all pertinent facts which are within the knowledge of the licensee, including such facts which might affect the status of or title to real estate.
(d) A licensee may not undertake to draw or prepare documents fixing and defining the legal rights of the principals to a real estate transaction.
(e) In negotiating real estate transactions, the licensee may fill in forms for such transactions, using exclusively forms which have been approved and promulgated by the commission or such forms as are otherwise permitted by these rules.
(f) When filling in a form authorized for use by this section, the licensee may only fill in the blanks provided and may not add to or strike matter from such form, except that licensees shall add factual statements and

business details desired by the principals and shall strike only such matter as is desired by the principals and as is necessary to conform the instrument to the intent of the parties.

(g) A licensee may not add to a promulgated contract form factual statements or business details for which a contract addendum, lease or other form has been promulgated by the commission for mandatory use.

(h) Nothing in this section shall be deemed to prevent the licensee from explaining to the principals the meaning of the factual statements and business details contained in the said instrument so long as the licensee does not offer or give legal advice.

(i) It is not the practice of law as defined in this Act for a real estate licensee to complete a contract form which is either promulgated by the commission or prepared by the committee and made available for trial use by licensees with the consent of the commission.

(j) Contract forms prepared by the committee for trial use may be used on a voluntary basis after being approved by the commission.

(k) Contract forms prepared by the committee and approved by the commission to replace previously promulgated forms may be used by licensees on a voluntary basis prior to the effective date of rules requiring use of the replacement forms.

(l) Where it appears that, prior to the execution of any such instrument, there are unusual matters involved in the transaction which should be resolved by legal counsel before the instrument is executed or that the instrument is to be acknowledged and filed for record, the licensee shall advise the principals that each should consult a lawyer of the principal's choice before executing same.

(m) A licensee may not employ, directly or indirectly, a lawyer nor pay for the services of a lawyer to represent any principal to a real estate transaction in which the licensee is acting as an agent. The licensee may employ and pay for the services of a lawyer to represent only the licensee in a real estate transaction, including preparation of the contract, agreement, or other legal instruments to be executed by the principals to the transactions.

(n) A licensee shall advise the principals that the instrument they are about to execute is binding on them.

(o) Forms approved or promulgated by the commission may be reproduced only from the following sources:

> *(1) numbered copies obtained from the commission, whether in a printed format or electronically reproduced from the files available on the commission's web site;*
>
> *(2) printed copies made from copies obtained from the commission;*
>
> *(3) legible photocopies made from such copies; or*
>
> *(4) computer-driven printers following these guidelines:*
>
>> *(A) The computer file or program containing the form text must not allow the end user direct access to the text of the form and may only permit the user to insert language in blanks in the forms or to strike through language at the direction of the parties to the contract.*
>>
>> *(B) Typefaces or fonts must appear to be identical to those used by the commission in printed copies of the particular form.*
>>
>> *(C) The text and number of pages must be identical to that used by the commission in printed copies of the particular form.*

(D) The spacing, length of blanks, borders and placement of text on the page must appear to be identical to that used by the commission in printed copies of the form.

(E) The name and address of the person or firm responsible for developing the software program must be legibly printed below the border at the bottom of each page in no less than six point type and in no larger than 10 point type.

(p) Forms approved or promulgated by the commission must be reproduced on the same size of paper used by the commission with the following changes or additions only:

(1) The business name or logo of a broker, organization or printer may appear at the top of a form outside the border.

(2) The broker's name may be inserted in any blank provided for that purpose.

Owner Disclosure Requirements

Section 5.008 of the Texas Property Code requires "a seller of residential property comprising not more than one dwelling unit located in this state to give to the purchaser of the property" a written notice of the property's condition. Form OP-H, Seller's Disclosure of Property Condition (see Figure 1.2), contains the language required by the Property Code.

Notice that TREC seller's disclosure is an optional form, not a promulgated form. The disclosure is required of the seller, but the Property Code does not dictate which form the seller needs to use. All the information on this form is required by the Property Code and is also on the Texas Association of REALTORS® (TAR) Seller's Disclosure of Property Condition form as well as some of the REALTOR® associations' and some brokers' forms. TAR forms also include additional disclosure items.

Sellers can limit their future liability by disclosing everything they know about the property. Even things that have been repaired or replaced need to be disclosed on the notice.

The seller's disclosure is discussed in paragraph 7B of the TREC-promulgated contract forms; we will use the One to Four Family Residential Contract as an example. Paragraph 7B (see Figure 1.3) gives the parties three choices for negotiations.

Paragraph 7B(1) is the easiest disclosure option and probably the best choice. In order for this to be available, the listing agent must have the form completed in advance. Many agents take a blank seller disclosure form in their listing packet and get the seller to complete it as soon as they list the property. Then they are ready to provide it when a buyer becomes interested.

Buyers need to review the seller's disclosure notice before making an offer. That way, buyers know what they are making an offer on "in its present condition" and can negotiate appropriately.

FIGURE 1.2

Seller's Disclosure of Property Condition

EQUAL HOUSING OPPORTUNITY

10-23-2013

APPROVED BY THE TEXAS REAL ESTATE COMMISSION (TREC)

SELLER'S DISCLOSURE OF PROPERTY CONDITION

CONCERNING THE PROPERTY AT _____
(Street Address and City)

THIS NOTICE IS A DISCLOSURE OF SELLER'S KNOWLEDGE OF THE CONDITION OF THE PROPERTY AS OF THE DATE SIGNED BY SELLER AND IS NOT A SUBSTITUTE FOR ANY INSPECTIONS OR WARRANTIES THE PURCHASER MAY WISH TO OBTAIN. IT IS NOT A WARRANTY OF ANY KIND BY SELLER OR SELLER'S AGENTS.

Seller ☐ is ☐ is not occupying the Property. If unoccupied, how long since Seller has occupied the Property? _____

1. The Property has the items checked below [Write Yes (Y), No (N), or Unknown (U)]:

_____ Range	_____ Oven	_____ Microwave
_____ Dishwasher	_____ Trash Compactor	_____ Disposal
_____ Washer/Dryer Hookups	_____ Window Screens	_____ Rain Gutters
_____ Security System	_____ Fire Detection Equipment	_____ Intercom System
	_____ Smoke Detector	
	_____ Smoke Detector-Hearing Impaired	
	_____ Carbon Monoxide Alarm	
	_____ Emergency Escape Ladder(s)	
_____ TV Antenna	_____ Cable TV Wiring	_____ Satellite Dish
_____ Ceiling Fan(s)	_____ Attic Fan(s)	_____ Exhaust Fan(s)
_____ Central A/C	_____ Central Heating	_____ Wall/Window Air Conditioning
_____ Plumbing System	_____ Septic System	_____ Public Sewer System
_____ Patio/Decking	_____ Outdoor Grill	_____ Fences
_____ Pool	_____ Sauna	_____ Spa _____ Hot Tub
_____ Pool Equipment	_____ Pool Heater	_____ Automatic Lawn Sprinkler System
_____ Fireplace(s) & Chimney (Wood burning)		_____ Fireplace(s) & Chimney (Mock)
_____ Natural Gas Lines		_____ Gas Fixtures
_____ Liquid Propane Gas	_____ LP Community (Captive)	_____ LP on Property
Garage: _____ Attached	_____ Not Attached	_____ Carport
Garage Door Opener(s):	_____ Electronic	_____ Control(s)
Water Heater:	_____ Gas	_____ Electric
Water Supply: _____ City	_____ Well _____ MUD	_____ Co-op

Roof Type: _____ Age: _____ (approx.)

Are you (Seller) aware of any of the above items that are not in working condition, that have known defects, or that are in need of repair? ☐ Yes ☐ No ☐ Unknown. If yes, then describe. (Attach additional sheets if necessary): _____

_____

_____

_____

TREC No. OP-H

FIGURE 1.3

Paragraph 7B of the One to Four Family Residential Contract

B. SELLER'S DISCLOSURE NOTICE PURSUANT TO §5.008, TEXAS PROPERTY CODE (Notice):
(Check one box only)
❑ (1) Buyer has received the Notice.
❑ (2) Buyer has not received the Notice. Within _____ days after the effective date of this
contract, Seller shall deliver the Notice to Buyer. If Buyer does not receive the Notice,
Buyer may terminate this contract at any time prior to the closing and the earnest money
will be refunded to Buyer. If Seller delivers the Notice, Buyer may terminate this contract
for any reason within 7 days after Buyer receives the Notice or prior to the closing,
whichever first occurs, and the earnest money will be refunded to Buyer.
❑ (3)The Seller is not required to furnish the notice under the Texas Property Code.

Paragraph 7B(2) is for the buyer's agent who is preparing an offer but has not been able to get a completed seller's disclosure from the listing agent. The buyer can make an offer and ask the seller to provide the notice within a certain number of days. The risk for the sellers is that even if they deliver the disclosure within the proper time frame, the buyer can terminate the contract, for any reason, within seven days and receive the earnest money back. If the sellers never deliver it, the buyer has a right to terminate and receive the earnest money back up to the day of closing.

Paragraph 7B(3) is for the seller, who (by law) is not required to furnish the notice. Contrary to popular belief, investors and relocation companies are required to provide the notice. As per Section 5.008(e) of the Texas Property Code, the notice is not required for transactions

(1) pursuant to a court order or foreclosure sale;
(2) by a trustee in bankruptcy;
(3) to a mortgagee by a mortgagor or successor in interest, or to a beneficiary of a deed of trust by a trustor or successor in interest;
(4) by a mortgagee or a beneficiary under a deed of trust who has acquired the real property at a sale conducted pursuant to a power of sale under a deed of trust or a sale pursuant to a court ordered foreclosure or has acquired the real property by a deed in lieu of foreclosure;
(5) by a fiduciary in the course of the administration of a decedent's estate, guardianship, conservatorship, or trust;
(6) from one co-owner to one or more other co-owners;
(7) made to a spouse or to a person or persons in the lineal line of consanguinity of one or more of the transferors;
(8) between spouses resulting from a decree of dissolution of marriage or a decree of legal separation or from a property settlement agreement incidental to such a decree;
(9) to or from any governmental entity;
(10) of a new residence of not more than one dwelling unit which has not previously been occupied for residential purposes; or
(11) of real property where the value of any dwelling does not exceed five percent of the value of the property.

Section 5.008 also states the following:

(c) A seller or seller's agent shall have no duty to make a disclosure or release information related to whether a death by natural causes, suicide, or accident unrelated to the condition of the property occurred on the property

or whether a previous occupant had, may have had, has, or may have AIDS, HIV related illnesses, or HIV infection.

(d) The notice shall be completed to the best of seller's belief and knowledge as of the date the notice is completed and signed by the seller. If the information required by the notice is unknown to the seller, the seller shall indicate that fact on the notice, and by that act is in compliance with this section.

(f) The notice shall be delivered by the seller to the purchaser on or before the effective date of an executory contract binding the purchaser to purchase the property. If a contract is entered without the seller providing the notice required by this section, the purchaser may terminate the contract for any reason within seven days after receiving the notice.

Section 5.008(g) of the Property Code also provides definitions for two terms in the seller disclosure notice:

(1) "Blockable main drain" means a main drain of any size and shape that a human body can sufficiently block to create a suction entrapment hazard.

(2) "Main drain" means a submerged suction outlet typically located at the bottom of a swimming pool or spa to conduct water to a recirculating pump.

As stated previously, failure to provide the disclosure can produce negative results for the seller. When the seller fails to provide and the buyer of a previously occupied single-family residence fails to receive the seller disclosure as required by Section 5.008 of the Texas Property Code, the contract may be terminated at the sole option of the buyer and is therefore voidable at the option of the buyer.

■ DECEPTIVE TRADE PRACTICES ACT

Real estate agents must use extreme care to deliver information that is accurate, complete, and completely accurate. The **Deceptive Trade Practices Act (DTPA)** is a consumer protection act which protects the public from

- ■ any false, misleading or deceptive act; and
- ■ a licensee taking advantage of the consumer's lack of knowledge, ability, experience, or capacity to a grossly unfair degree (i.e., an unconscionable act).

The primary difference between an action brought under DTPA and any other civil suit is that treble damages and mental anguish are available in the DTPA action. Additionally, court costs and attorneys' fees may be added. The main distinction between treble damages, or simply actual damages, is the word knowingly. If the real estate agent used a misleading statement without the knowledge of its falsity, then the treble damages may not be awarded.

The most likely trap for the real estate practitioner is the omission or commission of a material fact. Of the two most popular problems, the act of omission is the most prevalent, either by knowing or not knowing.

The treble damages portion can be defeated by offering to settle for an amount which is greater than that awarded in the suit.

■ SUMMARY

Real estate in Texas is governed by state law. The Texas Real Estate License Act (TRELA) and the TREC Rules are enforced by the Texas Real Estate Commission (TREC).

The Broker-Lawyer Committee drafts and edits contract forms for use by real estate licensees, and TREC approves and promulgates them.

Real estate licensees must use the promulgated forms except in specific exempted cases. Failure to use these forms where required might lead to the suspension or revocation of one's license for the unauthorized practice of law.

Promulgated contract forms cannot be altered except as a requirement of the parties.

The Texas Property Code requires most sellers of residential property (with some exceptions) to provide to the purchaser a written notice of the property's condition. TREC has provided a form for this purpose.

The Deceptive Trade Practices Act (DTPA) protects consumers from licensees who knowingly make false or deceptive statements.

CHAPTER 1 REVIEW QUESTIONS

1. The purpose of the Texas Real Estate License Act (TRELA) is to
   a. protect real estate licensees.
   b. protect real estate brokers from unscrupulous salespeople.
   c. protect the public.
   d. keep the cost of real estate services under control.

2. The Texas Deceptive Trade Practices Act (DTPA) is a consumer protection law which protects the public from
   a. false or misleading acts.
   b. deceptive acts.
   c. unconscionable acts.
   d. all of these.

3. Which action might leave a licensee open to a charge of practicing law without a license?
   a. Licensee advises the seller that the property probably won't sell because it is overpriced.
   b. Licensee advises the buyer in writing that a title policy, as well as a survey, should be obtained.
   c. Licensee advises both the seller and the buyer that, in his opinion, title to the subject property is encumbered.
   d. Licensee adds factual statements and business details to a promulgated form as requested by the client.

4. In which of the following situations is a licensee NOT required to use a contract promulgated by the Texas Real Estate Commission (TREC)?
   a. The licensee's broker provides an alternative contract.
   b. The licensee is working as his father's agent to sell his father's house.
   c. The buyer's attorney has drafted a contract that the buyer insists on using.
   d. The buyer doesn't like the TREC contract and asks the licensee to draft a different sales contract.

5. What should a licensee do in transactions for which there is no TREC promulgated contract?
   a. Change an existing TREC-promulgated contract to meet the needs of this transaction.
   b. Write a contract according to the wishes of the principal.
   c. Ask the buyer and the seller to work together to draft a contract.
   d. Use a form prepared by the Broker-Lawyer Committee and made available for trial use by licensees with the consent of TREC.

6. The Texas Deceptive Trade Practices Act (DTPA) has two features that are designed to deter wrongdoers. These two features are
   a. treble damages and a mental anguish award.
   b. actual damages and a minimum punitive award of $1 million.
   c. 10 times actual damages and attorneys' fees.
   d. treble damages and actual damages.

7. The Texas Property Code Section 5.008 requires all of the following to provide a seller's disclosure EXCEPT
   a. one spouse to another in a divorce proceeding.
   b. an out-of-state investor who has never seen the property.
   c. a sale in which the improvements are worth less than half of the land assessment.
   d. a local investor who has never lived in the property.

8. Section 5.008 of the Texas Property Code requires
   a. most sellers of residential property to provide the buyer with a written notice of the property's condition.
   b. all sellers of residential property to provide the buyer with a written notice of the property's condition.
   c. most sellers of residential property to provide the buyer with TREC Form OP-H, Seller's Disclosure of Property Condition.
   d. all sellers of residential property to provide the buyer with TREC Form OP-H, Seller's Disclosure of Property Condition.

9. Which of the following is *NOT* a promulgated form adopted by the Texas Real Estate Commission (TREC)?
   a. A contract for the sale of a farm
   b. A contract for the resale of a condominium
   c. A contract for the sale of a five-unit residential building
   d. A contract for the sale of a duplex

10. If the disclosure is provided to the buyer after the contract is fully executed, the
    a. buyer may terminate the contract within ten days after receipt of the disclosure.
    b. buyer may terminate the contract within seven days after receipt of the disclosure.
    c. buyer has no right to terminate the contract.
    d. seller is required to pay all of the buyer's closing costs.

CHAPTER 2

Basics of Real Estate Law

■ **LEARNING OBJECTIVES** *When you have completed this chapter, you will be able to*

- ■ **define** land, real estate, and real property;

- ■ **describe** the rights individuals can have in the ownership and use of real estate;

- ■ **give** examples of real and personal property;

- ■ **describe** and identify fixtures and trade fixtures;

- ■ **review** the characteristics of real property;

- ■ **compare** the ways that title can be held in co-ownership: tenancy in common, joint tenancy, tenancy by the entirety, and community property;

- ■ **explain** the different ways property can be owned by married couples;

- ■ **describe** the ways in which various business organizations may own property; and

- ■ **compare** the condominium, cooperative, town-house, and time-share forms of property ownership.

■ KEY TERMS

air rights	joint tenancy	severance
annexation	land	situs
appurtenance	limited liability company (LLC)	subsurface rights
area preference	limited partnership	surface rights
assessment	manufactured housing	tenancy in common
beneficiary	nonhomogeneity	time-share
bundle of legal rights	partition	time-share estate
common elements	partnership	time-share use
community property	personal property	title
condominium	proprietary lease	trade fixture
co-ownership	real estate	trust
cooperative	real property	trustee
corporation	right of survivorship	trustor
fixture	separate property	water rights
general partnership	severalty	
improvement		

■ REAL PROPERTY AND THE LAW

Real estate is a market like any other. Real property is a product, and the broker or the licensee is the salesperson. The sales agreement is a contract with all its many elements. Before beginning the study of the law of contracts, it is important to establish a foundation of understanding of basic real estate law. Real estate licensees are generally not attorneys and must always be cautious to not appear to be providing legal advice. However, providing a client with basic information regarding various aspects of real estate law is not only appropriate but is also an important part of fulfilling the fiduciary duty to protect the best interests of the client. This chapter reviews many of the precepts of real estate law that are covered in the first prelicensing course that real estate professionals are required to take. Hopefully, this chapter will serve as a review and as preparation for delving further into basic contract law.

■ LAND, REAL ESTATE, AND REAL PROPERTY

The terms *land*, *real estate*, and *real property* are often used interchangeably. To most people, they mean the same thing. Strictly speaking, however, the terms refer to different aspects of ownership interests in land. To fully understand the nature of real estate and the laws that affect it, real estate licensees must be aware of the subtle yet important differences in meaning of these words.

Land

Land is defined as the earth's surface extending downward to the center of the earth and upward to infinity, including permanent natural objects, such as trees and water (see Figure 2.1).

FIGURE 2.1

Land, Real Estate, and Real Property

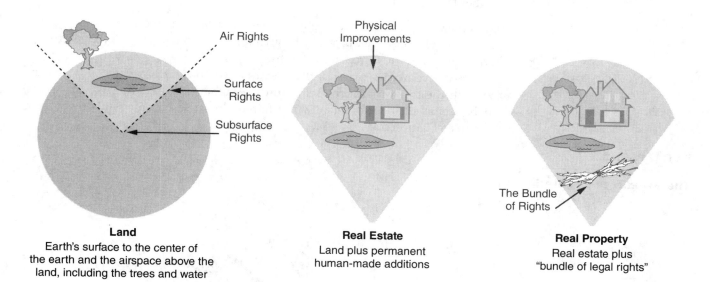

Land
Earth's surface to the center of the earth and the airspace above the land, including the trees and water

Real Estate
Land plus permanent human-made additions

Real Property
Real estate plus "bundle of legal rights"

Land includes not only the surface of the earth but also the underlying soil. It refers to things that are naturally attached to the land, such as boulders and plants. It includes the minerals and substances that lie far below the earth's surface. Land even includes the air above the earth, all the way into space. These are known respectively as the subsurface and the airspace. Most of the earth's surface, of course, is not land at all, but water. Special state and local laws govern the ownership of the wetter parts of the earth, including lakes and rivers.

Real Estate

Real estate is defined as land at, above, and below the earth's surface, plus all things permanently attached to it, whether natural or artificial (see Figure 2.1).

The term *real estate*, or *realty*, is similar to the term *land* but includes not only the natural components of the land but also all permanent man-made improvements on and to the land. An **improvement** is any artificial thing attached to the land, such as a building or a fence, as well as infrastructures, such as sewers.

Real Property

The term *real property* is the broadest of all. It includes both land and real estate. **Real property** is defined as the interests, benefits, and rights that are automatically included in the ownership of land and real estate (see Figure 2.1).

Real property includes the earth's surface, subsurface, and airspace, including all things permanently attached to it by nature or people, and the legal rights innate to the ownership of a parcel of real estate.

Traditionally, ownership rights of real property are described as a **bundle of legal rights**. These rights include the

- right of possession,
- right to control the property (within the framework of the law),

- right of enjoyment (to use the property in any legal manner),
- right of exclusion (to keep others from entering or using the property), and
- right of disposition (to sell, will, transfer, or otherwise dispose of or encumber the property).

The concept of a bundle of rights comes from old English law. In the Middle Ages, a seller transferred property by giving the purchaser a handful of earth or a bundle of bound sticks from a tree on the property. After accepting the bundle, the purchaser became the owner of the tree from which the sticks came and the land to which the tree was attached. Because the rights of ownership (like the sticks) can be separated and individually transferred, the sticks became symbolic of those rights (see Figure 2.2).

FIGURE 2.2

The Bundle of Legal Rights

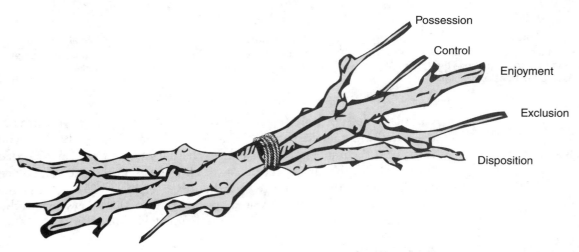

The word **title**, as it relates to real property, has two meanings: (1) the right to or ownership of the land, including the owner's bundle of legal rights; and (2) evidence of that ownership by a deed. Title refers to ownership of real property, not to a printed document. The document by which the owner transfers title to the real property is the deed.

Real property is often coupled with the word *appurtenance*. An **appurtenance** (runs with the land) is a right or privilege associated with the property, although not necessarily a part of it. Typical appurtenances include parking spaces in multiunit buildings, easements, water rights, and other improvements. An appurtenance is connected to the property, and ownership of the appurtenance normally transfers to the new owner when the property is sold.

IN PRACTICE   When people talk about buying or selling homes, office buildings, and land, they usually call these things *real estate*. For all practical purposes, the term *real estate* is synonymous with *real property* as defined here. In everyday usage, real estate includes the legal rights of ownership specified in the definition of real property. Sometimes people use the term *realty* instead.

Subsurface, Air, and Water Rights   **Surface rights** refer to the use of the surface of the earth. **Subsurface rights** are the rights to the natural resources below the earth's surface. An owner may transfer surface rights without transferring subsurface rights.

■ **FOR EXAMPLE**   A landowner sells the rights to any oil and gas found beneath the owned farm to an oil company. Later, the same landowner sells the remaining interests (the surface, air, and limited subsurface rights) to a buyer, reserving the rights to any coal that may be found and to pasture on the land. This buyer sells the remaining land to yet another buyer but retains the farmhouse, stable, and pasture. After these sales, four parties have ownership interests in the same real estate: (1) the original landowner owns all the coal; (2) the oil company owns all the oil and gas; (3) the first buyer owns the farmhouse, stable, and pasture; and (4) the second buyer owns the rights to the remaining real estate (see Figure 2.3).

FIGURE 2.3

Surface and Subsurface Rights

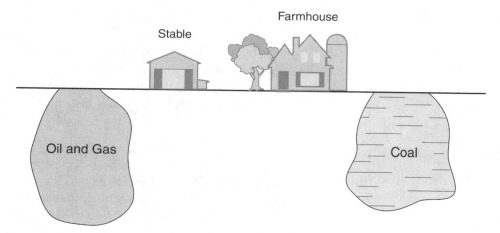

Air rights, the rights to use the space above the earth, may be sold or leased independently, provided the rights have not been preempted by law. Air rights can be an important part of real estate, particularly in large cities, where air rights over railroads must be purchased or leased to construct office buildings, hotels, or other multistory structures. To construct such a building, the developer must purchase not only the air rights but also numerous small portions of the land's surface for the building's foundation supports.

Before air travel was common, a property's air rights were considered unlimited, extending upward into the farthest reaches of outer space. Today, the courts permit reasonable interference with these rights, such as what is necessary for aircraft (and presumably spacecraft), as long as the owner's right to use and occupy the land is not unduly lessened. Government and airport authorities often purchase adjacent air rights to provide approach patterns for air traffic.

With the continuing development of solar power, air rights—and, more specifically, light or solar rights—are being closely examined by the courts. A new tall building that blocks sunlight from a smaller existing building may be held to be interfering with the smaller building's right to sunlight, particularly if systems in the smaller building are solar powered. Air and solar rights are regulated by state and local laws and ordinances.

Water rights are special common-law rights held by owners of land adjacent to rivers, lakes, or oceans and are restrictions on the rights of land ownership. Water rights are particularly important in drier western states, where water is a scarce and valuable public commodity (see Chapter 4).

■ REAL PROPERTY VS. PERSONAL PROPERTY

Property may be classified as either real or personal. **Personal property** is all the property that can be owned and that does not fit the definition of real property. An important distinction between the two is that personal property is movable. Items of personal property, also called chattels, include such tangibles as chairs, tables, clothing, money, bonds, and bank accounts.

Manufactured Housing

Manufactured housing is defined as dwellings that are built off-site and transported to a building lot where they are installed or assembled. Manufactured housing includes both modular and completed units generally referred to in the past as mobile homes. Use of the term *mobile homes* was phased out with the passage of the National Manufactured Housing Construction and Safety Standards Act of 1976, when manufactured homes became federally regulated. Nevertheless, the term *mobile home* is still commonly used by the public.

The distinction between real and personal property of a manufactured home is not always obvious. Manufactured housing may be considered personal property, even though its mobility may be limited to a single trip to a park or development to be hooked up to utilities. Manufactured housing may also be considered real property if it becomes permanently affixed to the land. The classification of real or personal property becomes significant when financing is involved. State law may vary with regard to registration of title to the property.

Section 1201.2055 of the Texas Occupations Code addresses the status of manufactured housing as real or personal property:

> (a) In completing an application for the issuance of a statement of ownership and location, an owner of a manufactured home shall indicate whether the owner elects to treat the home as personal property or real property. An owner may elect to treat a manufactured home as real property only if the home is attached to:
>> (1) real property that is owned by the owner of the home; or
>> (2) land leased to the owner of the home under a long-term lease, as defined by department rule.
> (b) Repealed by Acts 2009, 81st Leg., R.S., Ch. 77, Sec. 15(2), eff. September 1, 2009.
> (c) If the department issues a statement of ownership and location to an owner who has elected to treat a manufactured home as personal property, the statement of ownership and location on file with the department is evidence of ownership of the home. A lien, charge, or other encumbrance on a home treated as personal property may be made only by filing the appropriate document with the department.
> (d) If an owner elects to treat a manufactured home as real property, the department shall issue to the owner a certified copy of the statement of ownership and location that on its face reflects that the owner has elected to treat the manufactured home as real property at the location listed on the statement. Not later than the 60th day after the date the department issues a certified copy of the statement of ownership and location to the owner, the owner must:
>> (1) file the certified copy in the real property records of the county in which the home is located; and

(2) notify the department and the chief appraiser of the applicable appraisal district that the certified copy has been filed.

(e) A real property election for a manufactured home is not considered to be perfected until a certified copy of the statement of ownership and location has been filed and the department and the chief appraiser of the applicable appraisal district have been notified of the filing as provided by Subsection (d).

(f) Repealed by Acts 2011, 82nd Leg., R.S., Ch. 46, Sec. 8(1), eff. September 1, 2011.

(g) After a real property election is perfected under Subsection (e):

> *(1) the home is considered to be real property for all purposes; and*
>
> *(2) no additional issuance of a statement of ownership and location is required with respect to the manufactured home, unless:*
>
> > *(A) the home is moved from the location specified on the statement of ownership and location;*
> >
> > *(B) the real property election is changed; or*
> >
> > *(C) the use of the property is changed as described by Section 1201.216.*

(h) The provisions of this chapter relating to the construction or installation of a manufactured home or to warranties for a manufactured home apply to a home regardless of whether the home is considered to be real or personal property.

(i) Notwithstanding the 60-day deadline specified in Subsection (d), if the closing of a mortgage loan to be secured by real property including the manufactured home is held, the loan is funded, and a deed of trust covering the real property and all improvements on the property is recorded and the licensed title company or attorney who closed the loan failed to complete the conversion to real property in accordance with this chapter, the holder or servicer of the loan may apply for a statement of ownership and location electing real property status, obtain a certified copy of the statement of ownership and location, and make the necessary filings and notifications to complete such conversion at any time provided that:

> *(1) the record owner of the home, as reflected on the department's records, has been given at least 60 days' prior written notice at:*
>
> > *(A) the location of the home and, if it is different, the mailing address of the owner as specified in the department records; and*
> >
> > *(B) any other location the holder or servicer knows or believes, after a reasonable inquiry, to be an address where the owner may have been or is receiving mail or is an address of record;*
>
> *(2) such notification shall be given by certified mail; and*
>
> *(3) the department by rule shall require evidence that the holder or servicer requesting such after-the-fact completion of a real property election has complied with the requirements of this subsection.*

Manufactured housing, when appropriately converted to real property, may be financed as any other real property. A single wide may be moved and financed, but a double wide may not. The reason has to do with the ability to "mate" the two halves so that they don't leak. The Texas Department of Housing & Community Affairs, Manufactured Housing Division requires the movers of manufactured homes to register the move. They must inform the outgoing state of its location and where it is going.

As of July 2014, over 56,000 single and double wide manufactured homes were sold in the United States. Many of these buyers were looking for land to install the units, which gives the real estate agent a great business opportunity to explore. The trend of these purchases is down from 2002, when 174,000 were sold.

Plants

Trees and crops generally fall into one of two classes:

■ Trees, perennial shrubbery, and grasses that do not require annual cultivation are called fructus naturales. These items are considered real estate.

■ Annually cultivated crops such as fruit, vegetables, and grain are called emblements, or fructus industriales, and are generally considered personal property.

■ **FOR EXAMPLE** A farmer who sells his farm won't have to dig up growing corn plants and haul them away unless the sales contract says so. The farmer can return and harvest the corn when it's ready. Perennial crops, such as orchards or vineyards, are not personal property and so transfer with the land.

An item of real property can become personal property by **severance**, or separating from the land. For example, a growing tree is real estate until the owner cuts it down, literally severing it from the property. Similarly, an apple becomes personal property once it is picked from a tree.

It is also possible to change personal property into real property through the process called **annexation**. For example, if a landowner buys cement, stones, and sand and mixes them into concrete to construct a sidewalk across the land, the landowner has converted personal property (cement, stones, and sand) into real property (a sidewalk).

Real estate licensees need to know whether property is real or personal. An important distinction arises when the property is transferred from one owner to another. Real property is conveyed by deed, while personal property is conveyed by a bill of sale or receipt.

Classifications of Fixtures

In considering the differences between real and personal property, it is necessary to distinguish between a fixture and personal property.

Fixtures A **fixture** is personal property that has been so affixed to land or a building that, by law, it becomes part of the real property. Examples of fixtures are heating systems, elevator equipment in highrise buildings, radiators, kitchen cabinets, light fixtures, and plumbing. Almost any item that has been added as a permanent part of a building is considered a fixture.

Legal Tests of a Fixture The overall test used to determine whether an item is a fixture (real property) or personal property is a question of intent (see Figure 2.4). Did the person who installed the item intend it to remain permanently on the property or to be removable in the future? In determining intent, courts use the following three basic tests:

■ *Method of annexation*: How permanent is the method of attachment? Can the item be removed without causing damage to the surrounding property?

■ *Adaptation to real estate*: Is the item being used as real property or personal property? For example, a refrigerator is usually considered personal property. However, if a refrigerator has been adapted to match the kitchen cabinetry, it becomes a fixture.

■ *Agreement*: What is the annexor's intention?

FIGURE 2.4

Legal Tests of a Fixture

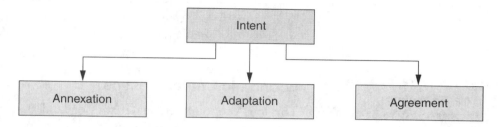

Although these tests may seem simple, court decisions have been complex and inconsistent. Property that appears to be permanently affixed has sometimes been ruled to be personal property, while property that seems removable has been ruled a fixture. It is important that an owner clarify what is to be sold with the real estate at the very beginning of the sales process so that the details may be correctly included in the sales contract.

IN PRACTICE   At the time a property is listed, the seller and the listing agent should discuss which items to include in the sale. The written sales contract between the buyer and the seller should specifically list all articles that are being included in the sale, particularly if any doubt exists as to whether they are personal property or fixtures (for example, built-in bookcases, chandeliers, ceiling fans, or exotic shrubbery). This specificity will avoid a misunderstanding between the parties that might result in the collapse of the transaction and expensive lawsuits. The most commonly disputed items between buyers and sellers are draperies, light fixtures, and appliances.

Trade Fixtures   A special category of fixtures includes property used in the course of business. An article owned by a tenant and attached to a rented space or building or used in conducting a business is a **trade fixture**. Some examples of trade fixtures are bowling alleys, store shelves, and barroom and restaurant equipment. Agricultural fixtures, such as chicken coops and tool sheds, are also included in this category. Trade fixtures must be removed on or before the last day the property is rented. The tenant is responsible for any damage caused by the removal of a fixture. Trade fixtures that are not removed become the real property of the landlord.

■ FOR EXAMPLE   A pizza parlor leases space in a small shopping center. The restaurateur bolted a large iron oven to the floor of the unit. When the pizza parlor goes out of business or relocates, the restaurateur will be able to remove the pizza oven if the bolt holes in the floor can be repaired. The oven is a trade fixture. On the other hand, if the pizza oven was brought into the restaurant in pieces, welded together, and set in concrete, the restaurateur might not be able to remove it without causing structural damage. In that case, the oven might become a fixture.

Trade fixtures differ from other fixtures in the following ways:

■ Fixtures belong to the owner of the real estate, but trade fixtures are usually owned and installed by a tenant for the tenant's use.

■ Fixtures are considered a permanent part of a building, but trade fixtures are removable. Trade fixtures may be attached to a building so they appear to be fixtures.

Legally, fixtures are real property, so they are included in any sale or mortgage. Trade fixtures, however, are considered personal property and are not included in the sale or mortgage of real estate, except by special agreement.

■ CHARACTERISTICS OF REAL PROPERTY

Real property possesses seven basic characteristics that define its nature and affect its use. These characteristics fall into two broad categories—economic and physical.

Economic Characteristics

The four economic characteristics of land that affect its value as a product in the marketplace are scarcity, improvements, permanence of investment, and area preference.

Scarcity   Only about a quarter of the earth's surface is dry land; the rest is water. The total supply of land, then, is not limitless. While a considerable amount of land remains unused or uninhabited, the supply in a given location or of a particular quality is generally considered finite.

Improvements   Building an improvement on one parcel of land can affect the land's value and use, as well as that of neighboring tracts and whole communities. For example, constructing a new shopping center or selecting a site for a nuclear power plant or toxic waste dump can dramatically change the value of land in a large area.

Permanence of Investment   The capital and labor used to build an improvement represent a large fixed investment. Although even a well-built structure can be razed to make way for a newer building, improvements such as drainage, electricity, water, and sewerage remain. The return on such investments tends to be long term and relatively stable.

Area Preference   **Area preference**, or **situs** ("to place"), is commonly called "location, location, location." This economic characteristic refers not only to geography but also to people's preference for a specific area. Area preference is based on several factors, such as convenience, reputation, and history. It is the unique quality of these preferences that results in the different price points for similar properties. Location is often considered the single most important economic characteristic of land.

■   **FOR EXAMPLE**   A river runs through a town, dividing it more or less in half. Houses on the north side of the river sell for an average of $170,000. On the south side of the river, identical houses sell for more than $200,000. The only difference is that homebuyers think that the area south of the river is a better neighborhood, even though no obvious difference exists between the two equally pleasant sides of town.

Schools also can contribute to area preference. With the diversity of quality education, many home buyers are selecting neighborhoods with high quality schools. This is true for elementary, middle, and high schools. It is not unusual for an adjoining neighborhood to have a 20% reduction in home prices because of a lesser quality school than the other.

Four Economic Characteristics of Real Estate

- Scarcity
- Improvements
- Permanence of investment
- Location or area preference

Physical Characteristics

Land has three physical characteristics: immobility, indestructibility, and uniqueness.

Immobility   It is true that some of the substances of land are removable and that topography can be changed, but the geographic location of any given parcel of land can never be changed. It is fixed, immobile.

Indestructibility   Land is also indestructible. This permanence of land, coupled with the long-term nature of improvements, tends to stabilize investments in real property.

The fact that land is indestructible does not change the fact that the improvements on land depreciate and can become obsolete, which may dramatically reduce the land's value. This gradual depreciation should not be confused with the knowledge that the economic desirability of a given location can change.

Uniqueness   Uniqueness, or **nonhomogeneity**, is the concept that no two parcels of property are the same or in the same location. The characteristics of each property, no matter how small, differ from those of every other. An individual parcel has no substitute because each is unique.

■ FORMS OF REAL ESTATE OWNERSHIP

Licensees may provide buyers the information necessary for them to determine the type of ownership that best fits their needs. Providing information does not put the licensee at risk of practicing law. What the licensee may not do is advise the buyers which form of ownership to take. The choice of ownership affects the ability to transfer the real estate, has tax implications, and decides rights to future claims.

Although the available forms of ownership are controlled by state laws, a fee simple estate may be held in three basic ways:

- In *severalty*, where title is held by one individual or corporation
- In *co-ownership*, where title is held by two or more individuals
- In *trust*, where a neutral individual holds title for the benefit of another

Ownership in Severalty

Ownership in **severalty** occurs when property is owned by one individual or corporation. The term comes from the fact that a sole owner is severed or cut off from other owners. The severalty owner has sole rights to the ownership and sole discretion to sell, will, lease, or otherwise transfer part or all the ownership rights to another person.

Co-Ownership

When title to one parcel of real estate is held by two or more individuals, those parties are called co-owners. Most states commonly recognize various forms of **co-ownership**. Individuals may co-own property as tenants in common, joint tenants, or tenants by the entirety, or they may co-own it as community property (see Figure 2.5). The differences in the types of co-ownership only become apparent when the property is conveyed or one of the owners dies.

FIGURE 2.5

Forms of Co-ownership

Co-ownerships	Property Held	Property Conveyed
Tenancy in common	Each tenant holds a fractional undivided interest.	The tenants can convey or devise their individual interest, but not the entire interest.
Joint tenancy	Unity of ownership. Created by intentional act; unities of possession, interest, time, title.	Possible right of survivorship; cannot be conveyed to heirs.
Community property	Husband and wife are equal partners in marriage. Real or personal property acquired during marriage is community property.	Conveyance requires signature of both spouses. No right of survivorship; when one spouse dies, survivor owns one-half of community property. Other one-half is distributed according to will or, if no will, according to state law.

Tenancy in Common   A parcel of real estate may be owned by two or more people as tenants in common. In a **tenancy in common**, each tenant holds an undivided fractional interest in the property. Although a tenant in common may hold one-half or one-third interest in a property, the physical property is not divided into a specific half or third. The co-owners have unity of possession, meaning that they are entitled to possession of the whole property. It is the ownership interest, not the property, that is divided.

The deed creating a tenancy in common may or may not state the fractional interest held by each co-owner. If no fractions are stated, the tenants are presumed to hold equal shares. For example, if five people hold title, each would own an undivided one-fifth interest.

Because the co-owners own separate interests, they can sell, convey, mortgage, or transfer their individual interest without the consent of the other co-owners.

However, no individual tenant may transfer the ownership of the entire property. When one co-owner dies, the tenant's undivided interest passes according to the co-owner's will, heirs, or living trust (see Figure 2.6).

FIGURE 2.6

Tenancy in Common

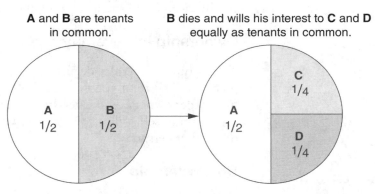

A and B are tenants in common.

B dies and wills his interest to C and D equally as tenants in common.

When two or more people acquire title to real estate and the deed does not indicate the form of the tenancy, the new owners are usually determined to have acquired title as tenants in common.

Joint Tenancy   Most states (including Texas) recognize some form of **joint tenancy** in property owned by two or more people.

Joint tenancy includes the **right of survivorship**. Upon the death of a joint tenant, the deceased's interest transfers directly to the surviving joint tenant or tenants. Essentially, there is one less owner.

With each successive death of a joint tenant, the surviving joint tenants keep acquiring the deceased tenant's interest equally. The last survivor takes title in severalty and has all the rights of sole ownership, including the right to pass the property to any heirs (see Figure 2.7).

FIGURE 2.7

Joint Tenancy with Right of Survivorship

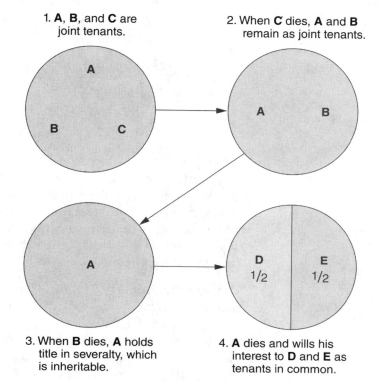

1. **A**, **B**, and **C** are joint tenants.

2. When **C** dies, **A** and **B** remain as joint tenants.

3. When **B** dies, **A** holds title in severalty, which is inheritable.

4. **A** dies and wills his interest to **D** and **E** as tenants in common.

IN PRACTICE   The form under which title should be taken should be discussed with an attorney. Remember that licensees may not give legal advice or engage in the practice of law.

Creating Joint Tenancies   A joint tenancy can be created only by the intentional act of conveying a deed or giving the property by will or living trust. It cannot be implied or created by operation of law. The deed must specifically state the parties' intention to create a joint tenancy, and the parties must be explicitly identified as joint tenants.

To create joint tenancy, four groups or unities are needed:

- Unity of possession—all joint tenants holding an undivided right to possession
- Unity of interest—all joint tenants holding equal ownership interests
- Unity of time—all joint tenants acquiring their interests at the same time
- Unity of title—all joint tenants acquiring their interests by the same document

Terminating Joint Tenancies   A joint tenancy is destroyed when any one of the four unities of joint tenancy is terminated. A joint tenant is free to convey interest in the jointly held property, but doing so destroys the unities of time and title. The new owner cannot become a joint tenant. Rights of other joint tenants, however,

Memory Tip

The Four Unities

The four unities necessary to create a joint tenancy may be remembered by the acronym PITT:
1. Possession
2. Interest
3. Time
4. Title

are unaffected. For example, if A, B, and C hold title as joint tenants and A conveys her interest to D, then D will own an undivided one-third interest in severalty as tenant in common with B and C, who continue to own their undivided two-thirds interest as joint tenants (see Figure 2.8).

FIGURE 2.8

Combination of Tenancies

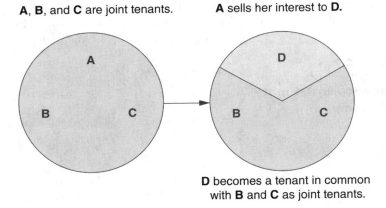

A, B, and C are joint tenants.   A sells her interest to D.

D becomes a tenant in common with B and C as joint tenants.

Termination of Co-ownership by Partition Suit   Partition is a legal way to dissolve the relationship when the parties do not voluntarily agree to its termination. If the court determines that the land cannot be divided physically into separate parcels without destroying its value, the court will order the real estate sold. The proceeds of the sale will then be divided among the co-owners according to their fractional interests.

Community Property Rights   Community property laws are based on the idea that a husband and wife, rather than merging into one entity, are equal partners in the marriage. Under community property laws, any property acquired during a marriage is considered to be obtained by mutual effort. Community property law varies widely among the states, but they all recognize two kinds of property: separate property and community property.

Separate property is real or personal property that was owned solely by either spouse before the marriage, acquired by gift or inheritance during the marriage, and purchased with separate funds during the marriage. Separate property can be mortgaged or conveyed by the owning spouse without the signature of the nonowning spouse.

Community property consists of real and personal property acquired by either spouse during the marriage. Any conveyance or encumbrance of community property requires the signatures of both spouses. Spouses can will their half of the community property to whomever they desire, but upon the death of one spouse, the surviving spouse automatically owns one-half of the remaining property. If one spouse dies without a will, the other half is inherited by the surviving spouse or by the decedent's other heirs, depending on state law. In Texas, if one spouse dies without a will and the heirs are common to both spouses (e.g., no stepchildren), the surviving spouse inherits the decedent's half of the property. If the heirs are not common to both spouses, the decedent's half of the property is split among the decedent's heirs.

Trusts

A **trust** is a device by which one person transfers ownership of property to someone else to hold or manage for the benefit of a third party. Perhaps a grandfather wishes to ensure the college education of his granddaughter, so he transfers his oil field to the grandchild's mother. He instructs the mother to use its income to pay for the grandchild's college tuition. In this case, the grandfather is the **trustor**—the person who creates the trust. The granddaughter is the **beneficiary**—the person who benefits from the trust. The mother is the **trustee**—the party who holds legal title to the property and is entrusted with carrying out the trustor's instructions regarding the purpose of the trust. The trustee's power and authority are limited by the terms of the trust agreement, will, or deed in trust.

IN PRACTICE   The legal and tax implications of setting up a trust are complex and vary widely from state to state. Attorneys and tax experts should always be consulted on the subject of trusts.

Most states (including Texas) allow real estate to be held in trust. Depending on the type of trust and its purpose, the trustor, trustee, and beneficiary can all be either people or legal entities, such as corporations. Trust companies are corporations set up for this specific purpose.

■ OWNERSHIP OF REAL ESTATE BY BUSINESS ORGANIZATIONS

A business organization is a legal entity that exists independently of its members. Ownership by a business organization makes it possible for many people to hold an interest in the same parcel of real estate. Investors may be organized to finance a real estate project in various ways. Some provide for the real estate to be owned by the entity; others provide for direct ownership by the investors.

Partnership

A **partnership** is an association of two or more persons who carry on a business for profit as co-owners. In a **general partnership**, all the partners participate in the operation and management of the business and share full liability for business losses and obligations. A **limited partnership** consists of one or more general partners plus a number of limited partners. The business is run by the general partner or partners. The limited partners are not legally permitted to participate, and each can be held liable for business losses only to the amount invested. The limited partnership is a popular method of organizing investors because it permits investors with small amounts of capital to participate in large real estate projects with predetermined maximum personal risk.

General partnerships are dissolved and must be reorganized if one partner dies, withdraws, or goes bankrupt. In a limited partnership, however, the partnership agreement may provide for the continuation of the organization following the death or withdrawal of one of the partners.

Corporations

A **corporation** is a legal entity—an artificial person—created under the authority of the laws of the state from which it receives its charter. A corporation is managed and operated by its board of directors. The charter sets forth the powers of the corporation, including its right to buy and sell real estate (based on a resolution by the board of directors). Because the corporation is a legal entity, it can own real estate in severalty or as a tenant in common. Some corporations are permitted by their charters to purchase real estate for any purpose; others are limited to purchasing only the land necessary to fulfill the entities' corporate purposes.

As a legal entity, a corporation continues to exist until it is formally dissolved. The death of one of the officers or directors does not affect title to property owned by the corporation.

After the corporation is formed, it is automatically an S corporation for IRS tax purposes. The corporation can file for C status if it wishes. The S corporation has the same tax attributes as an LLC or partnership, in that all profits and losses are passed to the shareholder.

The reason for these elaborate processes is to avoid personal liability, but it may be a futile attempt if the corporate formalities are not kept. This includes meetings, minutes, resolutions, votes, et cetera. Without these formalities, it is possible to "pierce the corporate veil" and attack the shareholder individually. One of the more popular ways is to insure the directors and officers with D&O insurance, but care must be given to the policy provisions because there are certain things that are generally not covered—fraud being at the top of the list.

Many investors are forming fancy entities, using a combination of limited partnerships coupled with LLCs and corporations to hold properties, sometimes forming these for each individual property. The new thinking for many is to hold the property individually and insure with a large blanket liability policy.

Limited Liability Companies

The **limited liability company (LLC)** is a form of business organization that combines the most attractive features of limited partnerships and corporations. The members of an LLC enjoy the limited liability offered by a corporate form of ownership and the tax advantages of a partnership. The structure and methods of establishing a new LLC, or of converting an existing entity to the LLC form, vary from state to state.

■ CONDOMINIUMS, COOPERATIVES, TOWN HOUSES, AND TIME-SHARES

A growing urban population, diverse lifestyles, changing family structures, and heightened mobility created a demand for new forms of ownership. Condominiums, cooperatives, town houses, and time-share arrangements are four types of property ownership that address society's changing real estate needs.

See Figure 2.9 for a comparison chart of these types of property ownership.

FIGURE 2.9

Four Types of Property Ownership

Type	Condomium	Cooperative	Time-Share
Description	Single units are located in lowrise and highrise complexes.	Single units are located in lowrise and highrise complexes.	Multiple purchasers buy interests in real estate—usually resort or hotel property. Each purchaser has the right to use their unit for a set time each year.
Ownership	Owners have fee title to interior space of units and share title to common areas.	Tenants own shares in a corporation, partnership, or trust that holds title to the building. Tenants have proprietary leases and the right to occupy their respective units.	Time-share estate is a fee simple interest. Time-share use agreement is personal property that expires after a specified time period.
Transfer	Single units are transferred by deed, will, or living trust.	Shares are personal property. Shareholders may sell or transfer shares. Transfer of shares may be restricted by bylaws.	An interest in a time-share estate may be conveyed by deed or will by the owner. An interest in time-share use is personal property that may or may not be transferable according to the contract.
Governed By	Declaration of condominium and elected board of directors (HOA)	Bylaws of the corporation and elected board of directors or trustees	Developer

Condominium Ownership

The **condominium** form of ownership has become increasingly popular throughout the United States. Condominium laws, often called horizontal property acts, have been enacted in every state (in Texas, this is the Uniform Condominium Act, which is Chapter 82 of the Texas Property Code). Under these laws, the owner of each unit holds a fee simple title to the unit. The individual unit owners also own a specified share of the undivided interest in the remainder of the building and land, called **common elements**. Common elements typically include such items as land, courtyards, lobbies, the exterior structure, hallways, elevators, stairways, and the roof, as well as recreational facilities such as swimming pools, tennis courts, and golf courses. The individual unit owners own these common elements as tenants in common. State law usually provides that unit owners do not have the same right to partition that other tenants in common have. Condominium ownership is not restricted to highrise buildings. Lowrises, town houses, and detached structures can all be condominiums.

Owning a Condominium   Once the property is established as a condominium, each unit becomes a separate parcel of real estate that is owned in fee simple and may be held by one or more persons in any type of ownership or tenancy recognized by state law. A condominium unit may be mortgaged like any other parcel of real estate and may be sold whenever desired (see Figure 2.10).

FIGURE   2.10

Condominium Ownership

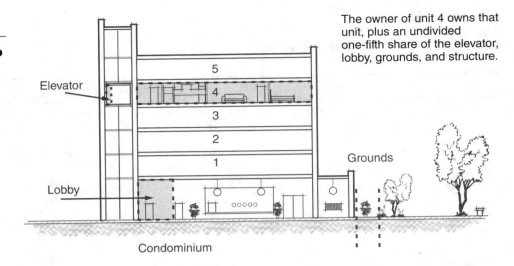

The owner of unit 4 owns that unit, plus an undivided one-fifth share of the elevator, lobby, grounds, and structure.

Real estate taxes are assessed and collected on each unit as an individual property. Default in the payment of taxes or a mortgage loan by one unit owner may result in a foreclosure sale of that owner's unit.

IN PRACTICE   Before buying a condominium, the buyer should do as much background research as possible. Examining association fees and rules are critical so that the buyer understands condominium ownership. Most states allow a time frame in which the buyer either receives and approves all documents or can be released from the contract.

Operation and Administration   The condominium property is administered by a homeowners association (HOA), which is made up of unit owners. The association can be governed by a board of directors or another official entity and can manage the property on its own or hire a property manager.

The HOA is responsible for the maintenance, repair, cleaning, and sanitation of the common elements and structural portions of the property. It must also maintain fire, extended-coverage, and liability insurance.

The expenses of maintaining and operating the building are paid by the unit owners in the form of fees and assessments that are imposed and collected by the HOA. Recurring fees (called condo fees) are paid by each unit owner. The fees may be due monthly, quarterly, semiannually, or annually, depending on the provisions of the bylaws. Depending on state law, if the fees are not paid, the association may seek a court-ordered judgment to have the delinquent owner's unit sold to cover the outstanding amount or to place a lien on the property.

Assessments are special payments required of unit owners to address some specific expense, such as a new roof. Assessments are structured like condo fees: Owners of larger units pay proportionately higher assessments than smaller units.

Cooperative Ownership

In a **cooperative**, a corporation holds title to the land and the building. The corporation then offers shares of stock to prospective tenants. The price the corporation sets for each apartment becomes the price of the stock. The purchaser becomes a shareholder in the corporation by virtue of stock ownership and receives a **proprietary lease** to the apartment for the life of the corporation. Because stock is personal property, the cooperative tenant-owners do not own real estate, as is the case with condominiums. Instead, they own an interest in a corporation that has only one asset: the building.

Operation and Management   The operation and management of a cooperative are determined by the corporation's bylaws. Through their control of the corporation, the shareholders of a cooperative control the property and its operation. They elect officers and directors who are responsible for operating the corporation and its real estate assets. Individual shareholders are obligated to abide by the corporation's bylaws.

An important issue in most cooperatives is the method by which shares in the corporation may be transferred to new owners. For example, the bylaws may require that the board of directors approve any prospective shareholders. In some cooperatives, a tenant-owner must sell the stock back to the corporation at the original purchase price so that the corporation realizes any profits when the shares are resold.

■ **FOR EXAMPLE**   In often publicized events, a controversial celebrity may attempt to move into a highly exclusive cooperative apartment building and is blocked by the cooperative's board. In refusing to allow a controversial personality to purchase shares, the board can cite the unwanted publicity and media attention other celebrity tenants might suffer.

Unlike in a condominium association, which has the authority to impose a lien on the title owned by someone who defaults on maintenance payments, the burden of any defaulted payment in a cooperative falls on the remaining shareholders. For this reason, approval of prospective tenants by the board of directors frequently involves financial evaluation. If the corporation is unable to make mortgage and tax payments because of shareholder defaults, the property might be sold by court order in a foreclosure suit. This would destroy the interests of all shareholders, including those who have paid their assessments.

Time-Share Ownership

Time-share ownership permits multiple purchasers to buy interests in real estate and is most common with resort property ownership. Each purchaser receives the right to use the facilities for a certain period. A time-share estate includes a fee simple interest in a specific unit; a time-share use is a contract under which the developer owns the real estate and establishes the rules for use of the property.

With a **time-share estate**, the owner's occupancy and use of the property are limited to the contractual period purchased—for example, the 17th complete week, Sunday through Saturday, of each calendar year. The owner is assessed for maintenance and common area expenses based on the ratio of the ownership period to the total number of ownership periods in the property. Time-share estates theoretically never end because they are real property interests. However, the physical life of the improvements is limited and must be looked at carefully when considering such a purchase.

The principal difference between a time-share estate and a **time-share use** lies in the interest transferred to an owner by the developer of the project. A time-share use consists of the right to occupy and use the facilities for a certain number of years. At the end of that time, the owner's rights in the property terminate. In effect, the developer has sold only a right of occupancy and use to the owner, not a fee simple interest.

Some time-sharing programs specify certain months or weeks of the year during which the owner can use the property. Others provide a rotation system under which the owner can occupy the unit during different times of the year in different years. Some include a swapping privilege for transferring the ownership period to another property to provide some variety for the owner. Time-shared properties typically are used 50 weeks each year, with the remaining two weeks reserved for maintenance of the improvements.

IN PRACTICE   The laws governing the development and sale of time-share units are complex and vary substantially from state to state. In addition, the sale of time-share properties may be subject to federal securities laws, as well as a state's real estate commission oversight. In many states, time-share properties are now subject to subdivision requirements.

■ LAWS AFFECTING REAL ESTATE

Laws Affecting Real Estate

- Contract law
- General property law
- Agency law
- Real estate license law
- Federal regulations
- Federal, state, and local tax laws
- Zoning and land-use laws
- Federal, state, and local environmental regulations

The unique nature of real estate has given rise to an equally unique set of laws and rights. Even the simplest real estate transaction involves a body of complex laws that includes the law of contracts, the general property law, the law of agency, and specific state real estate license law. Federal regulations, such as environmental laws, as well as federal, state, and local tax laws, also play an important role in real estate transactions. State and local land-use and zoning laws also have a significant effect on the practice of real estate.

A real estate licensee cannot be an expert in all areas of real estate law. However, licensees should know and understand some basic principles. Perhaps most important is the ability to recognize problems that should be referred to a competent attorney. Only attorneys are trained and licensed to prepare documents defining or transferring rights in property and to give advice on matters of law. Under no circumstances may real estate brokers or real estate salespeople act as attorneys, unless they are also licensed attorneys representing clients in that capacity.

Real Estate License Laws

Because real estate brokers and real estate salespeople are involved with other people's real estate and money, the need for regulation of their activities has long been recognized. The purpose of real estate license law is to protect the public from fraud, dishonesty, and incompetence in real estate transactions. All 50 states, the District of Columbia, and all Canadian provinces have passed laws that require real estate brokers and real estate salespeople to be licensed. Although state license laws are similar in many respects, they differ in some details, such as the amount and type of prelicensing and continuing education required.

■ SUMMARY

Land

- is the earth's surface, where water rights are held by owners of land adjacent to rivers, lakes, or oceans;
- extends downward to the center of the earth, where subsurface rights include mineral rights and other natural resources that can be transferred separately from surface rights;

- stretches upward to infinity, where air rights can be sold separately from surface rights with some limitations to enable air travel; and
- includes things naturally attached (*fructus naturales*) to the land, such as trees and crops that do not need cultivation and perennial crops, orchards, and vineyards.

Real estate includes land at, above, and below the earth's surface, plus all things permanently attached to the land, both natural and man-made.

Real property includes

- both land and real estate; and
- the bundle of legal rights:
  — right of possession,
  — right to control the property,
  — right of enjoyment,
  — right of exclusion, and
  — right of disposition.

Title is the right to ownership of the land, and evidence of ownership is provided by a written document, a deed, by which title is transferred.

Appurtenance is a right or privilege associated with real property and is normally conveyed to the new owner when the property is sold.

Personal property (chattel) includes

- movable items, such as furniture, cash, and bonds;
- manufactured homes, unless permanently affixed to land;
- emblements (*fructus industriales*), annual plantings or crops of grains, vegetables, and fruit;
- items of real property that become personal property by severance; and
- items of personal property can become real property by attachment (e.g., construction materials).

A fixture is personal property that has been affixed to the land or to a building so that by law it becomes part of the real property.

Legal tests for a fixture include the following:

- Method of annexation—not easily removable
- Adaptation to real estate—ordinarily considered a permanent addition
- Agreement of the parties—what is the annexor's intention?

Trade fixtures include property attached to the structure but used in the course of business, such as

- personal property, if removed by tenant and the premises are returned to original condition before the lease expires; and
- real property, if left behind by tenant. The landlord can acquire this type of property by accession.

The characteristics of real estate include the following:

- Economic
  — Scarcity
  — Improvements
  — Permanence of investment
  — Location (most important)

- Physical
  — Immobility
  — Indestructibility
  — Nonhomogeneity, or uniqueness

Forms of real estate ownership include the following:

- Severalty—title held by one individual
- Co-ownership—title held by two or more individuals, may be:
  — Tenancy in common, where each tenant holds
    - an undivided fractional interest with unity of possession—a right to occupy entire property; and
    - a right to sell, convey, mortgage, transfer, or pass by will.
  — Joint tenancy is where tenants enjoy the four unities (PITT):
    - Unity of possession—all joint tenants have undivided right to possession.
    - Unity of interest—all joint tenants own an equal interest.
    - Unity of time—all joint tenants acquire their interest at the same time.
    - Unity of title—title is conveyed to all joint tenants by the same document.

Joint tenants may also enjoy the right of survivorship; upon the death of a joint tenant, interest passes to the other joint tenant or tenants. Termination of joint tenancy is created when any one of the four unities is destroyed.

  — Community property is generally property acquired during marriage that is not separate property.
    - Separate property is property owned by one spouse before marriage, or by inheritance or gift.
    - Community property requires the signatures of both spouses to be conveyed. After the death of one spouse, the other spouse owns one-half of community property and the other half is distributed according to deceased spouse's will or according to state law of intestate succession.

- Trusts—one person (trustor) transfers ownership of property to a trustee to manage for benefit of a third party (beneficiary).

A partnership is an association of two or more persons who carry on a business for profit as co-owners in a general or a limited partnership, as provided by state law.

- In a general partnership, all partners participate in operation and management and share full liability for losses and obligations.
- A limited partnership has both general partners and limited partners.
  — Limited partners do not participate in running the business and are only liable for business losses up to the amount of the individual's investment.

A limited liability company (LLC) may offers its members the following benefits:

- Limited liability offered by a corporate form of ownership
- Tax advantages of a partnership (no double taxation)
- Flexible management structure without corporation requirements or restrictions on limited partnership

A corporation is chartered by the state and managed and operated by a board of directors; able to buy and sell real estate; and exists until formally dissolved.

Condominium laws of each state outline the following:

■ The condominium owner holds fee simple title to the airspace of a unit, as well as an undivided share in the remainder of the building and land, called the common elements.

■ Common elements are owned by condominium unit owners as tenants in common.

■ The condominium is administered by a homeowners association of unit owners that may decide to hire an outside property management firm.

■ Maintenance of common elements is funded by fees charged to each unit owner; default on payment does not affect other unit owners.

■ Condominium units may be mortgaged, sold, or willed to heirs.

■ Unit owners may be assessed to address specific expenses.

■ In a cooperative, title to the land and the building is held by a corporation that sells shares of stock to prospective tenants.

■ A purchaser of stock becomes a shareholder in the corporation and receives a proprietary lease to the apartment for the life of the corporation.

■ Stock is owned as personal property and not real estate.

■ The lender may accept stock as collateral for financing, which expands the pool of potential owners.

■ The IRS treats a cooperative the same as houses or condominiums for tax purposes.

A time-share permits the sale of a leasehold interest (time-share use) or deeded ownership (time-share estate) that allows occupancy during a specific period. Time-share ownership permits multiple purchasers to buy interests in real estate, a form of ownership most commonly found with resort property.

Laws that affect real estate include

■ contracts, property, agency, and real estate licensing, where all states require real estate brokers and salespeople to be licensed with requirements differing from state to state;

■ state and local land-use and zoning laws; and

■ federal and state environmental regulations and tax laws.

CHAPTER 2 REVIEW QUESTIONS

1. Real estate generally includes all the following *EXCEPT*
   a. trees.
   b. air rights.
   c. annual crops.
   d. mineral rights.

2. When an owner of real estate sells the property to someone else, which of the sticks in the bundle of legal rights is the owner, as seller, using?
   a. Exclusion
   b. Legal enjoyment
   c. Control
   d. Disposition

3. The buyer and the seller of a home are debating whether a certain item is real or personal property. The buyer says it is real property and should convey with the house; the seller says it is personal property and would not convey without a separate bill of sale. In determining whether an item is real or personal property, a court would *NOT* consider which of the following?
   a. The cost of the item when it was purchased
   b. Whether its removal would cause severe damage to the real estate
   c. Whether the item is clearly adapted to the real estate
   d. Any relevant agreement of the parties in their contract of sale

4. A buyer purchased a parcel of land and immediately sold the mineral rights to an oil company. The buyer gave up which of the following?
   a. Air rights
   b. Surface rights
   c. Subsurface rights
   d. Occupancy rights

5. A homeowner is building a new enclosed front porch on his home. A truckload of lumber that the homeowner purchased has been left in the driveway for use in building the porch. At this point, the lumber is considered
   a. real property because it will be permanently affixed to the existing structure.
   b. personal property.
   c. personal property waiting to become a fixture.
   d. a trade or chattel fixture.

6. A man owns one of 20 town houses in fee simple, along with a 5% ownership share in the parking facilities, recreation center, and grounds. What kind of property does he own?
   a. Cooperative
   b. Condominium
   c. Time-share
   d. Land trust

7. According to some states, any real property that either spouse of a married couple owns at the time of the marriage remains separate property. Further, any real property acquired by either spouse during the marriage (except by gift or inheritance) belongs to both of them equally. What is this form of ownership called?
   a. Partnership
   b. Joint tenancy
   c. Tenancy by the entirety
   d. Community property

8. A person lives in an apartment building. The land and structures are owned by a corporation, with one mortgage loan securing the entire property. Like the other residents, this person owns stock in the corporation and has a lease to the apartment. This type of ownership is called
   a. condominium.
   b. planned unit development.
   c. time-share.
   d. cooperative.

9. A married couple co-owns a farm and has right of survivorship. This arrangement is MOST likely
    a. severalty ownership.
    b. community property.
    c. a tenancy in common.
    d. a tenancy by the entirety.

10. Which of the following is NOT a form of co-ownership?
    a. Tenancy in common
    b. Ownership in severalty
    c. Tenancy by the entirety
    d. Community property

CHAPTER 3

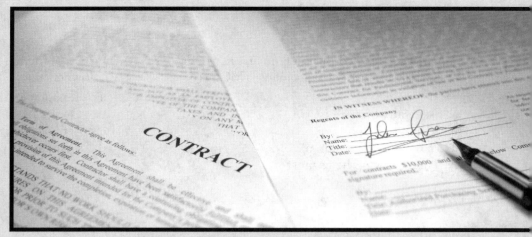

Contracts Used in Real Estate

■ **LEARNING OBJECTIVES** *When you have completed this chapter, you will be able to*

■ **distinguish** between express and implied, bilateral and unilateral, and executed and executory contracts;

■ **explain** the difference in valid, void, voidable and unenforceable contracts;

■ **identify** the essential elements of a valid contract;

■ **explain** the difference between an assignment and a novation;

■ **give** examples of what constitutes a breach of contract;

■ **list** reasons for a termination of a contract;

■ **describe** the types of contracts used in the real estate business;

■ **describe** different types of listings and how they may be terminated;

■ **identify** the information needed for a listing agreement;

■ **compare** a listing agreement and a buyer agency agreement;

■ **define** types of leasehold estates;

■ **summarize** the requirements and general conditions of a valid lease and how it may be discharged;

■ **describe** different leases and when they are used; and

■ **discuss** the potential use of an option and a land contract.

■ KEY TERMS

acceptance	express contract	offeror
assignment	gross lease	oil and gas lease
bilateral contract	ground lease	open listing
breach of contract	implied contract	option
buyer agency agreement	land contract	percentage lease
consent	lease	rescission
consideration	leasehold estate	reversionary right
contract	lease purchase	revocation
counteroffer	legally competent	right of first refusal
estate at sufferance	lessee	security deposit
estate at will	lessor	statute of frauds
estate for years	month-to-month tenancy	sublease
estate from period to period	multiple listing service (MLS)	time is of the essence
		unenforceable contract
exclusive-agency listing	net lease	unilateral contract
exclusive-right-to-sell listing	net listing	valid contract
	novation	void contract
executed contract	offer	voidable contract
executory contract	offeree	

■ REAL ESTATE CONTRACTS

The real estate market is driven by contracts. Both listing and buyer representation agreements are contracts. Options, escrow agreements, and leases are all contracts. And of course the offer to purchase is the first step in finalizing a sales contract. Whatever aspect of the real estate business is involved, licensees will be dealing with contracts. It is important to know how a contract is created, what it means, what is required for the parties, and what kinds of actions can end it.

■ CONTRACT LAW

A **contract** is a voluntary agreement or promise between legally competent parties, supported by legal consideration, to perform (or refrain from performing) some legal act. The definition may be easier to understand if its various parts are examined separately.

A contract must be

- voluntary—no one may be forced into a contract;
- an agreement or a promise—a contract is essentially a promise or set of promises;
- made by legally competent parties—the parties must be viewed by the law as capable of making a legally binding promise;
- supported by legal consideration—a contract must be supported by some valuable thing that induces a party to enter into the contract and that must be legally sufficient to support a contract; and
- for a legal act—no one may enter a legal contract for something illegal.

Licensees use many types of contracts and agreements to carry out their responsibilities to sellers, buyers, and the public. The area of law that governs such agreements is called contract law.

IN PRACTICE   Real estate licensees are required to use preprinted, pre-approved forms provided by TREC. Remember that licensees cannot practice law without a license. Both the buyer and the seller have the option of selecting their own attorney. See Chapter 1 for a list of promulgated forms.

Express and Implied Contracts

Depending on how a contract is created, it is either express or implied. In an **express contract**, the parties state the terms and show their intentions in words, either oral or written. Most real estate contracts are express contracts; they have been committed to writing. Under the **statute of frauds**, certain types of contracts must be in writing to be enforceable in a court of law. In an **implied contract**, the agreement of the parties is demonstrated by their acts and conduct.

IN PRACTICE   When someone enters a restaurant and orders a meal, there is an implied contract that the customer will pay the bill when it comes. A student signing up for a three-month food plan at a college makes an express contract.

Bilateral and Unilateral Contracts

Contracts are classified as either bilateral or unilateral. In a **bilateral contract**, both parties promise to do something; one promise is given in exchange for another. A real estate sales contract is a bilateral contract because the seller promises to sell a parcel of real estate and transfer title to the property to the buyer, who promises to pay a certain sum of money for the property. An exclusive-right-to-sell listing contract is a bilateral contract.

Bilateral contract

■ *Bi* means two—must have two promises.

A **unilateral contract,** on the other hand, is a one-sided agreement. One party makes a promise to entice a second party to do something. The second party is not legally obligated to act. However, if the second party does comply, the first party is obligated to keep the promise.

Unilateral contract

■ *Uni* means one—has only one promise.

■ **FOR EXAMPLE**   A homeowner offers to pay a commission to a broker to find a buyer for a property. The broker is not obligated to find a buyer. The property owner is only obligated to pay a commission to the broker who finds a buyer. This is a unilateral contract.

Executed and Executory Contracts

A contract may be classified as either executed or executory, depending on whether the agreement is performed. An **executed contract** is one in which all parties have fulfilled their promises; the contract has been performed. An **executory contract** exists when one (or both) party still has an act to perform. A sales contract is an executory contract from the time it is signed until closing; ownership has not yet changed hands, and the seller has not received the sales price. At closing, the sales contract is executed.

Figure 3.1 highlights the issues involved in the formation of a contract—issues talked about in detail in this chapter.

FIGURE 3.1

Contract Issues

Preformation	Formation	Post-formation
Essential Elements	**Classification**	**Discharge**
Offer and acceptance, consideration, legal purpose, consent, legal capacity	Valid, void, voidable, enforceable, unenforceable, express, implied, unilateral, bilateral, executory, executed	Performance, breach, remedies (damages, specific performance, rescission)

Elements of a Contract

■ Offer and acceptance
■ Consideration
■ Consent
■ Legal purpose
■ Legally competent parties

Essential Elements of a Valid Contract

A contract must meet certain minimum requirements to be considered legally valid. The following are the basic essential elements of a contract.

Offer and Acceptance   There must be an offer made by one party that is accepted by the other. The person who makes the offer is the **offeror**. The person to whom an offer is made is the **offeree**. This requirement is also called mutual assent. It means that there must be a "meeting of the minds"; that is, there must be complete agreement between the parties about the purpose and terms of the contract. Courts look to the "objective intent of the parties" to determine whether they intended to enter into a binding agreement. Most states require that the offer and acceptance be in writing. The wording of the contract must express all the agreed terms and must be clearly understood by the parties.

An **offer** is a promise made by one party, requesting something in exchange for that promise. The offer is made with the intention that the offeror will be bound to the terms if the offer is accepted. The terms of the offer must be definite and specific and must be communicated to the offeree.

An **acceptance** is a promise by the offeree to be bound by the exact terms proposed by the offeror. The acceptance must be communicated to the offeror. Proposing any deviation from the terms of the offer is considered a rejection of the original offer. This is called a **counteroffer**. The counteroffer must be accepted by both parties for a contract to exist.

Besides being terminated by a counteroffer, an offer may be terminated by the offeree's outright rejection of it. Alternatively, an offeree may fail to accept the offer before it expires. The offeror may revoke the offer at any time before acceptance. This **revocation** must be communicated to the offeree by the offeror, either directly or through the parties' agents. The offer is revoked if the offeree learns of the revocation and observes the offeror acting in a manner that indicates that the offer no longer exists. For example, if a buyer gives a seller three days to accept an offer and on the third day the buyer's broker calls the seller's broker and cancels the offer, the offer is now void.

Consideration   The contract must be based on consideration. **Consideration** is something of legal value offered by one party and accepted by another as an inducement to perform or to refrain from performing some act. There must be a definite statement of consideration in a contract to show that something of value was given in exchange for the promise. Consideration is some interest or benefit accruing to one party, or some loss or responsibility by the other party.

Consideration must be "good and valuable between the parties." The courts do not inquire into the adequacy of consideration. Adequate consideration ranges from as little as a promise of "love and affection" to a substantial sum of money. Anything that has been bargained for and exchanged is legally sufficient to satisfy the requirement for consideration. The only requirements are that the parties agree and that no undue influence or fraud has occurred.

Consent   A contract that complies with all the basic requirements may still be either void or voidable. A contract must be entered into with **consent** as a free and voluntary act of each party. Each party must be able to make a prudent and knowledgeable decision without undue influence. A mistake, misrepresentation, fraud, undue influence, or duress would deprive a person of that ability. If any of these circumstances is present, the contract is voidable by the injured party. If the other party were to sue for breach, the injured party could use lack of voluntary assent as a defense.

Legal Purpose   A contract must be for a legal purpose—that is, even with all the other elements (consent, competent parties, consideration, and offer and acceptance) present. A contract for an illegal purpose or an act against public policies is not a valid contract.

Legally Competent Parties   All parties to the contract must be **legally competent**, meaning they must be of legal age and have enough mental capacity to understand the nature or consequences of their actions in the contract. In most states, 18 is the age of contractual capacity.

Validity of Contracts   A contract can be described as valid, void, voidable, or unenforceable, depending on the circumstances.

A **valid contract** meets all the essential elements that make it legally sufficient, or enforceable, and is binding in a court of law.

A **void contract** has no legal force or effect because it lacks some or all the essential elements of a contract. A contract that is void was never a legal contract. For example, the use of a forged name in a listing contract would make the contract void.

A **voidable contract** appears on the surface to be valid but may be rescinded or disaffirmed by one or both parties based on some legal principle. A voidable contract is considered by the courts to be valid if the party who has the option to disaffirm the agreement does not do so within a period of time. A contract with a minor, for example, is voidable. A contract entered into by a mentally ill person is usually voidable during the mental illness and for a reasonable period after the person has recovered. If a contract was made under duress, with misrepresentation, under the influence, with intent to defraud, or with a minor, it is also voidable.

IN PRACTICE   Mental capacity to enter into a contract is not the same as medical sanity. The test is whether the individual in question is capable of understanding her actions. A person may suffer from a mental illness but clearly understand the significance of her actions. Such psychological questions require consultation with experts.

The most common situation today occurs with the more senior members of society who may be experiencing some difficulty remembering and/or communicating details. Agents should use great care when it is apparent that some mental faculties may be impaired. Although caution should be used when encouraging the customer/client to

---

Validity of Contracts

■ *Valid*—has all legal elements and is fully enforceable
■ *Void*—lacks one or all elements and has no legal force or effect
■ *Voidable*—has all legal elements and may be rescinded or disaffirmed
■ *Unenforceable*—has all legal elements and is enforceable only between the parties

have loved ones or trusted advisers be present, it is generally a safe harbor for the agent. Good notes of meetings and documentation will be very helpful if there should be a problem with a second-guessing relative or friend in the future.

An **unenforceable contract** may also appear on the surface to be valid; however, neither party can sue the other to force performance. For example, an oral agreement for the sale of a parcel of real estate would be unenforceable. Because the statute of frauds requires that real estate sales contracts be in writing, the defaulting party could not be taken to court and forced to perform. There is, however, a distinction between a suit to force performance and a suit for damages, which is permissible in an oral agreement. An unenforceable contract is said to be "valid as between the parties." This means that once the agreement is fully executed and both parties are satisfied, neither has reason to initiate a lawsuit to force performance.

■ DISCHARGE OF CONTRACTS

A contract is discharged when the agreement is terminated. The most desirable case is when a contract terminates because it was completely performed, with all its terms fulfilled. Contracts may be terminated for other reasons, such as a party's breach or default.

Performance of a Contract

Each party has certain rights and duties to fulfill. The question of when a contract must be performed is an important factor. Many contracts call for a specific time by which the agreed acts must be completely performed. Furthermore, some contracts provide that **time is of the essence**, which means that the contract must be performed within a specified time. A party who fails to perform on time is liable for breach of contract.

IN PRACTICE   When a "time is of the essence" clause is used in a contract, the parties may want to consult an attorney. The ramifications of a breach of a contract in which "time is of the essence" is used can be significant. For example, a buyer might lose escrow funds, or the seller might lose the right to enforce the contract.

When a contract does not specify a date for performance, the acts it requires should be performed within a reasonable time. The interpretation of what constitutes a reasonable time depends on the situation. Courts have sometimes declared contracts invalid because they did not contain a time or date for performance.

Assignment

Assignment refers to a transfer of rights or duties under a contract. Generally rights and obligations may be assigned to a third party. Obligations may be delegated, but the original party remains primarily liable unless specifically released. Most contracts have a clause to either allow or forbid assignment.

Novation

Substitution of a new contract for an existing contract is called **novation**. The new agreement may be between the same parties, or a new party may be substituted for either. The parties' intent must be to discharge the old obligation. For example, when a real estate purchaser assumes the seller's existing mortgage loan, the lender may choose to release the seller and substitute the buyer as the party primarily liable for the mortgage debt. Or when there are many changes to a real estate contract and it is faxed several times, the contract may no longer be legible. Novation occurs when a new, clear contract with all the accepted changes is signed by all the parties. However difficult to read, the original contract should always be saved in case of any later disagreement over the terms agreed upon.

Breach of Contract

A contract may be terminated if it is breached by one of the parties. A **breach of contract** is a violation of any of the terms or conditions of a contract without legal reason. Some breaches are curable, while others are not. The courts generally allow a defaulting party reasonable time to cure if there is no undue burden or hardship on the other party. For example, a tenant pays late but will not be evicted even though there would be a monetary penalty for the breach. An example of a breach that is not curable is when the buyer, who has signed a buyer-broker agreement, buys a property with another agent. While not curable, there is a remedy for the breach that may involve a small claims action up to $10,000.

Statute of Limitations   Every state limits the time during which parties to a contract may bring legal suit to enforce their rights. In Texas, the statute of limitations is four years for breach of contract. The statute of limitations varies for different legal actions, and any rights not enforced within the applicable period are lost.

Other Reasons for Termination   Contracts may also be discharged or terminated when any of the following occur:

- Partial performance of the terms, along with a written acceptance by the party for whom acts have not been done or to whom money is owed. For example, if the parties agree that the work performed is close enough to completion, they can agree that the contract is discharged even if some minor elements remain unperformed.
- Substantial performance, in which one party has substantially performed on the contract but does not complete all the details exactly as the contract requires. Such performance may be enough to force payment, with certain adjustments for any damages suffered by the other party. For example, where a newly constructed addition to a home is finished except for polishing the brass doorknobs, the contractor is entitled to the final payment.
- Impossibility of performance, in which an act required by the contract cannot be legally accomplished.
- Mutual agreement of the parties to cancel the contract.
- Operation of law—such as in the voiding of a contract by a minor—as a result of fraud, due to the expiration of the statute of limitations, or because a contract was altered without the written consent of all parties involved.
- Rescission—one party may cancel or terminate the contract as though it had never been made. Cancellation terminates a contract without a return to the original position. **Rescission**, however, returns the parties to their original positions before the contract, so any monies exchanged must be returned. Rescission is normally a contractual remedy for a breach, but a contract may also be rescinded by the mutual agreement of the parties.

■ CONTRACTS USED IN THE REAL ESTATE BUSINESS

The written agreements most commonly used by licensees are

- listing agreements and buyer agency agreements,
- real estate sales contracts,
- options agreements,
- escrow agreements,
- leases,
- land contracts or contracts for deed, and
- exchange agreements.

Many states have specific guidelines for when and how real estate licensees may prepare contracts for their consumers. These guidelines are created by state real estate officials, court decisions, or statutes. A licensee may be permitted to fill in the blanks on certain approved preprinted documents, such as sales contracts, as directed by the client. No separate fee may be charged for completing the forms. The practice of law includes preparing legal documents, such as deeds and mortgages, and offering advice on legal matters; a real estate licensee who is not a licensed attorney cannot practice law.

Contract Forms

The contracts for the sale of residential real estate are promulgated by TREC and must be used if prepared by real estate agents. They are:

- Unimproved Property Contract
- One to Four Family Residential Contract (Resale)
- New Home Contract (Incomplete Construction)
- New Home Contract (Completed Construction)
- Farm and Ranch Contract
- Residential Condominium Contract (Resale)

Exchange The purpose of an exchange is to defer taxes to some other time, as the tax will be lessened or absent. For many estates, deferring until death will result in no tax if the estate is exempt from the federal estate tax. The property will then get a stepped-up basis and the heirs will start the cost recovery (depreciation) at the current market value. This issue becomes important when agents are giving aggressive or conservative opinions of value for an estate because the size of the estate must be balanced with the issue of basis.

An exchange agreement is different from a purchase in the sense that equities are being exchanged and the properties are just the vehicle to effect the transfer. There are three different exchange situations which require three different forms.

1. Simultaneous exchange
2. Delayed exchange
3. Reverse exchange

Great care must be given to the preparation of the contract because the operative words in the exchange are IRS. In an audit, the IRS will look for both form and substance.

IN PRACTICE   It is essential that both parties to a contract understand exactly what they are agreeing to. Poorly drafted documents, especially those containing extensive legal language, may be subject to various interpretations and may lead to litigation. The parties to a real estate transaction may wish to have sales contracts and other legal documents examined by a lawyer to ensure that the agreements accurately reflect their intentions. When preprinted forms do not sufficiently cover special provisions in a transaction, the parties should have an attorney draft an appropriate contract. When a failed transaction ends up in the courtroom, the first question the judge will ask is, "What does it say in writing?"

Commercial Contracts

TREC does not provide promulgated forms for commercial transactions, though the Texas Association of REALTORS® provides these forms for its members.

Listing and Buyer Agency Agreements

A listing agreement is an employment contract. It establishes the rights and obligations of the broker as agent and the seller as principal. A buyer agency contract establishes the relationship between a buyer and the buyer's agent.

IN PRACTICE If a contract contains any ambiguity, the courts generally interpret the agreement against the party who prepared it.

■ LISTING AGREEMENTS

Under both the law of agency and state license laws, only a licensed real estate broker is authorized to represent others to list, buy, sell, exchange, or lease property. Stage agency law defines the specific duties required of an agent representing a client. (Any party to the transaction that is not represented by the agent is a customer.) Even though the real estate salesperson may perform most, if not all, of the listing services, the listing remains with the broker.

A listing agreement is an employment contract between a broker and a seller for the real estate professional services of the broker. All states, either by their statutes of fraud or by specific rules from their real estate licensing authorities, require that the listing agreement be in writing to be enforceable in court.

Types of Listing Agreements

Several types of listing agreements exist. The type of contract determines the specific rights and obligations of the parties (see Figure 3.2).

FIGURE 3.2

Types of Listing Agreements

Exclusive Right to Sell	Exclusive Agency	Open Listing
One broker	One broker	Multiple brokers
Broker is paid regardless of who sells the house.	Broker is paid only if the broker is procuring cause.	Only selling broker is paid.
	Seller retains the right to sell without obligation.	Seller retains the right to sell without obligation.

Exclusive-Right-to-Sell Listing

■ One authorized broker-agent receives a commission.
■ Seller pays broker-agent regardless of who sells property.

Exclusive Right-to-Sell Listing In an **exclusive-right-to-sell listing**, one broker is appointed as the seller's sole agent. The broker is given the exclusive right, or authorization, to market the seller's property. If the property is sold while the listing is in effect, the seller must pay the broker a commission, regardless of who sells the property. Sellers benefit from this form of agreement because the broker feels freer to spend time and money actively marketing the property.

Exclusive-Agency Listing   In an **exclusive-agency listing**, one broker is authorized to act as the exclusive agent of the principal. However, the seller retains the right to sell the property without the obligation to pay the broker.

Open Listing   In an **open listing** (also called in some areas a nonexclusive listing), the seller retains the right to employ any number of brokers as agents. The seller is only obligated to pay a commission to the broker who successfully produces a ready, willing, and able buyer. If the seller personally sells the property without the aid of any of the brokers, the seller is not obligated to pay a commission. The terms of an open listing still must be negotiated and put in writing

Special Listing Provisions

Multiple Listing   A multiple-listing clause may be included in a listing. It is used by brokers who are members of a local **multiple listing service (MLS)**.

The MLS offers advantages to brokers, sellers, and buyers. Brokers develop a sizable inventory of properties to be sold and are assured a portion of the commission if they list property or participate in the sale of another broker's listing. Sellers gain because the property is exposed to a larger market. Buyers gain because of access to the variety of properties on the market.

The contractual obligations among the member brokers of an MLS vary widely. Most MLSs require that a broker turn over new listings to the service within a specific, fairly short period after the broker obtains the listing. Under the provisions of an MLS, a participating broker makes a unilateral offer of cooperation and compensation to other member brokers. An offer of cooperation is not an offer of compensation. Absent the offer of compensation in MLS, there should be an agreement between brokers that states the amount and terms of payment. In some commercial transactions (such as leases), payments are made periodically rather than up front.

IN PRACTICE   Technology has enhanced the benefits of MLS membership. In addition to providing instant access to information about the status of listed properties, an MLS often offers a broad range of other useful information about mortgage loans, real estate taxes and assessments, and municipalities and school districts. They are equally helpful to the licensee in preparing a competitive market analysis to determine the value of a particular property before suggesting an appropriate range of listing price to the seller. Computer-assisted searches also help buyers select properties that best meet their needs.

Net Listing   A **net listing** provision specifies that the seller will receive a net amount of money from any sale, with the excess going to the listing broker as commission. The broker is free to offer the property at any price greater than that net amount. Because a net listing can create a conflict of interest between the broker's fiduciary responsibility to the seller and the broker's profit motive, it is illegal in many states and discouraged in others.

Termination of Listings

A listing agreement may be terminated under the following circumstances:

- When the agreement's purpose is fulfilled, such as when a ready, willing, and able buyer has been found
- When the agreement's term expires

Open Listing

- There are multiple agents.
- Only the selling agent is entitled to a commission.
- The seller retains the right to sell independently without obligation.

Net Listing

- The broker is entitled to any amount exceeding the seller's stated net profit.

- If the property is destroyed or its use is changed by some force outside the owner's control, such as a zoning change or condemnation by eminent domain
- If title to the property is transferred by operation of law, as in the case of the owner's bankruptcy or foreclosure
- If the broker and the seller mutually agree to cancel the listing
- If either the broker or the seller dies or becomes incapacitated (if the salesperson dies or becomes incapacitated, the listing is still valid)

In most states, failing to specify a definite termination date in a listing is grounds for the suspension or revocation of a real estate license.

Some listing contracts contain a broker protection clause. This clause provides that the property owner will pay the listing broker a commission if, within a specified number of days after the listing expires, the owner sells the property to someone the broker originally introduced to the owner.

While listing agreements are required to have a definite termination date, agency does not, and may be terminated at any time by either party. If a seller, for any or no reason, terminates the agent's agency, the agent must immediately cease all marketing. The agent should remove

- the lock box,
- the yard sign,
- the listing from the MLS, and
- the listing from the agent's website.

Should the property sell during the term of the listing agreement, the agent must not take any action that would block the sale in a residential transaction. If there are issues regarding the commission, it is best to let a judge decide, with the help of an attorney. In commercial transactions, it is possible to have an attorney file a lis pendens which will help resolve the dispute.

The Listing Process

Before signing a contract, the broker and the seller must discuss a variety of issues. The seller's main concerns typically are the selling price of the property and the net proceeds. This is the broker's opportunity to explain the various types of listing agreements, the ramifications of different agency relationships, and the marketing services the broker provides. The seller and the listing broker must agree on the amount of compensation to be paid for providing a ready, willing, and able buyer and whether the compensation may be shared with an assisting broker.

Information Needed for Listing Agreements

Obtaining as many facts as possible about the property is particularly important when the listing will be shared with other brokers through the MLS who will rely on the information taken by the listing agent.

The information needed for a listing agreement generally includes the

- names and relationship of the owners;
- street address and legal description of the property;
- size, type, age, and construction of the house;
- number of rooms and their sizes;
- dimensions of the lot;

- current (or most recent year's) property taxes;
- neighborhood amenities (schools, parks and recreational areas, churches, and public transportation);
- real property, if any, to be removed from the premises by the seller and any personal property to be included in the sale for the buyer;
- any additional information that would make the property more appealing and marketable; and
- required disclosures regarding property conditions.

Additional financial information that the listing agent will need but that does not necessarily appear in the MLS includes

- any existing loans, including the name and address of each lender, the type of loan, the loan number, the loan balance, the interest rate, the monthly payment which includes principal, interest, taxes, and insurance (PITI), whether the loan may be assumed by the buyer and under what circumstances, and whether the loan may be prepaid without penalty;
- the possibility of seller financing;
- the amount of any outstanding special assessments and whether they will be paid by the seller or assumed by the buyer; and
- the zoning classification of the property.

Disclosures

Most states have enacted disclosure laws requiring agents to disclose whose interests they legally represent. It is important that the seller be informed of the company's policies regarding single agency, dual agency, and buyer agency. Some states also have designated agency where two agents from the same company may participate in the same transaction while maintaining their agency relationship with either the buyer or the seller. Other states may allow for a facilitator or transaction broker that has no agency responsibility to either party.

The seller must also disclose property conditions as required by law in most states. These disclosures cover a wide range of structural, mechanical, and other conditions. Frequently, the laws require that the seller complete a standardized form.

The Listing Contract Form

Some brokers have attorneys draft listing contract forms for their firm, while others use forms prepared by the MLS, state, or local REALTOR® associations. A separate information sheet (also called a profile or data sheet) is prepared for submission to the MLS. The profile sheet contains all the details regarding the property, compensation to assisting brokers, and special property features. Licensees should carefully review the specific forms used in their market area and refer to their law for any specific requirements.

Generally, the listing contract should contain the following information:

- Whether the broker may place a sign on the property and advertise. The sign should address when the property can be shown, allowing reasonable notice to the seller.
- The brokerage company name, the employing broker, and if appropriate, the salesperson taking the listing

- The proposed sales price. The seller's proceeds will be reduced by unpaid real estate taxes, special assessments, mortgage debts, and any other outstanding obligations.
- Any personal property that will convey, as well as items of real or personal property that the seller expects to remove at the time of the sale. Items that may later become points of negotiation include major appliances, swimming pool and spa equipment, fireplace accessories, storage sheds, window treatments, stacked firewood, and stored heating oil.
- Any leased equipment—security systems, cable television boxes, water softeners, special antennas—that will be left with the property. The seller is responsible for notifying the equipment's lessor of the change of property ownership.
- A full legal description. The buyer's agent will refer to this information when preparing an offer to purchase.
- An anticipated closing date. The listing agreement should allow adequate time for the paperwork involved (including the buyer's qualification for any financing).
- A closing attorney, title company, or escrow company, all of which should be considered and retained as soon as possible. The closing agent will complete the settlement statements, disburse the funds, and file documents to be recorded and sent to the IRS.
- Evidence of ownership. A warranty deed, title insurance policy, or abstract of title with an attorney's opinion can be used for proof of title.
- All existing liens to be paid in full by the seller unless being assumed by the buyer
- The circumstances under which a commission will be paid, which must be specifically stated in the contract. The fee can be either a percentage or a flat rate and is usually paid at closing by the closing agent.
- The circumstances under which the contract can be terminated
- Warranties by the owner. The owner is responsible for certain assurances and disclosures. Depending on the type of deed being offered, the seller may be responsible for purchasing title insurance. Unless the property is being sold as is, all working systems and appliances must be in normal working condition.
- A home warranty, if offered, that covers plumbing, electrical and heating systems, water heaters, duct work, and major appliances. Coverage, deductibles, limitations, and exclusions in the contract should be clearly stated.
- Nondiscrimination (equal opportunity) wording. The seller must understand that the property will be shown and offered without regard to the race, color, religion, national origin, sex, familial status, or handicap of the prospective buyer. State or local law may include additional protected classes.
- Signatures of all parties who have a legal interest in the property. If one or more of the owners is married, the spouse's consent and signature is required in most states to release any marital rights.
- Whether the property is in the possession of a tenant, along with the terms of the tenancy. Instructions should be included on how the property is to be shown to prospective buyers.
- Prior permission to enter into an intermediary relationship

■ BUYER AGENCY AGREEMENTS

Like a listing agreement, a **buyer agency agreement** is an employment contract. In this case, the broker is employed as the buyer's agent; the buyer, rather than the seller, is the principal or client. The purpose of the agreement is to find a suitable property. A buyer's broker must protect the buyer's interests at all points in the transaction.

Buyer Representation Issues

Before signing a buyer agency agreement, a broker and a buyer must discuss several issues. The licensee should explain the forms of agency available and the parties' rights and responsibilities under each type. The specific services provided to a buyer-client should be clearly explained.

Compensation issues also need to be addressed. Buyer's agents may be compensated in the form of a flat fee for services, an hourly rate, or a percentage of the purchase price, or by sharing the commission paid by the seller to the listing broker. The agent may require a retainer fee at the time the agreement is signed to cover initial expenses to be applied as a credit toward any fees due at the closing.

As in any agency agreement, the source of compensation does not determine the relationship. A buyer's agent may be compensated by either the buyer or the seller. Issues of compensation are always negotiable.

■ LEASING REAL ESTATE

A **lease** is a contract between an owner of real estate (the **lessor**) and a tenant (the **lessee**). A lease is a contract to transfer the lessor's rights to exclusive possession and use of the property to the tenant for a specified period. The lease establishes the length of time the contract is to run and the amount the lessee is to pay for use of the property, plus other rights and obligations of the parties.

In effect, the lease agreement combines two contracts. A lease is (1) a conveyance of a possession of the real estate and (2) a contract to pay rent and assume other obligations. The lessor grants the lessee the right to occupy the real estate and use it for purposes stated in the lease. In return, the landlord receives payment for use of the premises and retains a **reversionary right** to possession after the lease term expires.

The statute of frauds in Texas requires lease agreements for more than one year to be in writing to be enforceable. In general, oral leases for one year or less that can be performed within a year of their making are enforceable. Written leases should be signed by both the lessor and the lessee.

IN PRACTICE   Even though an oral lease may be enforceable, it is always better practice to put lease agreements in writing. A written lease provides concrete evidence of the terms and conditions to which the parties have agreed.

■ LEASEHOLD ESTATES

A tenant's right to possess real estate for the term of the lease is called a **leasehold** (less-than-freehold) **estate**. Just as there are several types of freehold (ownership) estates, there are different kinds of leasehold estates (see Figure 3.3).

FIGURE   3.3

Leasehold Estates

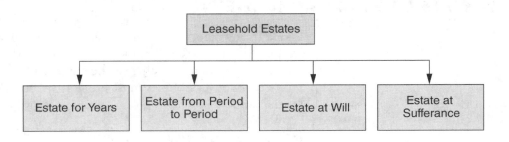

Estate for Years

Estate (Tenancy) for Years

■ Any definite period

An **estate for years** is a leasehold estate that continues for a definite period and always has specific starting and ending dates. When the estate expires, the lessee is required to vacate the premises and surrender possession to the lessor. No notice is required because the lease agreement states a specific expiration date.

Estate from Period to Period

Estate from Period to Period (Periodic Tenancy)

■ Indefinite term
■ Automatically renewing

An **estate from period to period** is created when the landlord and tenant enter into an agreement for an indefinite time with no specific termination date. Such a tenancy is usually created initially to run for a definite amount of time—for example, month to month, week to week, or year to year—but the tenancy continues indefinitely until proper notice of termination is given. A **month-to-month tenancy**, for example, is created when a tenant takes possession with no definite termination date and pays monthly rent. Periodic tenancy is often used in residential leases.

■ **FOR EXAMPLE**   A landlord and a tenant have agreed that the apartment can be rented by the month without specifying the number of months the lease will run. The lease simply continues until either the landlord or the tenant gives proper notice to terminate.

Estate at Will

Estate (Tenancy) at Will

■ Indefinite term
■ Possession with landlord's consent

An **estate at will** gives the tenant the right to possess property with the landlord's consent for an unspecified or uncertain term; it continues until it is terminated by either party giving proper notice. An estate at will is automatically terminated by the death of either the landlord or the tenant.

■ **FOR EXAMPLE**   A landlord tells a tenant that at the end of the lease someone else will be moving into the apartment. The landlord gives the tenant the option to continue to rent until the new tenant is ready to move. If the tenant agrees, a tenancy at will is created.

Estate at Sufferance

Estate (Tenancy) at Sufferance

■ Tenant's previously lawful possession continued without landlord's consent

An **estate at sufferance** arises when a tenant who lawfully possessed real property continues in possession of the premises without the landlord's consent after the rights expire. A tenant who "holds over" or fails to surrender possession is responsible for the payment of monthly rent at the existing terms and rate.

If a lease does not contain a holdover clause, state law typically offers three options:

■ The landlord can accept rent offered by the tenant, thereby creating a new tenancy under conditions of the original lease.

■ The landlord can treat the tenant as a tenant at sufferance by either object-ing to the tenant holding over or informing the tenant of such treatment, thus creating a month-to-month or periodic tenancy.

■ The landlord can treat the tenant as a trespasser and proceed with an evic-tion and damages action. Under this situation, the landlord must comply with the notice-to-quit requirements in the lease and the state laws regard-ing the landlord-tenant relationship. Texas requires a three-day notice to vacate the property before filing a Forcible Entry and Detainer. However, the Property Code does not use the term *notice to quit*.

■ LEASE AGREEMENTS

Most states require no special wording to establish the landlord-tenant relation-ship, but an agency disclosure may be required. For example, an agent represent-ing the landlord would have to disclose to a potential tenant that the agent is representing the landlord and has no responsibility to the tenant. The law of the state where the real estate is located must be followed to ensure the validity of the lease.

Requirements of a Valid Lease

A lease is a contract between the lessor (landlord) and the lessee (tenant). To be valid, a lease must meet the following requirements, which are essentially the same as in any other contract:

■ *Capacity to contract.* The parties must have the legal capacity to contract.
■ *Legal objectives.* The objectives of the lease must be legal.
■ *Offer and acceptance.* The parties must reach a mutual agreement on all the terms of the contract.
■ *Consideration.* The lease must be supported by valid consideration.

The leased premises should be clearly described. For most residential leases, the street address or the apartment number is usually sufficient. If supplemental space is part of the rental, it should be clearly identified. If the lease covers land, such as a ground lease, then a legal description should be used.

IN PRACTICE   Preprinted lease agreements are usually better suited to residential leases. Commercial leases are generally more complex, have different legal requirements, and may include complicated calculations of rent and mainte-nance costs. Drafting a commercial lease—or even a complex residential lease, for that matter—may constitute the practice of law. Unless the real estate licensee is also an attorney, legal counsel should be sought.

Possession and Use of Premises

The lessor, as the owner of the real estate, is usually bound by the "covenant of quiet enjoyment" that the lessee can occupy the premises without interference from the owner or anyone else. The lease usually stipulates the conditions under which the landlord may enter the property to perform maintenance, to make repairs, or for other stated purposes.

A lessor may restrict a lessee's use of the premises through provisions included in the lease, such as, "the property shall be used strictly as a residence and for no other purpose." Use restrictions are particularly common in leases for stores or commercial space. In the absence of such clear limitations, a lessee may use the premises for any lawful purpose.

Term of Lease

The term of a lease, the period for which the lease will run, should be stated precisely, including the beginning and ending dates together with a statement of the total period of the lease. For example, a lease might run "for a term of 10 years beginning June 1, 2015, and ending May 31, 2025."

Security Deposit

Tenants are often required to provide a **security deposit**, which is held by the landlord during the lease term. The security deposit is used if the tenant defaults on payment of rent or destroys the premises. State law may govern how security deposits are to be held, maximum amounts, whether interest must be paid, and how and when they are returned. In Texas, a security deposit must be returned or accounted for on or before the 30th day after the tenant surrenders the residential premises, or the 60th day for commercial premises. All or part of the deposit may be retained if no new address is given, or if money is owed and not disputed. It may not be used by the tenant for the last month's rent.

IN PRACTICE   A lease should specify whether a payment is a security deposit or an advance on rent. If it is a security deposit, the tenant may apply it to the final month's rent. Failure to return or properly account for the security deposit(s) may expose the agency (if they hold the deposit under a property management agreement) or the owner to treble damages for the amount unreasonably withheld, plus court costs and attorneys fees. The general rule is that the deposit may be offset by damage caused by the tenant, less normal wear and tear.

Improvements

Neither the landlord nor the tenant is required to make any improvements to the leased property. A tenant may make improvements with the landlord's permission, but any alterations usually become the property of the landlord. In commercial leases, tenants are permitted to install trade fixtures that are required to conduct their business. Trade fixtures may be removed before the lease expires, provided the tenant restores the premises to the previous condition.

Accessibility

The federal Fair Housing Act makes it illegal to discriminate against prospective tenants on the basis of physical disability. Tenants with disabilities must be permitted to make reasonable modifications to a property at their own expense. However, if the modifications would interfere with a future tenant's use, the landlord may require that the premises be restored to their original condition at the end of the lease term.

Maintenance of Premises

Most states require a lessor of residential property to maintain dwelling units in a habitable condition. Landlords must make any necessary repairs to common areas, such as hallways, stairs, and elevators, and maintain safety features, such as fire sprinklers and smoke alarms. The tenant must return the premises in the same condition they were received, with allowances for ordinary wear and tear.

Destruction of Premises

The obligation to pay rent for damaged or destroyed premises differs depending on the type of property and the lease. Tenants are not generally required to continue to pay rent after the leased premises are destroyed.

Assignment and Subleasing

When a tenant transfers all leasehold interests to another person, the lease has been assigned. The new tenant is legally obligated for all the promises the original tenant made in the lease.

When a tenant transfers some leasehold interests by leasing them to a new tenant, the original tenant has **subleased** (or sublet) the property. The original tenant remains responsible for rent being paid by the new tenant and for any damage done to the rental during the lease term. Assignment and subleasing should be in writing and are only allowed when a lease specifically permits them.

Options

Some leases grant the lessee the option to purchase the leased premises at a pre-determined price within a certain period. The lease might also contain a **right of first refusal** clause, allowing the tenant the opportunity to buy the property before the owner accepts an offer from another party.

IN PRACTICE   All the general statements concerning provisions of a lease are controlled largely by the terms of the agreement and state law. Landlord-tenant laws vary from state to state. Recent federal legislation requires a landlord to notify a tenant if the landlord is at risk of foreclosure on the property.

■ TYPES OF LEASES

The manner in which rent is determined indicates the type of lease that is put into effect. There are three basic types of leases: gross lease, net lease, and percentage lease (see Figure 3.4).

FIGURE 3.4

Types of Leases

Type of Lease	Lessee	Lessor
Gross lease	Pays basic rent	Pays property charges (taxes, repairs, insurance, etc.)
Net lease	Pays basic rent plus all or most property charges	May pay some property charges
Percentage lease (commercial and industrial)	Pays basic rent plus a percent of gross sales (may pay property costs)	Often pays property charges (taxes, repairs, insurance, etc.)

In a **gross lease**, the tenant pays a fixed rent, and the landlord pays all taxes, insurance, repairs, utilities, and maintenance connected with the property. Residential and commercial office leases are most often gross leases.

In a **net lease**, the tenant pays all or most of the property charges in addition to the rent. The monthly rental is net income for the landlord after operating costs have been paid. This lease is most often associated with large commercial and industrial leases.

Either a gross lease or a net lease may be a **percentage lease**. This type of lease is generally used for retail business leases. The rent is based on a minimum fixed rental fee plus a percentage of the gross income received by the tenant doing business on the leased property.

Other Types of Leases

Variable Lease   Some leases allow for increases in the rental charges during the lease periods. A graduated lease provides for specified rent increases at set future dates. Another is the index lease, which allows rent to be increased or decreased periodically based on changes in the consumer price index or some other indicator.

Ground Lease   When a landowner leases unimproved land to a tenant who agrees to erect a building on the land, the lease is usually called a **ground lease**. It is most often used in commercial property development. They often run for terms of 50 to 99 years.

Sandwich Lease   When a tenant subleases to a new tenant (sublessee), the original lease between the original tenant (who becomes the sublessor) and the landlord is called a sandwich lease.

Oil and Gas Lease   When an oil company leases land to explore for oil and gas, a special lease agreement must be negotiated with the landowner receiving a cash payment for executing the lease. If no well is drilled within the period stated in the lease, the lease expires. However, most **oil and gas leases** permit the oil company to continue its rights for another year by paying another flat rental fee. If oil or gas is found, the landowner usually receives a percentage of its value as a royalty. As long as oil or gas is obtained in significant quantities, the lease continues indefinitely.

Lease Purchase   A **lease purchase** is used when a tenant wants to purchase the property but is unable to do so at present. In this arrangement, the purchase agreement is the primary consideration, and the lease is secondary. Part of the periodic rent may be applied toward the purchase price at the time the property goes to settlement.

Executory Contract   An **executory contract**, for our purposes, is any contract for the sale of real estate which has unperformed obligations in excess of 180 days, on both sides, involving a personal residence. Any contract, such as a contract for deed, lease option, and the like, are subject to the rules contained in Section 5 of the Texas Property Code. A reading of the statutes will inspire the parties to comply with the spirit and letter of the act because failure to do so can and will result in severe penalties.

Sale and Leaseback   This is an arrangement whereby the owners and occupiers of property sell to an investor, lease it back, and maintain their occupancy. This technique is usually done in commercial transactions for two main reasons. The first is to raise capital for business operations, expansion, and/or to pay short-term debt. The second has to do with accounting, when a depreciated asset can be sold to bolster the net worth when required for various reasons.

■ DISCHARGE OF LEASES

As with any contract, a lease is discharged when the contract terminates. Termination can occur when all parties have fully performed their obligations under the agreement. In addition, the parties may agree to cancel the lease. A tenant who simply abandons leased property, however, remains liable for the terms of the lease—including the rent. The lease does not generally terminate if the parties die unless it is a lease from the owner of a life estate or is a tenancy at will. The heirs of a deceased landlord are bound by the terms of existing valid leases.

In general, if leased real estate is sold or otherwise conveyed, the new landlord takes the property subject to the rights of the tenants. A lease agreement may, however, contain language that permits a new landlord to terminate existing leases given proper notice. A tenancy may also be terminated by operation of law, as in a bankruptcy or condemnation proceeding.

■ OPTIONS

Options are used to give a buyer time to assess his ability or desire to proceed with a purchase. Option time and fees vary with the market conditions at the time of the contract. An option gives the buyer the right to proceed but not the obligation. On the other hand, it gives the seller an obligation to sell, but he cannot require the buyer to perform.

Residential   The most-used form is the TREC-promulgated One to Four Family Residential Contract (Resale). Paragraph 23 of the form provides the buyer an option for a stated fee and time period, which is generally $100 to $500 for 7 to 10 days. This period is most often used to give the buyer time to get a home inspection, negotiate repairs, and evaluate the purchase. If the buyer decides not to proceed, the buyer must affirmatively terminate the contract (there is a form for such purpose). The mere lapse of time does not automatically terminate the contract.

Commercial   The option period in commercial transactions is generally longer, usually from 30 to 90 days. If there are to be zoning changes, then the period would reflect the process that is required by the zoning authority. The amount of option fee varies depending upon market conditions, but generally is several thousand dollars.

Long Term   Options may be for any period and may involve initial option fees and possibly periodic option amounts. One to three years is not unusual in long-term options. These differ from first right of refusal in that they have a fixed purchase price, even if that price is based on an increase in price as time goes by. The most popular index for price variation is the Consumer Price Index (CPI).

Real estate can be sold under a **land contract**, also called a contract for deed, an installment contract, a land sales contract, or articles of agreement for warranty deed. Under a typical land contract, the seller (also called the vendor) retains legal title. The buyer (called the vendee) takes possession and gets equitable title to the property. The buyer agrees to give the seller a down payment and pay regular monthly installments of principal and interest over a number of years. The buyer also agrees to pay real estate taxes, insurance premiums, repairs, and upkeep on the property. Although the buyer obtains possession under the contract, the seller is not obligated to execute and deliver a deed to the buyer until the terms of the contract have been satisfied. This frequently occurs when the buyer has made enough payments to obtain a real estate loan and pay off the balance due on the contract.

■ SALES CONTRACTS

The real estate sales contract is the most important document in the sale of real estate. It establishes the legal rights and obligations of the buyer and the seller. Depending upon the area, the contract may be called an offer to purchase, a contract of purchase and sale, a purchase agreement, an earnest money agreement, or a deposit receipt. A detailed discussion of the components of a sales contract will be covered in Chapter 5.

■ SUMMARY

A contract is a voluntary, legally enforceable promise between two competent parties to perform (or not perform) some legal act in exchange for consideration.

A contract may be

- express or implied by conduct of parties,
- required to be in writing to be enforceable in a court of law,
- bilateral (having obligations on both sides) or unilateral (a promise by one side that can be accepted or rejected by the other side),
- executed (all parties have fulfilled their promises) or executory (one or both parties still have an act to perform),
- void if one of the essential elements is missing, or
- voidable if it may be rescinded or disaffirmed by one or both parties.

The essential elements of a valid contract are as follows:

- Agreement or promise based on an offer by one party (offeror) that is accepted by the other (offeree)
- Mutual assent or meeting of the minds
- Counteroffer that terminates the original offer and initiates a new offer
- Legally competent parties of legal age who are able to understand the nature or consequences of their actions
- Supported by legal consideration,
  — something of legal value, which could be love and affection, and
  — free of undue influence or fraud
- Concerned with a legal act
- Can be valid, void, or voidable, depending on circumstances
  — Valid—contains all legal elements
  — Void—not legal force or effect
  — Voidable—may be rescinded by either party

Contracts may be discharged (completed) by the following:

- Performance, which completes the contract terms
- Partial performance, if agreeable to both parties
- Substantial performance, depending on circumstances
- Impossibility of performance (required acts cannot be legally accomplished)
- Assignment (transfer of rights to assignee or delegation of duties)
- Novation (substitutes a new contract or party for the original)

- Breach by one of the parties without legal cause
  — Liquidated damages clause may specify the amount the seller will receive if the buyer defaults.
- Failure to enforce contract within statute of limitations
- Mutual agreement of parties
- Operation of law, as when a contract is void from inception
- Rescission (cancellation) by one or both parties

Real estate contracts may be completed by real estate licensees if preprinted, standard contract forms are used. Real estate licensees who are not licensed attorneys may not practice law.

Contracts used in the real estate business include

- listing and buyer agency agreements,
- real estate sales contracts,
- option,
- leases, and
- land contracts.

Types of listing agreements include

- exclusive right-to-sell—broker paid whoever sells property,
- exclusive agency—broker exclusive agent for seller,
- open listing—multiple brokers,
- multiple listing—shared information with other brokers, and
- net listing—broker retains all over net amount to seller.

A listing agreement may be terminated when

- the agreement's purpose is fulfilled,
- the agreement's term expires,
- the property is destroyed,
- title to the property is transferred by operation of law (e.g., bankruptcy),
- the broker and the seller mutually agree to end the listing,
- either party dies or becomes incapacitated, and
- either the broker or the seller breaches the contract.

Disclosures of agency relationships and property condition are important consumer safeguards and may be required by state law. The listing contract form covers many issues.

A buyer agency agreement is similar to a listing agreement with a seller because it establishes a relationship between broker and buyer. A buyer agent may be compensated by the buyer or through the transaction.

Lease contracts give right of possession to the tenant in return for rent. These can be estate for years, estate from period to period, estate at will, or estate at sufferance. Requirements for a valid lease are essentially the same as for a valid contract. Lease should cover possession and use of premises, terms of lease, security deposit, improvements, accessibility, maintenance, destruction, assignment, and subleasing.

Types of leases include gross, net, and percentage. Other variations are variable, ground, sandwich, oil and gas, and a lease-purchase. The lease is discharged when the contract terminates. If the landlord dies or the property is sold, the tenant's rights are still protected.

An option gives an optionee the right to buy or lease a property within a certain amount of time and is only enforceable by the optionee.

Under a land contract, the seller retains title to the property until full payment is made. There is no mortgage; the buyer makes installment payments over time.

The sales contract is the most important document in the sale of real estate.

CHAPTER 3 REVIEW QUESTIONS

1. The Texas Real Estate Commission does *NOT* promulgate a form for which of the following situations?
   a. A sale of a 10-unit apartment building
   b. A duplex
   c. A resale condominium
   d. A 10-acre ranch

2. A contract is said to be bilateral if
   a. one of the parties is a minor.
   b. the contract has yet to be fully performed.
   c. only one party to the agreement is bound to act.
   d. all parties to the contract exchange binding promises.

3. Texas Property Code 5.008 does *NOT* require a property disclosure statement for
   a. a duplex.
   b. a seller who is over 65 years old.
   c. a seller who has never lived in nor seen the property.
   d. any of these.

4. A contract for deed for a period of two years is considered
   a. illegal.
   b. an executory contract.
   c. voidable.
   d. a good idea for commercial properties only.

5. Under the statute of frauds, all contracts for the sale of real estate must be
   a. originated by a real estate broker.
   b. on preprinted forms.
   c. in writing to be enforceable.
   d. accompanied by earnest money deposits.

6. A buyer signs a contract under which he is given the right to purchase a property for $30,000 any time in the next three months. The buyer pays the current owner $500 at the time that contract is signed. Which of the following *BEST* describes this agreement?
   a. Contingency
   b. Option
   c. Installment
   d. Sales

7. A seller has listed a property under an exclusive-agency listing with a broker. If the seller finds a buyer, the seller will owe the broker
   a. no commission.
   b. the full commission.
   c. a partial commission.
   d. only reimbursement for the broker's costs.

8. *MOST* states require that listing agreements contain
   a. a multiple listing service (MLS) clause.
   b. a definite contract termination date.
   c. an automatic extension clause.
   d. a broker protection clause.

9. A tenant's tenancy for years will expire in two weeks. The tenant plans to move to a larger apartment across town when the current tenancy expires. In order to terminate this agreement, the tenant must
   a. give the landlord immediate notice or the lease will automatically renew.
   b. give the landlord one week's prior notice or the lease will automatically renew.
   c. do nothing, because the agreement will terminate automatically at the end of the current term.
   d. sign a lease for the new apartment, which will automatically terminate the existing lease.

10. A tenancy in which the tenant continues in possession after the lease has expired, without the landlord's permission, is a
    a. tenancy for years.
    b. periodic tenancy.
    c. tenancy at will.
    d. tenancy at sufferance.

CHAPTER 4

Ownership Rights and Limitations

- **identify** the limitations on ownership rights that are imposed by governmental powers;

- **define** each of the types of freehold estates and the rights and limitations each conveys;

- **distinguish** between an estate and an encumbrance;

- **describe** the types of encumbrances that may impact a sales contract;

- **explain** how tax liens, mechanics' liens, and mortgage liens are applied;

- **give** examples of different types of easements and how they are created and terminated;

- **explain** how an easement, an encroachment, and a license impact the use of real estate; and

- **discuss** the types of water rights: riparian, littoral, and doctrine of prior appropriation.

■ KEY TERMS

accretion	encumbrance	life estate
ad valorem tax	erosion	lis pendens
avulsion	escheat	littoral rights
condemnation	estate in land	mechanic's lien
covenants, conditions, and restrictions (CC&Rs)	fee simple	mortgage lien
	fee simple defeasible	police power
deed restrictions	fee simple determinable	prior appropriation
easement	fee simple subject to condition subsequent	pur autre vie
easement appurtenant		remainder interest
easement by necessity	freehold estate	reversionary interest
easement by prescription	future interest	riparian rights
easement in gross	homestead	tacking
eminent domain	leasehold estate	taxation
encroachment	license	water rights
	lien	

■ INTERESTS IN REAL ESTATE

Ownership of a parcel of real estate is not necessarily absolute; it is dependent on the type of interest a person holds in the property. Keep in mind that the power of landowners to control their property relates to the landowners having a title to the property and the bundle of legal rights that accompanies the title. Even the most complete ownership the law allows is limited by public and private restrictions. These restrictions are intended to ensure that one owner's use or enjoyment of his property does not interfere with others' use or enjoyment of their property or with the welfare of the public.

A sales contract does not necessarily refer to any of the limitations on ownership described in this chapter. Existing liens are often not known until a title search is done in preparation for closing. An existing easement or encroachment may create a cloud on the title that will have to be resolved to the buyer's satisfaction before settlement.

■ GOVERNMENTAL POWERS

Memory Tip

Four Government Powers

■ Police power
■ Eminent domain
■ Taxation
■ Escheat

Individual ownership rights are subject to certain powers, or rights, held by federal, state, and local governments. These limitations on the ownership of real estate are imposed for the general welfare of the community and, therefore, supersede the rights or interests of the individual. Governmental powers include police power, eminent domain, taxation, and escheat.

Police Power

Every state has the power to enact legislation to preserve order, protect the public health and safety, and promote the general welfare of its citizens. That authority is called a state's **police power**. The state's authority is passed on to municipalities and counties through legislation called enabling acts. What is identified as being in the public interest can vary considerably from state to state and region to region. For example, a police power is used to enact environmental protection laws, zoning ordinances, and building codes. Regulations that govern the use, occupancy, size, location, and construction of real estate also fall within the police powers.

Eminent Domain

Eminent domain is the government's right to acquire private property for public use; condemnation is the actual process of taking property.

Eminent domain is the right of the government to acquire privately owned real estate for public use. **Condemnation** is the process by which the government exercises this right, by either judicial or administrative proceedings. In the taking of property, just compensation is to be paid to the owner, and the rights of the property owner are to be protected by due process of law. Ideally, the public agency and the owner of the property in question agree on compensation through direct negotiation, and the government purchases the property for a price considered fair by the owner.

Taxation

Taxation is a charge on real estate to raise funds to meet the public needs of a government. Taxes on real estate include annual real estate taxes assessed by governmental entities, including school districts; taxes on income realized by individuals and corporations on the sale of property; and special fees that may be levied for special projects. Nonpayment of taxes may give government the power to claim an interest in the property.

Escheat

Escheat (revert) is a process by which the state may acquire privately owned real or personal property. State laws provide for ownership to transfer, or **escheat**, to the state when an owner dies and leaves no heirs (as defined by the law) and there is no will or living trust instrument that directs how the real estate is to be distributed. In some states, real property escheats to the county where the land is located; in other states, it becomes the property of the state. Escheat is intended to prevent property from being ownerless or abandoned.

■ ESTATES IN LAND

Estates are an ownership interest and are transferred using a deed.

An **estate in land** defines the degree, quantity, nature, and extent of an owner's interest in real property. Many types of estates exist, but not all interests in real estate are estates. To be an estate in land, an interest must allow possession, meaning the holding and enjoyment of the property either now or in the future, and must be measured according to time. Historically, estates in land have been classified primarily by their length of time of possession.

Freehold estates last for an indeterminable length of time, such as for a lifetime or forever. A freehold estate continues for an indefinite period and may be passed along to the owner's heirs. A life estate is based on the lifetime of a person and ends when that individual dies. There are various types of freehold estates, which are illustrated in Figure 4.1. Non-freehold estates are those for which the length of time can be determined. These are called **leasehold estates**.

FIGURE 4.1

Freehold Estates

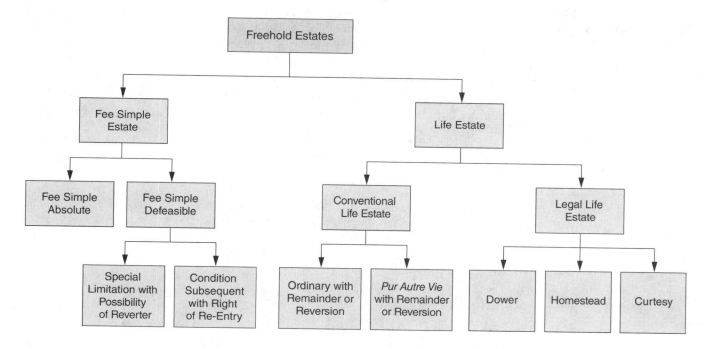

The type of freehold estate held by the seller does not usually present a problem for a potential purchaser but the following descriptions provide useful background information. A seller holding less than a fee simple estate may make conveyance of the title a problem that will require legal assistance.

Fee Simple Estate

A **fee simple** estate, or fee simple absolute, is the highest interest in real estate recognized by law. Fee simple ownership is ownership in which the holder is entitled to all rights to the property by law. This estate is intended to run forever; upon the death of its owner, it passes to the owner's heirs. It is limited only by public and private restrictions, such as zoning laws and restrictive covenants.

A **fee simple defeasible** estate is a qualified fee estate that is subject to the occurrence or nonoccurrence of some specified event. Two categories of defeasible estates exist: fee simple determinable and fee simple subject to a condition subsequent.

Fee Simple Determinable

- "So long as"
- "While"
- "During"

A **fee simple determinable** is a fee simple defeasible estate that may be inherited. This estate is qualified by a special limitation (which is an occurrence or event). The language used to distinguish a special limitation—words such as *so long as*, *while*, or *during*—is the key to creating this special limitation. The former owner retains a possibility of reverter. If the limitation is violated, the former owner (or heirs or successors) can reacquire full ownership with no need to go to the court. The deed is automatically returned to the former owner.

■ **FOR EXAMPLE**   When an owner gives land to a church, so long as the land is used for only religious purposes, it is called a fee simple determinable. The church has the full bundle of rights possessed by any property owner, but one of the "sticks" in the bundle is a control "stick." In this case, if the church ever decides to use the land for a nonreligious purpose, the original owner has the right to reacquire the land without going to court.

A **fee simple subject to a condition subsequent**, the second type of fee simple defeasible estate, is similar to a fee simple determinable in that an owner gives real estate on condition of ownership, but it differs in the way the estate will terminate if there is a violation to the condition. In fee simple determinable, the property reverts immediately to the original owner upon violation of the limitation. In fee simple subject to a condition subsequent, the estate does not automatically terminate upon violation of the condition of ownership. The owner has the right of reentry but must go through the court to assert this right.

The right of entry and possibility for reverter may never take effect. If they do, it will only be at some time in the future. Therefore, each of these rights is considered a **future interest**.

■ **FOR EXAMPLE**   Land given on the condition that there be no consumption of alcohol on the premises is a fee simple subject to a condition subsequent. If alcohol is consumed on the property, the former owner has the right to reacquire full ownership. It will be necessary for the former owner (or the heirs or successors) to go to court to assert that right.

Life Estate

A **life estate** is a freehold estate limited in duration to the life of the owner or the life of some other designated person or persons. Unlike other freehold estates, a life estate is not inheritable. It passes to future owners according to the provisions of the life estate.

A life tenant is not a renter like a tenant associated with a lease. A life tenant is entitled to the rights of ownership and can benefit from possession and ordinary use, as well as profits arising from ownership, just as if the individual were a fee simple owner. The life tenant's ownership may be sold, mortgaged, or leased, but it is always subject to the limitation of the life estate.

Pur Autre Vie   A life estate may also be based on the lifetime of a person other than the life tenant. Although a life estate is not considered an estate of inheritance, a life estate **pur autre vie** (for the life of another) provides for inheritance by the life tenant's heirs only until the death of the third party. A life estate pur autre vie is often created for people who are physically or mentally incapacitated in the hope of providing incentive for someone to care for them.

Remainder and Reversion   The fee simple owner who creates a life estate must plan for its future ownership. When the life estate ends, it is replaced by a fee simple estate. The future owner of the fee simple estate may be designated in one of two ways:

1. *Remainder interest*. The creator of the life estate may name a remainderman as the person to whom the property will pass when the life estate ends.
2. *Reversionary interest*. The creator of the life estate may choose not to name a remainderman. In that case, ownership is said to revert to the original owner upon the end of the life estate.

Legal Life Estate   A legal life estate is not created voluntarily by an owner. Rather, it is a form of life estate established by state law. It becomes effective automatically when certain events occur. Dower, curtesy, and homestead are the legal life estates currently used in some states. Community property states (like Texas) do not use dower and curtesy.

■ HOMESTEAD IN TEXAS

Under Texas **homestead** laws, a family or single person cannot be forced out of their home as a result of creditor claims. The one exception to this claim is a pre-existing real estate loan or mechanic's lien, which can foreclose for defaults and nonpayment. There is no limit on the amount of equity that is protected. If a homestead sits on less than 10 acres in an urban setting, then it is protected. In a rural situation, 200 acres and 100 acres are covered for a family and a single person, respectively.

Establishing a Texas homestead does not require any formal filing. One need only occupy exclusively to establish the deed. A family with a vacation home worth much more than their city home, wishing to claim the vacation home as their homestead, may have a problem. Weekend or occasional use (such as in the case of a vacation home) may not be enough to qualify if challenged by a creditor. In this situation, the family might have the urban home with little or no equity, with the lake house free and clear. In case of potential anticipated financial difficulties, a family would rearrange its finances accordingly. Even in this situation, despite some manipulation in the finances, the courts have applied the homestead laws liberally.

Refinancing the homestead may be done provided there is no "cash out" in homes with less than 20% equity. Texas is the only state that only allows combined loan to value (CLTV) up to 80%. If the home is worth $150,000, there is an existing loan of $75,000, and the owner wants to get a home equity line of credit (HELOC), the owner can only borrow the difference between 80% of value ($120,000), less the existing loan ($75,000)—$45,000.

Selling a homestead may be done without fear of judgment creditors being awarded the equity because the law allows the family or single person up to six months to find a replacement homestead.

■ ENCUMBRANCES

Physical Encumbrances
- Restrictions
- Easements
- Licenses

An **encumbrance** is a claim, charge, or liability that attaches to real estate. An encumbrance is not an estate, so it does not allow possession. An encumbrance may decrease the value or obstruct the use of the property. In essence, an encumbrance is a right or an interest held by someone other than the property owner that affects title to the real estate but does not necessarily prevent a transfer of title.

Liens

A **lien** is an encumbrance that is usually a monetary charge against property that provides security for a debt. If the obligation is not repaid, the lienholder is entitled to have the debt satisfied from the proceeds of a court-ordered sale of the debtor's property. Real estate taxes, mortgages, and mechanics' liens all represent possible liens against an owner's real estate.

A lien may be voluntary (mortgage debt) or involuntary (tax lien created by statute). Because a lien attaches to the property and would be binding to a new owner, the value of a property could be reduced. Real estate taxes and special assessments generally take priority over other types of liens. Otherwise, the priority of liens is set by state law.

Tax Lien   A general real estate tax is an **ad valorem tax** (Latin for *according to value*) charged by various government agencies and municipalities. Most state laws exempt properties such as schools, parks, houses of worship, hospitals, and government buildings. The percentage of value used for assessment of property and the tax rate applied varies from one locality to another. An outstanding tax lien would be paid first from the proceeds of a court-ordered sale of a property.

Mortgage Lien   A **mortgage lien** (or deed of trust lien in some states) is a voluntary lien given to a lender by a borrower as security for a real estate loan. Lenders generally require that the mortgage lien take first priority (except for a real estate tax lien).

Mechanic's Lien   A **mechanic's lien** is an involuntary lien that provides security for a person or company that has not been fully paid for labor performed or material furnished to improve real property. State law regarding the filing and priority of mechanics' liens varies from state to state. In many states, the sales contract must include cautionary language regarding the possibility of existing mechanic's liens.

Lis Pendens   When any suit affecting the title to real estate is filed, a special notice, knows as a **lis pendens** (Latin for *litigation pending*) is recorded. This notifies potential purchasers and lenders that there is a possible future lien on the property.

Deed Restrictions

Deed restrictions are private restrictions that affect the use of the land. Once placed in the deed by a previous owner, they "run with the land," limiting the use of the property and binding to all grantees.

Covenants, conditions, and restrictions (CC&Rs) are private agreements that affect land use. They may be enforced by an owner of real estate and included in the seller's deed to the buyer. Typically, however, restrictive covenants are imposed by a developer or subdivider to maintain specific standards in a subdivision. Such restrictive covenants are listed in the original development plans for the subdivision filed in the public record. Disclosure of CC&Rs is normally required for all condominium projects.

Easements

An **easement** is the right to use the land of another for a particular purpose. It may exist in any portion of the real estate, including the airspace above or a right-of-way across the land.

An **easement appurtenant** is attached to the ownership of one parcel and allows this owner the use of a neighbor's land. For an easement appurtenant to exist, two adjacent parcels of land must be owned by two different parties. The parcel over which the easement runs is called the servient tenement; the neighboring parcel that benefits is called the dominant tenement (see Figure 4.2).

FIGURE 4.2

Easement Appurtenant

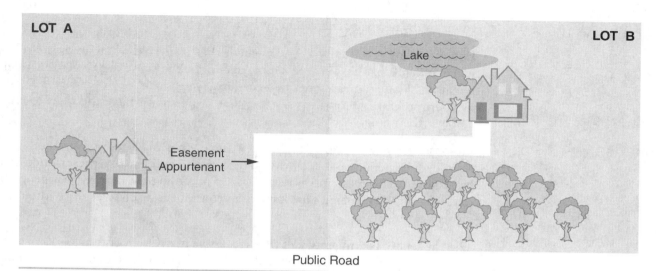

The owner of Lot B has an easement appurtenant across Lot A to gain access to his property from the public road. Lot B is dominant, and Lot A is servient.

This type of easement is an encumbrance on property and will transfer with the deed of the dominant tenement forever unless released legally.

An **easement in gross** is an individual or company interest in, or right to use, someone else's land (see Figure 4.3). A railroad's right-of-way is an easement in gross, as are the rights-of-way of utility easements.

FIGURE 4.3

Easement in Gross

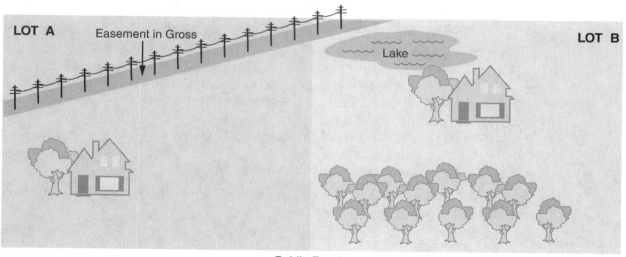

The utility company has an easement in gross across both parcels of land for its power lines.

Creating an Easement   An easement is created by a written agreement between the parties that establishes the easement right. The creation of an easement always involves two separate parties, one of whom is the owner of the land over which the easement runs. Two other ways for an easement to be created are easement by necessity and easement by prescription.

Easement by Necessity   An easement that is created when an owner sells a parcel of land that has no access to a street or public way except over the seller's remaining land is an **easement by necessity**. An easement by necessity is created by court order, based on the principle that owners must have the right to enter and exit their land.

Easement by Prescription   If the claimant has made use of another's land for a certain period as defined by state law, an **easement by prescription** may be acquired. The prescriptive period varies according to state law but generally requires that the claimant's use have been continuous, exclusive, and without the owner's permission.

The concept of **tacking** provides that successive periods of continuous occupation by different parties may be combined (tacked) to reach the required total number of years necessary to establish a claim for a prescriptive easement.

■ **FOR EXAMPLE**   A property is located in a state with a prescriptive period of 20 years. For the past 22 years, a neighbor has driven across the property's front yard several times a day to reach the neighbor's garage from a more comfortable angle. The neighbor has an easement by prescription.

For 25 years, another neighbor has driven across this same front yard two or three times a year to reach that neighbor's property when in a hurry. This neighbor does not have an easement by prescription because the use was not continuous.

For 15 years, the next-door neighbor parked a car on the same property, next to the garage. Six years ago, this neighbor sold the house to a person who continued to park a car next to garage. Last year, the new neighbor acquired an easement by prescription through tacking.

Terminating an Easement   An easement terminates

■ when the need no longer exists,
■ when the owner of either the dominant or the servient tenement becomes sole owner and the properties are merged under one legal description,
■ by the release of the right of easement to the owner of the servient tenement,
■ by the abandonment of the easement (the intention of the parties is the determining factor), or
■ by the nonuse of a prescriptive easement.

Note that an easement may not automatically terminate for these reasons. Certain legal steps may be required.

Licenses

A **license** is a personal privilege to enter the land of another for a specific purpose. A license differs from an easement in that it can be terminated or canceled. A license ends with the death of either party or with the sale of the land.

Encroachments

When a building, fence, or driveway illegally extends beyond the land of its owner or legal building lines, an **encroachment** occurs. An encroachment is usually disclosed by either a physical inspection of the property or a spot survey. If a building encroaches on adjoining land, the neighbor may be able to either recover damages or secure removal of the portion of the building that encroaches.

■ WATER RIGHTS

Whether for agricultural, recreational, or other purposes, waterfront real estate has always been desirable. Each state has strict laws that govern the ownership and use of water as well as the adjacent land. The laws vary among the states, but all are closely linked to climactic and topographical conditions. Where water is plentiful, states may rely on the simple parameters set by the common-law doctrines of riparian and littoral rights. Where water is scarce, a state may control all but limited domestic use of water, according to the doctrine of prior appropriation.

Riparian Rights

Riparian rights are common-law rights granted to owners of land along the course of a river, stream, or similar body of water. Although riparian rights are governed by laws that vary from state to state, they generally include the unrestricted right to use the water. As a rule, the only limitation on the owner's use is that such use cannot interrupt or alter the flow of the water or contaminate it in any way. In addition, an owner of land that borders a non-navigable waterway, (i.e., a body of water unsuitable for commercial boat traffic) owns the land under the water to the exact center of the waterway. Land adjoining commercially navigable rivers, on the other hand, is usually owned to the water's edge, with the state holding title to the submerged land (see Figure 4.4).

FIGURE 4.4

Riparian Rights

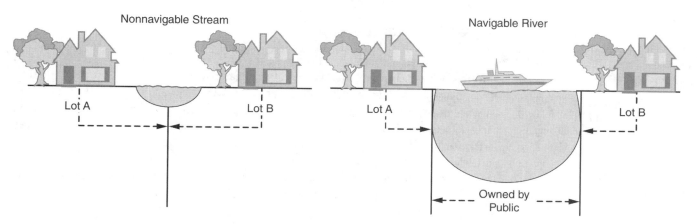

Littoral Rights

Closely related to riparian rights are the **littoral rights** of owners whose land borders commercially navigable lakes, seas, and oceans. Owners with littoral rights enjoy unrestricted use of available waters but own the land adjacent to the water only up to the average high-water mark. All land below this point is owned by the government.

Accretion, Erosion, and Avulsion

The amount of land an individual owns may be affected by the natural action of water. An owner is entitled to all land created through **accretion**—increases in the land resulting from the deposit of soil by the water's action.

On the other hand, an owner may lose land through erosion. **Erosion** is the gradual and imperceptible wearing away of the land by natural forces, such as wind, rain, and flowing water. Fortunately, erosion usually takes hundreds or even thousands of years to have any noticeable effect on a person's property. Flash floods or heavy winds, however, can increase the speed of erosion.

Avulsion is the sudden removal of soil by an act of nature. It is an event that causes the loss of land much less subtly than erosion. An earthquake or a mudslide, for example, can cause an individual's landholding to become much smaller very quickly.

Doctrine of Prior Appropriation

In states where water is scarce, ownership and use of water are often determined by the doctrine of **prior appropriation**. Under this doctrine, the right to use any water, with the exception of limited domestic use, is controlled by the state rather than by the landowner adjacent to the water.

To secure water rights in prior appropriation states, a landowner must demonstrate to a state agency that the owner's plans are for beneficial use, such as crop irrigation. If the state's requirements are met, the landowner receives a permit to use a specified amount of water for the limited purpose of the beneficial use. Although statutes governing prior appropriation vary from state to state, the priority of water rights is usually determined by the oldest recorded permit date.

Under some state laws, once granted, **water rights** attach to the land of the permit holder. The permit holder may sell a water right to another party. Issuance of a water permit does not grant access to the water source. All access rights-of-way over the land of another (easements) must be obtained from the property owner.

Mineral Rights

Texas is known for its rich treasures of oil and gas, with more than 1,294 oil fields alone. With billions of dollars of oil and gas royalties at stake, property owners are possessive about their mineral rights. However, so are buyers, and real estate agents must not only negotiate the property and minerals, but paper it according to the wishes of the parties. For a simple transaction where the seller is simply insisting on reserving some or all of the minerals, there is a promulgated form entitled Addendum for Reservation of Oil, Gas and Other Minerals. For more complex reservation, and when the minerals have been leased, real estate agents should advise the parties to seek competent legal counsel.

When real estate agents represent properties outside of city limits and in areas where there is oil and gas drilling activity and leases are in place, they must be cautious about the surface rights of the lease holders.

As in all transactions, agents must not undertake any assignment that they are not fully qualified and trained to do and without the approval of their broker or manager.

■ ENVIRONMENTAL ISSUES

Real estate agents must focus on contamination in and on properties. Additionally, agents are now required to understand the energy efficiency attributes of the properties that they are involved in selling and listing (see Figure 4.5).

FIGURE 4.5

Environmental Hazards

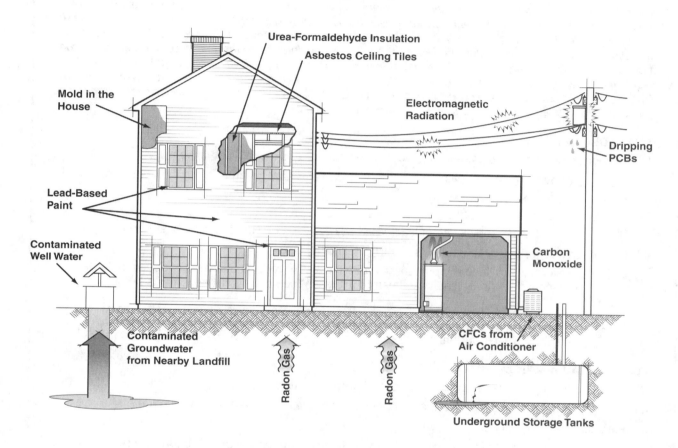

Residential Issues

Lead   If the home was built before 1978, a Disclosure of Information on Lead-Based Paint and/or Lead-Based Paint Hazards (see Figure 4.6) and the EPA pamphlet *Protect Your Family from Lead In Your Home* must be provided to prospective buyers and renters by the seller or landlord. The law now requires contractors to observe certain protocols when performing repairs, remodeling, and painting in homes, child-care facilities, and pre-schools. To learn more, visit http://www2.epa.gov/lead/.

FIGURE 4.6

Disclosure of Information on Lead-Based Paint and/or Lead-Based Paint Hazard

---

Disclosure of Information on Lead-Based Paint and/or Lead-Based Paint Hazards

Lead Warning Statement

Every purchaser of any interest in residential real property on which a residential dwelling was built prior to 1978 is notified that such property may present exposure to lead from lead-based paint that may place young children at risk of developing lead poisoning. Lead poisoning in young children may produce permanent neurological damage, including learning disabilities, reduced intelligence quotient, behavioral problems, and impaired memory. Lead poisoning also poses a particular risk to pregnant women. The seller of any interest in residential real property is required to provide the buyer with any information on lead-based paint hazards from risk assessments or inspections in the seller's possession and notify the buyer of any known lead-based paint hazards. A risk assessment or inspection for possible lead-based paint hazards is recommended prior to purchase.

Seller's Disclosure

(a) Presence of lead-based paint and/or lead-based paint hazards (check (i) or (ii) below):

    (i) _____ Known lead-based paint and/or lead-based paint hazards are present in the housing (explain).

    _____

    (ii) _____ Seller has no knowledge of lead-based paint and/or lead-based paint hazards in the housing.

(b) Records and reports available to the seller (check (i) or (ii) below):

    (i) _____ Seller has provided the purchaser with all available records and reports pertaining to lead-based paint and/or lead-based paint hazards in the housing (list documents below).

    _____

    (ii) _____ Seller has no reports or records pertaining to lead-based paint and/or lead-based paint hazards in the housing.

Purchaser's Acknowledgment (initial)

(c) _____ Purchaser has received copies of all information listed above.

(d) _____ Purchaser has received the pamphlet *Protect Your Family from Lead in Your Home.*

(e) Purchaser has (check (i) or (ii) below):

    (i) _____ received a 10-day opportunity (or mutually agreed upon period) to conduct a risk assessment or inspection for the presence of lead-based paint and/or lead-based paint hazards; or

    (ii) _____ waived the opportunity to conduct a risk assessment or inspection for the presence of lead-based paint and/or lead-based paint hazards.

Agent's Acknowledgment (initial)

(f) _____ Agent has informed the seller of the seller's obligations under 42 U.S.C. 4852(d) and is aware of his/her responsibility to ensure compliance.

Certification of Accuracy

The following parties have reviewed the information above and certify, to the best of their knowledge, that the information they have provided is true and accurate.

Seller	Date	Seller	Date
Purchaser	Date	Purchaser	Date
Agent	Date	Agent	Date

Indoor Air Quality (IAQ)   Many homeowners are purchasing better furnace filters and are changing them in the recommended time. This results in cost savings and increased comfort. Many utility companies in Texas will perform an inspection and energy audit at little or no cost to insure the best possible IAQ.

Understanding efficiency is also important. Where cooling is concerned, seasonal energy efficiency ratio (SEER) should be considered, balancing cost with energy savings. Where heating is concerned, the annual fuel utilization efficiency (AFUE) should be considered.

Commercial Issues

Many lenders of commercial properties require a Phase I environmental site assessment. This assessment involves a visual inspection of the property along with determining the historical use of the property. If the property is next to an old gas station, then the subject property may be suspect. If the property shows any signs of contamination, then a Phase II assessment will be required. This assessment involves soil samples and analysis to determine the significance of the contamination. If the contamination is toxic, then a Phase III assessment may be necessary, involving remediation.

■ SUMMARY

Governmental powers can be recalled by using the acronym *PETE*:

■ Police power is the state's authority—passed down to municipalities and counties through enabling acts—to enact nondiscriminatory legislation to
  — preserve order,
  — protect the public health and safety, and
  — promote the general welfare of citizens.
■ Eminent domain is the government's right to acquire privately owned real estate for a public or economically beneficial use through
  — condemnation, a process that begins with a judicial or an administrative proceeding, or
  — just compensation, which must be paid to the property owner.
■ Taxation is a charge on real estate to raise funds to meet public needs.
■ Escheat occurs when the deceased has no will or lawful heirs.

A freehold estate lasts for an indeterminable length of time:

■ Fee simple is the highest estate recognized by law.
■ Fee simple defeasible is a qualified estate subject to occurrence or nonoccurrence of some specified event.
■ Life estate is based on the lifetime of a person.

An encumbrance is a claim, charge, or liability that attaches to real estate. There are numerous types of encumbrances:

■ A monetary encumbrance is a lien. Liens are charges against property that provide security for a debt or obligation of the property owner. Specific liens include
  — Tax lien—based on ad valorem tax,
  — Mortgage lien—provides security for real estate loan, and
  — Mechanic's lien—provides security for company not paid for services or supplies

- Covenants, conditions, and restrictions (CC&Rs) are private agreements that affect the use of land.
- Easements are rights to use the land of another:
  - An appurtenant easement is said to run with the land when title is transferred.
  - An easement in gross is an individual or company interest in or right to use another's land.
  - An easement by necessity arises when land has no access to a street or public way.
  - An easement by prescription is acquired when a claimant has used another's land for 10 to 21 years. The use must be visible, open, and notorious.
  - An easement is usually created by written agreement between the parties.

An easement is terminated

- when the need no longer exists,
- when the owner of either the dominant or the servient tenement becomes the sole owner,
- when the owner of a servient tenement releases the right of easement,
- if the easement is abandoned, or
- by the nonuse of prescriptive easement.

License is a personal privilege to enter the land of another for a specific purpose.

Encroachment occurs when all or part of a structure illegally intrudes on the land of another or beyond legal building lines.

Water rights are determined by common law and statute:

- Riparian rights are common-law rights granted to owners of land along rivers, streams, or similar bodies of water.
- Littoral rights belong to owners of land that borders commercially navigable lakes, seas, and oceans.
- The doctrine of prior appropriation in some states provides that water use, aside from limited domestic use, is controlled by the state rather than the landowner adjacent to the water; to use the water, the landowner must demonstrate beneficial use of the water, such as irrigation of crops.

Environmental issues are as follows:

- Federal or state law may require certain environmental disclosure.
- Potential buyers may make contracts contingent on inspection for various hazardous substances.

CHAPTER 4 REVIEW QUESTIONS

1. A purchaser of real estate learns that his owner-ship rights could continue forever and that no other person can claim to be the owner or have any ownership control over the property. This person owns a
   a. fee simple interest.
   b. life estate.
   c. determinable fee.
   d. condition subsequent.

2. A person owned the fee simple title to a vacant lot adjacent to a hospital and was persuaded to make a gift of the lot. She wanted to have some control over its use, so her attorney prepared her a deed to convey ownership of the lot to the hospital "so long as it is used for hospital pur-poses." After completion of the gift, the hospital will own a
   a. fee simple absolute estate.
   b. license.
   c. fee simple determinable.
   d. leasehold estate.

3. Which of the following is NOT an example of governmental power?
   a. Dedication
   b. Police power
   c. Eminent domain
   d. Taxation

4. Which of the following is a legal life estate?
   a. Leasehold
   b. Fee simple absolute
   c. Homestead
   d. Determinable fee

5. An owner conveys ownership of her residence to her church but reserves for herself a life estate in the residence. The future interest held by the church is a
   a. pur autre vie.
   b. remainder.
   c. reversion.
   d. leasehold.

6. A homeowner may be allowed certain protec-tion from judgments of creditors as a result of the state's
   a. littoral rights.
   b. curtesy rights.
   c. homestead rights.
   d. dower rights.

7. The type of easement that is a right-of-way for a utility company's power lines is
   a. an easement in gross.
   b. an easement by necessity.
   c. an easement by prescription.
   d. a nonassignable easement.

8. A landowner has divided much of his land into smaller parcels and has recently sold a tract near a nature preserve that is landlocked and can-not be entered except through one of the other tracts. The buyer of that property will prob-ably be granted what type of easement by court action?
   a. Easement by necessity
   b. Easement in gross
   c. Easement by prescription
   d. Easement by condemnation

9. The highest interest a person may have in real estate is
   a. fee simple absolute.
   b. a life estate.
   c. determinable fee.
   d. estate for years.

10. A Phase I environmental site assessment is generally associated with
    a. remediation of lead-based paint in 1–4 fam-ily homes.
    b. the rules for remodeling any dwelling that houses or teaches children.
    c. a commercial property purchase.
    d. the process a developer must undergo before lots and/or houses may be sold.

CHAPTER 5

The Sales Contract

■ **LEARNING OBJECTIVES** *When you have completed this chapter, you will able to*

- ■ **list** the details included in a sales contract;
- ■ **describe** the process of offer and acceptance of a sales contract;
- ■ **explain** the process involved in making a counteroffer;
- ■ **define** statute of frauds and parole evidence and their use;
- ■ **identify** types of personal and financial information that may be included in the sales contract;
- ■ **describe** the three methods that are used for a legal description of property;
- ■ **discuss** the financing information that should be included in a contract;
- ■ **review** the purpose and disposition of an earnest money deposit; and
- ■ **discuss** the ramifications of default or breach of contract.

■ KEY TERMS

acceptance	liquidated damages	school section
base line	lot and block	section
commingling	metes and bounds	subdivision plat
contract of sale	monument	suit for specific
counteroffer	offer to purchase	performance
cross-hatch	plat map	survey
disclosure	point of beginning (POB)	tort
earnest money	preapproval letter	township
equitable title	principal meridian	township line
legal description	range	township tier
letter of intent (LOI)	rectangular survey system	

■ INTRODUCTION

A real estate sales contract contains the complete agreement between a buyer of a parcel of real estate and the seller. It is an offer to purchase real estate as soon as it has been prepared and signed by the purchaser. Depending on the state or locality, this agreement may be called an *offer to purchase, contract of purchase and sale, earnest money agreement, deposit receipt,* or other variations of these terms. While there are different contracts depending on the type of sale, the sales contract used most often in Texas is published by the Texas Real Estate Commission (TREC) and is called the One to Four Family Residential Contract (Resale) (see Figure 5.1). Whatever the document is called, when it has been prepared and signed by the purchaser, it is an offer to purchase the subject real estate. Both the public and licensees often refer to this offer to purchase as a "contract," but only after the document is accepted and signed by the seller, does it become a **contract of sale**, or sales contract.

The contract of sale is the most important document in the sale of real estate because it sets out in detail the agreement between the buyer and the seller and establishes the legal rights and obligations of both parties.

In addition to the essential elements required for any contract, details that typically appear in contracts for the purchase of property include

■ the sales price and terms;
■ a legal description of the land;
■ a statement of the kind and condition of the title and the form of deed to be delivered by the seller;
■ the kind of title evidence required, who will provide it, and how many defects in the title will be eliminated;
■ a statement of all the terms and conditions of the agreement between the parties; and
■ any contingencies.

■ THE PROCESS

Offer and Acceptance

Offer   A broker lists an owner's real estate for sale at whatever price and conditions the owner sets. When a prospective buyer is found, the buyer's agent helps that consumer prepare an **offer to purchase**. The offer is signed by the prospective buyer and presented by the listing broker to the seller. In states that allow dual agency, the same agent may represent both parties, both in preparing the offer to purchase and in making the presentation to the seller. Traditionally the listing broker makes all presentations to the seller, but on some occasions a buyer's agent may be permitted to make the presentation.

FIGURE 5.1

One to Four Family Residential Contract (Resale)

4-28-2014

PROMULGATED BY THE TEXAS REAL ESTATE COMMISSION (TREC)
ONE TO FOUR FAMILY RESIDENTIAL CONTRACT (RESALE)
NOTICE: Not For Use For Condominium Transactions

1. PARTIES: The parties to this contract are _____
(Seller) and _____(Buyer).
Seller agrees to sell and convey to Buyer and Buyer agrees to buy from Seller the Property defined
below.

2. PROPERTY: The land, improvements and accessories are collectively referred to as the "Property".
  A. LAND: Lot _____ Block_____, _____
    Addition, City of _____ , County of _____,
    Texas, known as _____
    (address/zip code), or as described on attached exhibit.
  B. IMPROVEMENTS: The house, garage and all other fixtures and improvements attached to the
    above-described real property, including without limitation, the following **permanently installed
    and built-in items,** if any: all equipment and appliances, valances, screens, shutters, awnings,
    wall-to-wall carpeting, mirrors, ceiling fans, attic fans, mail boxes, television antennas, mounts
    and brackets for televisions and speakers, heating and air-conditioning units, security and fire
    detection equipment, wiring, plumbing and lighting fixtures, chandeliers, water softener system,
    kitchen equipment, garage door openers, cleaning equipment, shrubbery, landscaping, outdoor
    cooking equipment, and all other property owned by Seller and attached to the above described
    real property.
  C. ACCESSORIES: The following described related accessories, if any: window air conditioning units,
    stove, fireplace screens, curtains and rods, blinds, window shades, draperies and rods, door keys,
    mailbox keys, above ground pool, swimming pool equipment and maintenance accessories,
    artificial fireplace logs, and controls for: (i) garage doors, (ii) entry gates, and (iii) other
    improvements and accessories.
  D. EXCLUSIONS: The following improvements and accessories will be retained by Seller and must
    be removed prior to delivery of possession:_____
    _____.

3. SALES PRICE:
  A. Cash portion of Sales Price payable by Buyer at closing .... $_____
  B. Sum of all financing described below (excluding any loan funding
    fee or mortgage insurance premium) .... $_____
  C. Sales Price (Sum of A and B).. $_____

4. FINANCING (Not for use with reverse mortgage financing): The portion of Sales Price not
payable in cash will be paid as follows: (Check applicable boxes below)
❑ A.THIRD PARTY FINANCING: One or more third party mortgage loans in the total amount of
    $_____ (excluding any loan funding fee or mortgage insurance premium).
  (1) Property Approval: If the Property does not satisfy the lenders' underwriting requirements for
    the loan(s) (including, but not limited to appraisal, insurability and lender required repairs),
    Buyer may terminate this contract by giving notice to Seller prior to closing and the earnest
    money will be refunded to Buyer.
  (2) Credit Approval: (Check one box only)
  ❑ (a) This contract is subject to Buyer being approved for the financing described in the attached
    Third Party Financing Addendum for Credit Approval.
  ❑ (b) This contract is not subject to Buyer being approved for financing and does not involve FHA
    or VA financing.
❑ B. ASSUMPTION: The assumption of the unpaid principal balance of one or more promissory notes
    described in the attached TREC Loan Assumption Addendum.
❑ C. SELLER FINANCING: A promissory note from Buyer to Seller of $_____, secured by
    vendor's and deed of trust liens, and containing the terms and conditions described in the attached
    TREC Seller Financing Addendum. If an owner policy of title insurance is furnished, Buyer shall
    furnish Seller with a mortgagee policy of title insurance.

Initialed for identification by Buyer_____ _____ and Seller _____ _____   TREC NO. 20-12

F I G U R E   5.1

One to Four Family Residential Contract (Resale) (Continued)

Contract Concerning _____ Page 2 of 9   4-28-2014
                                                (Address of Property)

5. EARNEST MONEY: Upon execution of this contract by all parties, Buyer shall deposit $_____ as earnest money with _____, as escrow agent, at _____ (address). Buyer shall deposit additional earnest money of $_____ with escrow agent within _____days after the effective date of this contract. If Buyer fails to deposit the earnest money as required by this contract, Buyer will be in default.

6. TITLE POLICY AND SURVEY:

A. TITLE POLICY: Seller shall furnish to Buyer at ❑ Seller's ❑ Buyer's expense an owner policy of title insurance (Title Policy) issued by _____ (Title Company) in the amount of the Sales Price, dated at or after closing, insuring Buyer against loss under the provisions of the Title Policy, subject to the promulgated exclusions (including existing building and zoning ordinances) and the following exceptions:
   (1) Restrictive covenants common to the platted subdivision in which the Property is located.
   (2) The standard printed exception for standby fees, taxes and assessments.
   (3) Liens created as part of the financing described in Paragraph 4.
   (4) Utility easements created by the dedication deed or plat of the subdivision in which the Property is located.
   (5) Reservations or exceptions otherwise permitted by this contract or as may be approved by Buyer in writing.
   (6) The standard printed exception as to marital rights.
   (7) The standard printed exception as to waters, tidelands, beaches, streams, and related matters.
   (8) The standard printed exception as to discrepancies, conflicts, shortages in area or boundary lines, encroachments or protrusions, or overlapping improvements: ❑(i) will not be amended or deleted from the title policy; ❑(ii) will be amended to read, "shortages in area" at the expense of ❑Buyer ❑Seller.

B. COMMITMENT: Within 20 days after the Title Company receives a copy of this contract, Seller shall furnish to Buyer a commitment for title insurance (Commitment) and, at Buyer's expense, legible copies of restrictive covenants and documents evidencing exceptions in the Commitment (Exception Documents) other than the standard printed exceptions. Seller authorizes the Title Company to deliver the Commitment and Exception Documents to Buyer at Buyer's address shown in Paragraph 21. If the Commitment and Exception Documents are not delivered to Buyer within the specified time, the time for delivery will be automatically extended up to 15 days or 3 days before the Closing Date, whichever is earlier. If, due to factors beyond Seller's control, the Commitment and Exception Documents are not delivered within the time required, Buyer may terminate this contract and the earnest money will be refunded to Buyer.

C. SURVEY: The survey must be made by a registered professional land surveyor acceptable to the Title Company and Buyer's lender(s). (Check one box only)
❑(1)Within _____ days after the effective date of this contract, Seller shall furnish to Buyer and Title Company Seller's existing survey of the Property and a Residential Real Property Affidavit promulgated by the Texas Department of Insurance (T-47 Affidavit). **If Seller fails to furnish the existing survey or affidavit within the time prescribed, Buyer shall obtain a new survey at Seller's expense no later than 3 days prior to Closing Date.** If the existing survey or affidavit is not acceptable to Title Company or Buyer's lender(s), Buyer shall obtain a new survey at ❑Seller's ❑Buyer's expense no later than 3 days prior to Closing Date.
❑(2)Within _____ days after the effective date of this contract, Buyer shall obtain a new survey at Buyer's expense. Buyer is deemed to receive the survey on the date of actual receipt or the date specified in this paragraph, whichever is earlier.
❑(3)Within _____ days after the effective date of this contract, Seller, at Seller's expense shall furnish a new survey to Buyer.

D. OBJECTIONS: Buyer may object in writing to defects, exceptions, or encumbrances to title: disclosed on the survey other than items 6A(1) through (7) above; disclosed in the Commitment other than items 6A(1) through (8) above; or which prohibit the following use or activity: _____
_____.
Buyer must object the earlier of (i) the Closing Date or (ii) _____ days after Buyer receives the Commitment, Exception Documents, and the survey. Buyer's failure to object within the time allowed will constitute a waiver of Buyer's right to object; except that the requirements in Schedule C of the Commitment are not waived by Buyer. Provided Seller is not obligated to incur any expense, Seller shall cure the timely objections of Buyer or any third party lender

Initialed for identification by Buyer_____ _____ and Seller _____ _____   TREC NO. 20-12

F I G U R E   5.1

One to Four Family Residential Contract (Resale) (Continued)

Contract Concerning _____ Page 3 of 9   4-28-2014
(Address of Property)

within 15 days after Seller receives the objections and the Closing Date will be extended as necessary. If objections are not cured within such 15 day period, this contract will terminate and the earnest money will be refunded to Buyer unless Buyer waives the objections.

E. TITLE NOTICES:

(1) ABSTRACT OR TITLE POLICY: Broker advises Buyer to have an abstract of title covering the Property examined by an attorney of Buyer's selection, or Buyer should be furnished with or obtain a Title Policy. If a Title Policy is furnished, the Commitment should be promptly reviewed by an attorney of Buyer's choice due to the time limitations on Buyer's right to object.

(2) MEMBERSHIP IN PROPERTY OWNERS ASSOCIATION(S): The Property ☐is ☐is not subject to mandatory membership in a property owners association(s). If the Property is subject to mandatory membership in a property owners association(s), Seller notifies Buyer under §5.012, Texas Property Code, that, as a purchaser of property in the residential community identified in Paragraph 2A in which the Property is located, you are obligated to be a member of the property owners association(s). Restrictive covenants governing the use and occupancy of the Property and all dedicatory instruments governing the establishment, maintenance, or operation of this residential community have been or will be recorded in the Real Property Records of the county in which the Property is located. Copies of the restrictive covenants and dedicatory instruments may be obtained from the county clerk. **You are obligated to pay assessments to the property owners association(s). The amount of the assessments is subject to change. Your failure to pay the assessments could result in enforcement of the association's lien on and the foreclosure of the Property.** Section 207.003, Property Code, entitles an owner to receive copies of any document that governs the establishment, maintenance, or operation of a subdivision, including, but not limited to, restrictions, bylaws, rules and regulations, and a resale certificate from a property owners' association. A resale certificate contains information including, but not limited to, statements specifying the amount and frequency of regular assessments and the style and cause number of lawsuits to which the property owners' association is a party, other than lawsuits relating to unpaid ad valorem taxes of an individual member of the association. These documents must be made available to you by the property owners' association or the association's agent on your request. **If Buyer is concerned about these matters, the TREC promulgated Addendum for Property Subject to Mandatory Membership in a Property Owners Association(s) should be used.**

(3) STATUTORY TAX DISTRICTS: If the Property is situated in a utility or other statutorily created district providing water, sewer, drainage, or flood control facilities and services, Chapter 49, Texas Water Code, requires Seller to deliver and Buyer to sign the statutory notice relating to the tax rate, bonded indebtedness, or standby fee of the district prior to final execution of this contract.

(4) TIDE WATERS: If the Property abuts the tidally influenced waters of the state, §33.135, Texas Natural Resources Code, requires a notice regarding coastal area property to be included in the contract. An addendum containing the notice promulgated by TREC or required by the parties must be used.

(5) ANNEXATION: If the Property is located outside the limits of a municipality, Seller notifies Buyer under §5.011, Texas Property Code, that the Property may now or later be included in the extraterritorial jurisdiction of a municipality and may now or later be subject to annexation by the municipality. Each municipality maintains a map that depicts its boundaries and extraterritorial jurisdiction. To determine if the Property is located within a municipality's extraterritorial jurisdiction or is likely to be located within a municipality's extraterritorial jurisdiction, contact all municipalities located in the general proximity of the Property for further information.

(6) PROPERTY LOCATED IN A CERTIFICATED SERVICE AREA OF A UTILITY SERVICE PROVIDER: Notice required by §13.257, Water Code: The real property, described in Paragraph 2, that you are about to purchase may be located in a certificated water or sewer service area, which is authorized by law to provide water or sewer service to the properties in the certificated area. If your property is located in a certificated area there may be special costs or charges that you will be required to pay before you can receive water or sewer service. There may be a period required to construct lines or other facilities necessary to provide water or sewer service to your property. You are advised to determine if the property is in a certificated area and contact the utility service provider to determine the cost that you will be required to pay and the period, if any, that is required to provide water or sewer service to your property. The undersigned Buyer hereby acknowledges receipt of the foregoing notice at or before the execution of a binding contract for the purchase of the real property described in Paragraph 2 or at closing of purchase of the real property.

Initialed for identification by Buyer_____ _____ and Seller _____ _____   TREC NO. 20-12

F I G U R E   5.1

One to Four Family Residential Contract (Resale) (Continued)

Contract Concerning _____ Page 4 of 9   4-28-2014
                                    (Address of Property)

   (7) PUBLIC IMPROVEMENT DISTRICTS: If the Property is in a public improvement district, §5.014, Property Code, requires Seller to notify Buyer as follows: As a purchaser of this parcel of real property you are obligated to pay an assessment to a municipality or county for an improvement project undertaken by a public improvement district under Chapter 372, Local Government Code. The assessment may be due annually or in periodic installments. More information concerning the amount of the assessment and the due dates of that assessment may be obtained from the municipality or county levying the assessment. The amount of the assessments is subject to change. Your failure to pay the assessments could result in a lien on and the foreclosure of your property.
   (8) TRANSFER FEES: If the Property is subject to a private transfer fee obligation, §5.205, Property Code, requires Seller to notify Buyer as follows: The private transfer fee obligation may be governed by Chapter 5, Subchapter G of the Texas Property Code.
   (9) PROPANE GAS SYSTEM SERVICE AREA: If the Property is located in a propane gas system service area owned by a distribution system retailer, Seller must give Buyer written notice as required by §141.010, Texas Utilities Code. An addendum containing the notice approved by TREC or required by the parties should be used.

 7. PROPERTY CONDITION:
   A. ACCESS, INSPECTIONS AND UTILITIES: Seller shall permit Buyer and Buyer's agents access to the Property at reasonable times. Buyer may have the Property inspected by inspectors selected by Buyer and licensed by TREC or otherwise permitted by law to make inspections. Seller at Seller's expense shall immediately cause existing utilities to be turned on and shall keep the utilities on during the time this contract is in effect.
   B. SELLER'S DISCLOSURE NOTICE PURSUANT TO §5.008, TEXAS PROPERTY CODE (Notice): (Check one box only)
   ❑ (1) Buyer has received the Notice.
   ❑ (2) Buyer has not received the Notice. Within _____ days after the effective date of this contract, Seller shall deliver the Notice to Buyer. If Buyer does not receive the Notice, Buyer may terminate this contract at any time prior to the closing and the earnest money will be refunded to Buyer. If Seller delivers the Notice, Buyer may terminate this contract for any reason within 7 days after Buyer receives the Notice or prior to the closing, whichever first occurs, and the earnest money will be refunded to Buyer.
   ❑ (3) The Seller is not required to furnish the notice under the Texas Property Code.
   C. SELLER'S DISCLOSURE OF LEAD-BASED PAINT AND LEAD-BASED PAINT HAZARDS is required by Federal law for a residential dwelling constructed prior to 1978.
   D. ACCEPTANCE OF PROPERTY CONDITION: "As Is" means the present condition of the Property with any and all defects and without warranty except for the warranties of title and the warranties in this contract. Buyer's agreement to accept the Property As Is under Paragraph 7D(1) or (2) does not preclude Buyer from inspecting the Property under Paragraph 7A, from negotiating repairs or treatments in a subsequent amendment, or from terminating this contract during the Option Period, if any.
   (Check one box only)
   ❑ (1) Buyer accepts the Property As Is.
   ❑ (2) Buyer accepts the Property As Is provided Seller, at Seller's expense, shall complete the following specific repairs and treatments: _____
   _____.
   (Do not insert general phrases, such as "subject to inspections" that do not identify specific repairs and treatments.)
   E. LENDER REQUIRED REPAIRS AND TREATMENTS: Unless otherwise agreed in writing, neither party is obligated to pay for lender required repairs, which includes treatment for wood destroying insects. If the parties do not agree to pay for the lender required repairs or treatments, this contract will terminate and the earnest money will be refunded to Buyer. If the cost of lender required repairs and treatments exceeds 5% of the Sales Price, Buyer may terminate this contract and the earnest money will be refunded to Buyer.
   F. COMPLETION OF REPAIRS AND TREATMENTS: Unless otherwise agreed in writing: (i) Seller shall complete all agreed repairs and treatments prior to the Closing Date; and (ii) all required permits must be obtained, and repairs and treatments must be performed by persons who are licensed to provide such repairs or treatments or, if no license is required by law, are commercially engaged in the trade of providing such repairs or treatments. At Buyer's election, any transferable warranties received by Seller with respect to the repairs and treatments will be transferred to Buyer at Buyer's expense. If Seller fails to complete any agreed repairs and treatments prior to the Closing Date, Buyer may exercise remedies under Paragraph 15 or extend the Closing Date up to 5 days if necessary for Seller to complete the repairs and treatments.
   G. ENVIRONMENTAL MATTERS: Buyer is advised that the presence of wetlands, toxic substances, including asbestos and wastes or other environmental hazards, or the presence of a threatened or endangered species or its habitat may affect Buyer's intended use of the

Initialed for identification by Buyer_____ _____ and Seller _____ _____   TREC NO. 20-12

FIGURE 5.1

One to Four Family Residential Contract (Resale) (Continued)

Contract Concerning _____ Page 5 of 9   4-28-2014
                                    (Address of Property)

Property. If Buyer is concerned about these matters, an addendum promulgated by TREC or required by the parties should be used.
  H. RESIDENTIAL SERVICE CONTRACTS: Buyer may purchase a residential service contract from a residential service company licensed by TREC. If Buyer purchases a residential service contract, Seller shall reimburse Buyer at closing for the cost of the residential service contract in an amount not exceeding $_____. Buyer should review any residential service contract for the scope of coverage, exclusions and limitations. **The purchase of a residential service contract is optional. Similar coverage may be purchased from various companies authorized to do business in Texas.**

8. **BROKERS' FEES:** All obligations of the parties for payment of brokers' fees are contained in separate written agreements.

9. **CLOSING:**
  A. The closing of the sale will be on or before _____, 20____, or within 7 days after objections made under Paragraph 6D have been cured or waived, whichever date is later (Closing Date). If either party fails to close the sale by the Closing Date, the non-defaulting party may exercise the remedies contained in Paragraph 15.
  B. At closing:
    (1) Seller shall execute and deliver a general warranty deed conveying title to the Property to Buyer and showing no additional exceptions to those permitted in Paragraph 6 and furnish tax statements or certificates showing no delinquent taxes on the Property.
    (2) Buyer shall pay the Sales Price in good funds acceptable to the escrow agent.
    (3) Seller and Buyer shall execute and deliver any notices, statements, certificates, affidavits, releases, loan documents and other documents reasonably required for the closing of the sale and the issuance of the Title Policy.
    (4) There will be no liens, assessments, or security interests against the Property which will not be satisfied out of the sales proceeds unless securing the payment of any loans assumed by Buyer and assumed loans will not be in default.
    (5) If the Property is subject to a residential lease, Seller shall transfer security deposits (as defined under §92.102, Property Code), if any, to Buyer. In such an event, Buyer shall deliver to the tenant a signed statement acknowledging that the Buyer has received the security deposit and is responsible for the return of the security deposit, and specifying the exact dollar amount of the security deposit.

10. **POSSESSION:**
  A Buyer's Possession: Seller shall deliver to Buyer possession of the Property in its present or required condition, ordinary wear and tear excepted: ❏upon closing and funding ❏according to a temporary residential lease form promulgated by TREC or other written lease required by the parties. Any possession by Buyer prior to closing or by Seller after closing which is not authorized by a written lease will establish a tenancy at sufferance relationship between the parties. **Consult your insurance agent prior to change of ownership and possession because insurance coverage may be limited or terminated. The absence of a written lease or appropriate insurance coverage may expose the parties to economic loss.**
  B. Leases:
    (1) After the Effective Date, Seller may not execute any lease (including but not limited to mineral leases) or convey any interest in the Property without Buyer's written consent.
    (2) If the Property is subject to any lease to which Seller is a party, Seller shall deliver to Buyer copies of the lease(s) and any move-in condition form signed by the tenant within 7 days after the Effective Date of the contract.

11. **SPECIAL PROVISIONS:**   (Insert only factual statements and business details applicable to the sale. TREC rules prohibit licensees from adding factual statements or business details for which a contract addendum, lease or other form has been promulgated by TREC for mandatory use.)

12. **SETTLEMENT AND OTHER EXPENSES:**
  A. The following expenses must be paid at or prior to closing:
    (1) Expenses payable by Seller (Seller's Expenses):
      (a) Releases of existing liens, including prepayment penalties and recording fees; release of Seller's loan liability; tax statements or certificates; preparation of deed; one-half of escrow fee; and other expenses payable by Seller under this contract.
      (b) Seller shall also pay an amount not to exceed $_____ to be applied in the

Initialed for identification by Buyer_____ _____ and Seller _____ _____   TREC NO. 20-12

F I G U R E   5.1

One to Four Family Residential Contract (Resale) (Continued)

Contract Concerning _____ Page 6 of 9   4-28-2014
(Address of Property)

following order: Buyer's Expenses which Buyer is prohibited from paying by FHA, VA, Texas Veterans Land Board or other governmental loan programs, and then to other Buyer's Expenses as allowed by the lender.

(2) Expenses payable by Buyer (Buyer's Expenses): Appraisal fees; loan application fees; adjusted origination charges; credit reports; preparation of loan documents; interest on the notes from date of disbursement to one month prior to dates of first monthly payments; recording fees; copies of easements and restrictions; loan title policy with endorsements required by lender; loan-related inspection fees; photos; amortization schedules; one-half of escrow fee; all prepaid items, including required premiums for flood and hazard insurance, reserve deposits for insurance, ad valorem taxes and special governmental assessments; final compliance inspection; courier fee; repair inspection; underwriting fee; wire transfer fee; expenses incident to any loan; Private Mortgage Insurance Premium (PMI), VA Loan Funding Fee, or FHA Mortgage Insurance Premium (MIP) as required by the lender; and other expenses payable by Buyer under this contract.

B. If any expense exceeds an amount expressly stated in this contract for such expense to be paid by a party, that party may terminate this contract unless the other party agrees to pay such excess. Buyer may not pay charges and fees expressly prohibited by FHA, VA, Texas Veterans Land Board or other governmental loan program regulations.

13. PRORATIONS: Taxes for the current year, interest, maintenance fees, assessments, dues and rents will be prorated through the Closing Date. The tax proration may be calculated taking into consideration any change in exemptions that will affect the current year's taxes. If taxes for the current year vary from the amount prorated at closing, the parties shall adjust the prorations when tax statements for the current year are available. If taxes are not paid at or prior to closing, Buyer shall pay taxes for the current year.

14. CASUALTY LOSS: If any part of the Property is damaged or destroyed by fire or other casualty after the effective date of this contract, Seller shall restore the Property to its previous condition as soon as reasonably possible, but in any event by the Closing Date. If Seller fails to do so due to factors beyond Seller's control, Buyer may (a) terminate this contract and the earnest money will be refunded to Buyer (b) extend the time for performance up to 15 days and the Closing Date will be extended as necessary or (c) accept the Property in its damaged condition with an assignment of insurance proceeds and receive credit from Seller at closing in the amount of the deductible under the insurance policy. Seller's obligations under this paragraph are independent of any other obligations of Seller under this contract.

15. DEFAULT: If Buyer fails to comply with this contract, Buyer will be in default, and Seller may (a) enforce specific performance, seek such other relief as may be provided by law, or both, or (b) terminate this contract and receive the earnest money as liquidated damages, thereby releasing both parties from this contract. If Seller fails to comply with this contract, Seller will be in default and Buyer may (a) enforce specific performance, seek such other relief as may be provided by law, or both, or (b) terminate this contract and receive the earnest money, thereby releasing both parties from this contract.

16. MEDIATION: It is the policy of the State of Texas to encourage resolution of disputes through alternative dispute resolution procedures such as mediation. Any dispute between Seller and Buyer related to this contract which is not resolved through informal discussion will be submitted to a mutually acceptable mediation service or provider. The parties to the mediation shall bear the mediation costs equally. This paragraph does not preclude a party from seeking equitable relief from a court of competent jurisdiction.

17. ATTORNEY'S FEES: A Buyer, Seller, Listing Broker, Other Broker, or escrow agent who prevails in any legal proceeding related to this contract is entitled to recover reasonable attorney's fees and all costs of such proceeding.

18. ESCROW:

A. ESCROW: The escrow agent is not (i) a party to this contract and does not have liability for the performance or nonperformance of any party to this contract, (ii) liable for interest on the earnest money and (iii) liable for the loss of any earnest money caused by the failure of any financial institution in which the earnest money has been deposited unless the financial institution is acting as escrow agent.

B. EXPENSES: At closing, the earnest money must be applied first to any cash down payment, then to Buyer's Expenses and any excess refunded to Buyer. If no closing occurs, escrow agent may: (i) require a written release of liability of the escrow agent from all parties, (ii) require payment of unpaid expenses incurred on behalf of a party, and (iii) only deduct from the earnest money the amount of unpaid expenses incurred on behalf of the party receiving the earnest money.

C. DEMAND: Upon termination of this contract, either party or the escrow agent may send a release of earnest money to each party and the parties shall execute counterparts of

Initialed for identification by Buyer_____ _____ and Seller _____ _____   TREC NO. 20-12

FIGURE 5.1

One to Four Family Residential Contract (Resale) (Continued)

Contract Concerning ______________________________ Page 7 of 9 4-28-2014
(Address of Property)

the release and deliver same to the escrow agent. If either party fails to execute the release, either party may make a written demand to the escrow agent for the earnest money. If only one party makes written demand for the earnest money, escrow agent shall promptly provide a copy of the demand to the other party. If escrow agent does not receive written objection to the demand from the other party within 15 days, escrow agent may disburse the earnest money to the party making demand reduced by the amount of unpaid expenses incurred on behalf of the party receiving the earnest money and escrow agent may pay the same to the creditors. If escrow agent complies with the provisions of this paragraph, each party hereby releases escrow agent from all adverse claims related to the disbursal of the earnest money.

D. DAMAGES: Any party who wrongfully fails or refuses to sign a release acceptable to the escrow agent within 7 days of receipt of the request will be liable to the other party for liquidated damages in an amount equal to the sum of: (i) three times the amount of the earnest money; (ii) the earnest money; (iii) reasonable attorney's fees; and (iv) all costs of suit.

E. NOTICES: Escrow agent's notices will be effective when sent in compliance with Paragraph 21. Notice of objection to the demand will be deemed effective upon receipt by escrow agent.

19. **REPRESENTATIONS:** All covenants, representations and warranties in this contract survive closing. If any representation of Seller in this contract is untrue on the Closing Date, Seller will be in default. Unless expressly prohibited by written agreement, Seller may continue to show the Property and receive, negotiate and accept back up offers.

20. **FEDERAL TAX REQUIREMENTS:** If Seller is a "foreign person," as defined by applicable law, or if Seller fails to deliver an affidavit to Buyer that Seller is not a "foreign person," then Buyer shall withhold from the sales proceeds an amount sufficient to comply with applicable tax law and deliver the same to the Internal Revenue Service together with appropriate tax forms. Internal Revenue Service regulations require filing written reports if currency in excess of specified amounts is received in the transaction.

21. **NOTICES:** All notices from one party to the other must be in writing and are effective when mailed to, hand-delivered at, or transmitted by facsimile or electronic transmission as follows:

To Buyer at:	______________________	To Seller at:	______________________
	______________________		______________________
Telephone:	( )	Telephone:	( )
Facsimile:	( )	Facsimile:	( )
E-mail:	______________________	E-mail:	______________________

22. **AGREEMENT OF PARTIES:** This contract contains the entire agreement of the parties and cannot be changed except by their written agreement. Addenda which are a part of this contract are (Check all applicable boxes):

- ☐ Third Party Financing Addendum for Credit Approval
- ☐ Seller Financing Addendum
- ☐ Addendum for Property Subject to Mandatory Membership in a Property Owners Association
- ☐ Buyer's Temporary Residential Lease
- ☐ Loan Assumption Addendum
- ☐ Addendum for Sale of Other Property by Buyer
- ☐ Addendum for Reservation of Oil, Gas and Other Minerals
- ☐ Addendum for "Back-Up" Contract
- ☐ Addendum for Coastal Area Property
- ☐ Environmental Assessment, Threatened or Endangered Species and Wetlands Addendum
- ☐ Seller's Temporary Residential Lease
- ☐ Short Sale Addendum
- ☐ Addendum for Property Located Seaward of the Gulf Intracoastal Waterway
- ☐ Addendum for Seller's Disclosure of Information on Lead-based Paint and Lead-based Paint Hazards as Required by Federal Law
- ☐ Addendum for Property in a Propane Gas System Service Area
- ☐ Other (list): ______________________

Initialed for identification by Buyer______ ______ and Seller _______ ______ TREC NO. 20-12

F I G U R E   5.1

One to Four Family Residential Contract (Resale) (Continued)

Contract Concerning _____ Page 8 of 9   4-28-2014
(Address of Property)

23. **TERMINATION OPTION:** For nominal consideration, the receipt of which is hereby acknowledged by Seller, and Buyer's agreement to pay Seller $_____ (Option Fee) within 3 days after the effective date of this contract, Seller grants Buyer the unrestricted right to terminate this contract by giving notice of termination to Seller within _____ days after the effective date of this contract (Option Period). If no dollar amount is stated as the Option Fee or if Buyer fails to pay the Option Fee to Seller within the time prescribed, this paragraph will not be a part of this contract and Buyer shall not have the unrestricted right to terminate this contract. If Buyer gives notice of termination within the time prescribed, the Option Fee will not be refunded; however, any earnest money will be refunded to Buyer. The Option Fee ❑will ❑will not be credited to the Sales Price at closing. **Time is of the essence for this paragraph and strict compliance with the time for performance is required.**

24. **CONSULT AN ATTORNEY BEFORE SIGNING:** TREC rules prohibit real estate licensees from giving legal advice. READ THIS CONTRACT CAREFULLY.

Buyer's
Attorney is: _____

Seller's
Attorney is: _____

_____

_____

Telephone: (___)_____

Telephone: (___)_____

Facsimile: (___)_____

Facsimile: (___)_____

E-mail: _____

E-mail: _____

EXECUTED the _____day of _____, 20____ (EFFECTIVE DATE).
(BROKER: FILL IN THE DATE OF FINAL ACCEPTANCE.)

_____
Buyer

_____
Seller

_____
Buyer

_____
Seller

The form of this contract has been approved by the Texas Real Estate Commission. TREC forms are intended for use only by trained real estate licensees. No representation is made as to the legal validity or adequacy of any provision in any specific transactions. It is not intended for complex transactions. Texas Real Estate Commission, P.O. Box 12188, Austin, TX 78711-2188, (512) 936-3000 (http://www.trec.texas.gov) TREC NO. 20-12. This form replaces TREC NO. 20-11.

TREC NO. 20-12

FIGURE 5.1

One to Four Family Residential Contract (Resale) (Continued)

Contract Concerning _____ Page 9 of 9   4-28-2014
                          (Address of Property)

BROKER INFORMATION
(Print name(s) only. Do not sign)

_____   _____
Other Broker Firm   License No.   Listing Broker Firm   License No.

represents ☐ Buyer only as Buyer's agent   represents ☐ Seller and Buyer as an intermediary
            ☐ Seller as Listing Broker's subagent   ☐ Seller only as Seller's agent

_____   _____
Name of Associate's Licensed Supervisor Telephone   Name of Associate's Licensed Supervisor Telephone

_____   _____
Associate's Name   Telephone   Listing Associate's Name   Telephone

_____   _____
Other Broker's Address   Facsimile   Listing Broker's Office Address   Facsimile

_____   _____
City   State   Zip   City   State   Zip

_____   _____
Associate's Email Address   Listing Associate's Email Address

                                              _____
                                              Selling Associate's Name   Telephone

                                              _____
                                              Name of Selling Associate's Licensed Supervisor Telephone

                                              _____
                                              Selling Associate's Office Address Facsimile

                                              _____
                                              City   State   Zip

                                              _____
                                              Selling Associate's Email Address

Listing Broker has agreed to pay Other Broker_____of the total sales price when the Listing Broker's fee is received. Escrow agent is authorized and directed to pay other Broker from Listing Broker's fee at closing.

OPTION FEE RECEIPT

Receipt of $_____ (Option Fee) in the form of _____ is acknowledged.

_____   _____
Seller or Listing Broker   Date

CONTRACT AND EARNEST MONEY RECEIPT

Receipt of ☐Contract and ☐$_____Earnest Money in the form of _____
is acknowledged.

Escrow Agent: _____   Date: _____

By: _____
                                              _____
                       Email Address
                                              Telephone (____)_____
_____
Address
                                              Facsimile: (____) _____
_____
City   State   Zip

TREC NO. 20-12

All offers should be in writing and presented to the property owner as quickly as is reasonably practical. The TREC Rules call for immediate presentation. Occasionally, a buyer's agent may make a verbal offer to a listing agent. In these situations, the agent should try to find out if the buyer will put the offer in writing. If not, the agent must submit the verbal offer to the seller. The seller then can make an election as to what to do. The choices are to

■ accept subject to the written contract containing all acceptable terms and conditions,
■ counter the offer subject to the written contract containing all acceptable terms and conditions, or
■ reject the offer.

A seller hires a real estate professional to be the greatest marketing person to get the highest possible price, which means screening in offers rather than screening out potentially good offers. While this approach happens most often in commercial deals, it can also be used in residential transactions. Remember, the statute of frauds only applies to the enforcement of the contract, and not the negotiation for the contract.

No real estate broker or salesperson has the right to withhold an offer from a property owner. To do so may result in suspension or revocation of one's license under the provisions of the Texas Real Estate License Act (TRELA) or, worse, result in an unpleasant lawsuit for tortious interference. A **tort** is an act that damages another individual and gives rise to legal action. A property owner may consider the licensee's failure to present an offer in a timely manner a tortious interference with the owner's ability to sell the property. Unless instructed otherwise by the owner, all offers must be presented. A seller's instruction not to present backup offers must be given to the licensee in writing.

Upon receipt of an offer, the seller can accept, reject, or make a counteroffer. The contract must be signed and in most cases, initialed on each page. The initialing of each page is to ensure that no one makes a change to the contract after signatures are obtained. If the offer is acceptable to the seller, the offer is signed and dated and returned to the buyer. It is now a contract of sale. If the offer is rejected, the offer is returned to the buyer marked "void."

Any change made to the original offer should be marked with a **cross-hatch**, leaving a space for the seller to initial and also for the buyer to initial if willing to accept the change. No blanks should ever be left in the contract document due to the risk that someone might insert something later that was not actually agreed upon by the buyer and the seller. A blank may be filled with "NA"—meaning not applicable—or a drawn line. If an entire paragraph is not applicable in a particular situation, a line may be drawn vertically through the paragraph or marked out line-by-line, and initialed in the margin. See Figure 5.2 for an illustration of cross-hatching.

FIGURE 5.2

Change Made to a Contract

9. CLOSING:
A. The closing of the sale will be on or before ___November ~~October~~-15___, 20_15_, or within 7 days after objections made under Paragraph 6D have been cured or waived, whichever date is later (Closing Date). If either party fails to close the sale by the Closing Date, the non-defaulting party may exercise the remedies contained in Paragraph 15.

A counteroffer is a new offer; it rejects the original offer.

Counteroffer Any change by the seller to the terms proposed by the buyer creates a **counteroffer**. The original offer ceases to exist because the seller has rejected it. The counteroffer is basically a new offer. The buyer may accept or reject the seller's counteroffer. If the buyer is willing to accept the changes made in the counteroffer, the buyer should initial at the crosshatch next to each change. Once the seller has been notified of the buyer's acceptance, the offer to purchase becomes a ratified contract. If the buyer is not willing to accept the changes made by the seller, the buyer should cross out the change and the crosshatch containing the seller's initials. The buyer may now make a different change marking with a crosshatch and buyer's initials. This new offer is then returned to the seller for acceptance, rejection, or an additional counteroffer.

The process may continue by making additional counteroffers. Any change in the last offer may result in a counteroffer until either the parties reach agreement or one party walks away.

An offer or counteroffer may be withdrawn at any time before it has been accepted. This is often a point of confusion when either buyer or seller has made a counteroffer that has not been accepted and the offering party wishes to withdraw the counter.

IN PRACTICE   A seller has listed his home for $250,000 and is not willing to convey the washer and dryer.

1. Offer: Buyer makes an offer of $200,000 and wants the washer and dryer included.
2. Counteroffer: Seller changes price to $230,000 and agrees to convey the washer and dryer.
3. Counteroffer: Buyer changes price to $215,000 but still wants the washer and dryer.

Seller makes no response for five days and buyer's agent notifies seller's agent that the offer is withdrawn. Seller now wants to accept the $215,000 offer, but it is too late.

Acceptance If the seller agrees to the original offer or a later counteroffer exactly as it is made and signs and initials the document, the offer has been accepted and a contract is formed. The seller's agent must advise the buyer's agent of the seller's acceptance. Some contracts may call for an attorney's approval before final acceptance.

An offer is not considered accepted until the person making the offer has been notified of the other party's **acceptance**. When the parties communicate through an agent or at a distance, questions may arise regarding whether an acceptance, rejection, or counteroffer has occurred. Though current technology allows for fast communication, a signed agreement that is faxed, for example, would not necessarily constitute adequate communication unless this is so specified in the contract. The agents should transmit all offers, acceptances, or other responses as soon as possible to avoid any questions of proper communication.

A copy of the signed contract must be provided to each party. In some states, a contract is not considered to be fully in force until a final signed copy is physically delivered to both parties.

Statute of Frauds

The statute of frauds states that certain contracts must be reduced to writing and signed by the party charged with the promise to enforce. These include

- contracts for the sale of real estate,
- a lease for real estate for longer than one year,
- any agreement for which performance time is greater than one year (options, first right of refusal, etc.), and
- commission agreements (listing or buyer representation, oil and gas leases).

If there is a conflict between the written contract and parole evidence, the courts have ruled that the written words will be controlling. Therefore, the agent must take great care not to make nor allow customers/clients to make any verbal promises to avoid any conflict in the future. This is one of the primary reasons that agents will keep sellers and buyers from meeting until after the closing.

The deed is the final agreement between the parties, which means that all unfulfilled promises that are not merged into the deed don't have to be kept. The one major exception to this rule is fraud. If a seller made promises to a buyer that the seller did not intend to keep in order to get the buyer to sign the contract, then the contract might be considered fraudulent inducement. In the case of fraud, a court may consider parole evidence to demonstrate the presence of fraud in the deal.

The One to Four Family Residential Contract (Resale) specifies certain accessories in paragraph 2C, which will be conveyed, with an opportunity to exclude in paragraph 2D those items the seller wishes to keep.

IN PRACTICE   The agent must take the time to thoroughly explain this section of the contract. The following items are often the source of conflict between sellers and buyers:

- Window coverings and curtain rods
- Unattached fireplace screens
- Above-ground pools and hot tubs
- Chandeliers

If a seller does not intend for an item to go with the house, then it should be removed prior to showings.

Letter of Intent

In many states, specific guidelines have been drawn, either by agreement between broker and lawyer associations, by court decision, or by statute, regarding the authority of real estate licensees to prepare documents for their clients and customers. As a rule, a real estate broker is not authorized to practice law, which can be construed to be the preparation of legal documents. Only a licensed attorney can prepare legal documents and give legal advice. However, a broker or salesperson acting on the behalf of the broker may be permitted to fill in the blanks of preprinted documents (such as sales contracts and leases).

In some states (not Texas), licensees may prepare a shorter document called a **letter of intent (LOI)**, instead of a complete sales contract. The binder states the essential terms of the offer. A more formal and complete contract of sale is drawn up once the seller accepts and signs the LOI. A LOI might also be used when the details of the transaction are too complex for the standard sales contract form. This is often the case with commercial transactions.

Equitable Title

When a buyer signs a contract to purchase real estate, the buyer does not receive title to the land. Title transfers only upon delivery and acceptance of a deed. However, after both buyer and seller have executed a sales contract, the buyer acquires an interest in the land. This interest is called **equitable title**. A person who holds equitable title has rights that vary from state to state.

In some states, equitable title may give the buyer an insurable interest in the property. In other cases, equitable title may give the buyer the right to legally require that the seller transfer the property to the buyer. If the parties decide to not go through with the purchase and sale, the buyer may be required to give the seller a quitclaim deed to release the buyer's equitable interest in the land. The developer of a mall shopping center might begin to initiate rental agreements with anchor stores for the project based on the developer's equitable interest in purchasing the land. Any such agreement should be made contingent on settlement of the property.

■ THE DOCUMENT

All real estate sales contracts can be divided into a number of separate parts. Although each form of contract contains these divisions, their location within a particular contract may vary depending on who has prepared the document. In addition to the sales price and terms being offered, sales contracts typically include information as described below.

Personal Information

Personal information for both the purchaser and the seller may include

- the purchaser's name and a statement of the purchaser's obligation to purchase the property, including how the purchaser intends to take title;
- the seller's name and a statement of the type of deed a seller agrees to give, including any covenants, conditions, and restrictions;
- a listing of any personal property that is to be left on the premises (e.g., appliances, lawn and garden equipment, window treatments);
- specific items that are to be removed by the seller (e.g., storage shed, firewood, trash);
- the transfer of any applicable warranties on heating and cooling systems or built-in appliances;
- the identification of any leased equipment to be transferred to the new owner (e.g., security system, cable service, water softener system);
- the purchaser's right to inspect the property shortly before the closing to ensure that all contract provisions have been met (usually called a walk-through);
- the method by which real estate taxes, rents, fuel costs, and any other expenses are to be prorated; and
- the transfer of payment for any special assessments.

Legal Description

A street address, while usually enough to find the location of a particular building, is not precise enough to describe legal ownership. Addresses change as streets are renamed, or rural roads might become public streets in growing communities. Sales contracts, deeds, and mortgages require a more specific description of property to be binding.

A **legal description** is a detailed way of describing a parcel of land. The description is based on information collected through a **survey**—the process by which boundaries are measured by calculating the dimensions and area to determine the exact location of a piece of land. Courts have stated that a description is legally sufficient if it allows a surveyor to locate the parcel. In this context, the term *locate* means that the surveyor must be able to define the exact boundaries of the property. A street address will not tell a surveyor how large the property is or where it begins and ends. Several alternative systems of identification have been developed to express a legal description of real estate. Although each method can be used independently, the methods may be combined in some situations. Some states use only one method; others use all three.

Metes-and-Bounds Method   **Metes-and-bounds** descriptions were used in the original 13 colonies and in those states that were being settled while the rectangular survey system was being developed. "Metes" means to measure, and "bounds" means linear directions. The method relies on a property's physical features to determine the boundaries and measurements of the parcel. A metes-and-bounds description starts at a designated place on the parcel, called the **point of beginning (POB)**. The POB is also the point of ending (POE), but often only the POB is used in describing the property. From there, the surveyor proceeds around the property's boundaries. The boundaries are recorded by referring to linear measurements, natural and artificial landmarks (called monuments), and directions. A metes-and-bounds description always ends back at the POB so that the tract being described is completely enclosed.

Monuments are fixed objects used to identify the POB, all corners of the parcel or ends of boundary segments, and the location of intersecting boundaries. In colonial times, a monument might have been a natural object such as a stone, a large tree, a lake, or a stream. It also might have been a street, a fence, or other marker. Today, monuments are iron pins or concrete posts placed by the U.S. Corps of Engineers, other government departments, or trained private surveyors. Measurements often include the words "more or less" because the location of the monuments is more important than the distances between them. Because monuments can be moved, surveyors give their final metes-and-bounds reference in terms of cardinal points and distance. They include the statement "to the point of beginning (POB)" to ensure closure and to remove questions if an error in footage prevents closure.

An example of a historical metes-and-bounds description of a parcel of land (see Figure 5.3) follows:

> *A tract of land located in Red Skull, Boone County, Virginia, described as follows: Beginning at the intersection of the east line of Jones Road and the south line of Skull Drive; then east along the south line of Skull Drive 200 feet; then south 15° east 216.5 feet, more or less, to the center thread of Red Skull Creek then northwesterly along the center line of said creek to its intersection with the east line of Jones Road; then north 105 feet, more or less, along the east line of Jones Road to the point of beginning.*

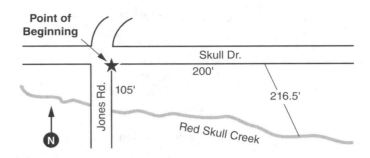

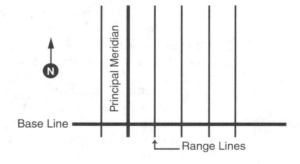

FIGURE 5.3

Metes-and-Bounds Tract

The directions of township lines and range lines may be easily remembered by thinking of the words this way:

Township lines
Range lines

FIGURE 5.4

Range Lines

Memory Tip

Township Numbering

Townships are numbered the same way a field is plowed. Remember: right to left, left to right, right to left.

Rectangular Survey System The **rectangular survey system**, sometimes called the government survey system, was established by Congress in 1785 to standardize the description of land acquired by the newly formed federal government. By dividing the land into rectangles, the survey provided land descriptions by describing the rectangle(s) in which the land was located. The system is based on two sets of intersecting lines: principal meridians and base lines. The **principal meridians** run north and south, and the **base lines** run east and west. Both are located by reference to degrees of longitude and latitude. Each principal meridian has a name or number and is crossed by a base line. Each principal meridian and its corresponding base line are used to survey a definite area of land, indicated on the map by boundary lines. There are 37 principal meridians in the United States.

The land on either side of a principal meridian is divided into six-mile-wide strips by lines that run north and south, parallel to the meridian. These north-south strips of land are called **ranges** (see Figure 5.4). They are designated by consecutive numbers east or west of the principal meridian. For example, Range 3 East would be a strip of land between 12 and 18 miles east of its principal meridian.

Lines running east and west, parallel to the base line and six miles apart, are called **township lines** (see Figure 5.5). They form strips of land called **township tiers**. These township tiers are designated by consecutive numbers north or south of the base line. For example, the strip of land between 6 and 12 miles north of a base line is Township 2 North.

FIGURE 5.5

Township Lines

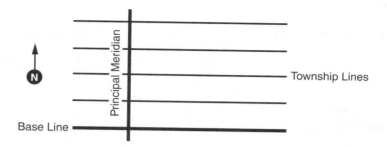

When the horizontal township lines and the vertical range lines intersect, they form squares. These township squares are the basic units of the rectangular survey system (see Figure 5.6). **Townships** are 6 miles square and contain 36 square miles (23,040 acres).

FIGURE 5.6

Townships in the Rectangular Survey System

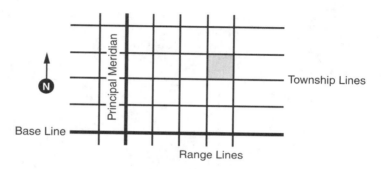

Each township is given a legal description. The township's description includes the following:

- Designation of the township tier in which the township is located
- Designation of the range strip
- Name or number of the principal meridian for that area

■ **FOR EXAMPLE**   In Figure 5.6, the shaded township is described as Township 3 North, Range 4 East of the principal meridian. This township is the third strip, or tier, north of the base line, and it designates the township number and direction. The township is also located in the fourth range strip (those running north and south) east of the principal meridian. Finally, reference is made to the principal meridian because the land being described is within the boundary of land surveyed from that meridian. This description is abbreviated as T3N, R4E 4th Principal Meridian.

Sections   Township squares are subdivided into sections and subsections called halves and quarters, which can be further divided. Each township contains 36 **sections.** Each section is one square mile or 640 acres, with 43,560 square feet in each acre. Sections are numbered 1 through 36, as shown in Figure 5.7. Section 1 is always in the northeast, or upper right-hand, corner. The numbering proceeds right to left to the upper left-hand corner. From there, the numbers drop down to the next tier and continue from left to right, then back from right to left. By law, each Section 16 was set aside for school purposes, and the sale or rental proceeds from this land were originally available for township school use. The schoolhouse was usually located in this section so it would be centrally located for all the students in the township. As a result, Section 16 is commonly called a **school section.**

FIGURE 5.7

Sections in a Township

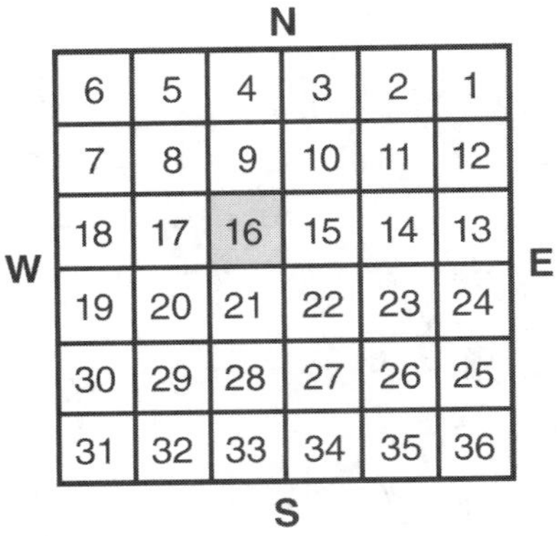

Math Shortcut

To calculate acres in a survey system description, multiply all the denominators and divide that number into 640 acres. For example, the SE¼ of SE¼ of SE¼ of Section 1 = 4 × 4 × 4 = 64; 640 ÷ 64 = 10 acres.

FIGURE 5.8

A Section

Sections are divided into halves (320 acres) and quarters (160 acres). In turn, each of those parts is further divided into halves and quarters. The southeast quarter of a section, which is a 160-acre tract, is abbreviated SE¼. The SE¼ of SE¼ of SE¼ of Section 1 would be a 10-acre square in the lower right-hand corner of Section 1 (see Figure 5.8).

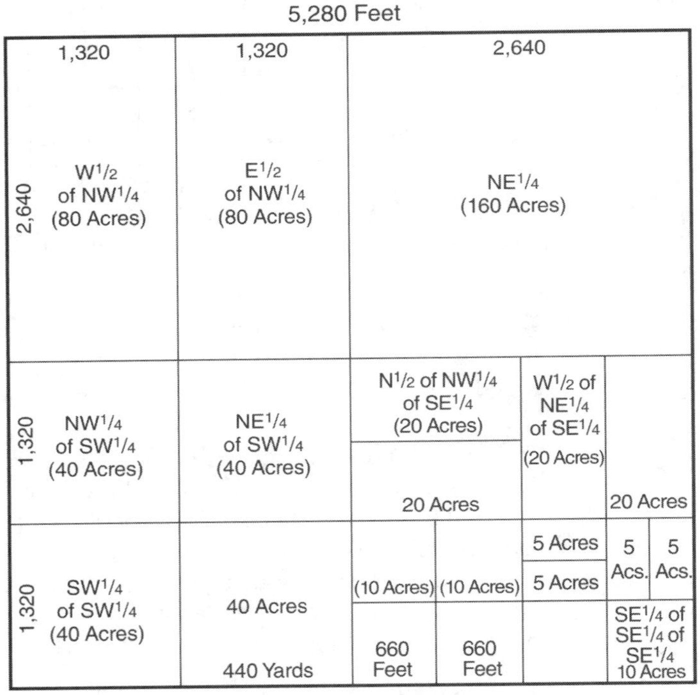

Legal descriptions should always include the name of the county and state in which the land is located because meridians often relate to more than one state and occasionally relate to two base lines. For example, the description "the southwest quarter of Section 10, Township 4 North, Range 1 West of the Fourth Principal Meridian" could refer to land in either Illinois or Wisconsin.

Metes-and-Bounds Descriptions Within the Rectangular Survey System
Land in states that use the rectangular survey system may also require a metes-and-bounds description. This usually occurs in one of three situations: (1) when describing an irregular tract, (2) when a tract is too small to be described by quarter-sections, or (3) when a tract does not follow the lot or block lines of a recorded subdivision or section, quarter-section lines, or other fractional section lines.

Lot-and-Block System The third method of legal description is the **lot-and-block (recorded plat) system**. This system uses lot and block numbers referred to in a **plat map** filed in the public records of the county where the land is located. The plat map is a map of a town, a section, or a subdivision, indicating the location and boundaries of individual properties. The lot-and-block system is used mostly in subdivisions and urban areas.

A lot-and-block survey is performed in two steps. First, a large parcel of land is described either by the metes-and-bounds method or by rectangular survey. Once this large parcel is surveyed, it is broken into smaller parcels. For each parcel described under the lot-and-block system, the "lot" refers to the numerical designation of any particular parcel. The "block" refers to the name of the subdivision under which the map is recorded.

The lot-and-block system starts with the preparation of a **subdivision plat** by a licensed surveyor or an engineer (see Figure 5.9). On this plat, the land is divided into numbered or lettered lots and blocks, and streets or access roads for public use are indicated. Lot sizes and street details must be described completely and must comply with all local ordinances and requirements. When properly signed and approved, the subdivision plat is recorded in the county in which the land is located. The plat becomes part of the legal description. In describing a lot from a recorded subdivision plat, three identifiers are used:

1. Lot and block number
2. Name or number of the subdivision plat
3. Name of the county and state

F I G U R E   5.9

Subdivision Plat Map of Block A

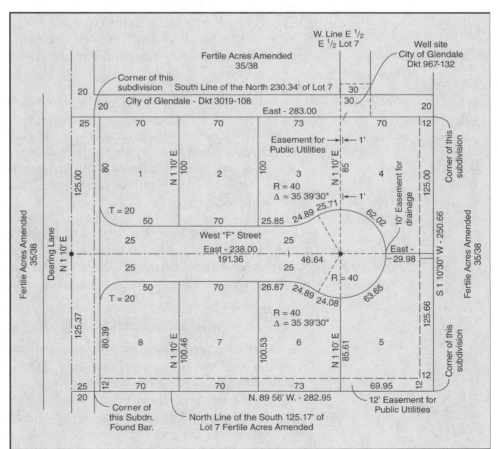

The following is an example of a lot-and-block description:

> *Lot 71, Happy Valley Estates 2, located in a portion of the southeast quarter of Section 23, Township 7 North, Range 4 East of the Seward Principal Meridian in _____ County, _____ [state].*

Some lot-and-block descriptions are not dependent on a government survey system and may simply refer to the plat recording in the land records of the county.

> *Lot 71, Happy Valley Estates 2, _____ County, _____ [state].*

Caution

Legal descriptions should not be altered or combined without adequate information from a surveyor or title attorney. Legal descriptions should be copied with extreme care. An incorrectly worded legal description in a sales contract may result in a conveyance of more or less land than the parties intended.

For example, damages suffered from an incorrect description could be extensive if buildings and improvements need to be moved because the land upon which the improvements were made is not owned. Often, even punctuation is extremely critical. Title problems can arise for the buyer who seeks to convey the property at a future date. Even if the contract can be corrected before the sale is closed, the licensee risks losing a commission and may be held liable for damages suffered by an injured party because of an improperly worded legal description.

■ FINANCING INFORMATION

The purchase price and how the purchaser intends to pay for the property, including earnest money deposits, additional cash from the purchaser, and the conditions of any mortgage financing, are all important elements of the financing portion of the contract.

The amount of the down payment is stated along with a brief description of the type of financing the purchaser is applying for. Some potential buyers might question why the seller needs to be made aware of the type of financing. The reason is that most sales contracts are automatically contingent on the purchaser being able to obtain financing. Because this has now been made a part of the contract, if the purchaser is unable to obtain the stated financing, the contract may become null and void.

IN PRACTICE   The contract states that the purchaser will obtain a Department of Veterans Affairs (VA) zero down-payment loan. Unfortunately, it turns out that the purchaser is not actually eligible for the VA loan and is unwilling to apply for any other type of financing, so the contract becomes void.

Other examples of situations where the purchaser might back out of the contract based on financial issues include the following scenarios:

- Purchaser applies for a 4% interest rate loan but the rate goes up to 6% and the purchaser no longer qualifies for the loan.
- Purchaser's application is rejected due to a prior bankruptcy, foreclosure, or other credit problems.
- Purchaser applies for a low down payment FHA loan but is rejected and is unwilling to apply for a conventional loan that requires a higher down payment.

Because of the risk to the seller if the purchaser is not able to obtain the financing described in the contract, it has become fairly common for a purchaser to provide the seller with a written letter of lender loan approval submitted along with the offer to purchase. This should be an actual **preapproval letter**, not just a prequalification. Many lenders will say someone is prequalified without doing a formal check of credit history, employment record, and cash available for down payment and closing costs.

A complete discussion of financing for the purchase of real property can be found in Chapter 7.

Earnest Money Deposit

It is customary, although not mandatory, for a purchaser to provide a deposit when making an offer to purchase real estate. This deposit, usually in the form of a check, is called **earnest money**. The earnest money deposit is evidence of the buyer's intention to carry out the terms of the contract in good faith. The check is given to the broker, who holds it in a special account.

The deposit amount is a matter to be agreed on by the parties. Under the terms of most listing agreements, a real estate broker is required to accept a reasonable amount as earnest money. As a rule, the deposit should be an amount sufficient to

- discourage the buyer from defaulting,
- compensate the seller for taking the property off the market, and
- cover any expenses the seller might incur if the buyer defaults.

A large earnest money deposit is usually looked on favorably by a seller, especially when multiple offers are being made. The one with a large earnest money deposit may be given preferential consideration.

This earnest money cannot be mixed with a broker's personal or business funds (called **commingling**). It must be retained in a special escrow account. (Exact regulations vary according to state law.) A separate escrow account does not have to be opened for each earnest money deposit received; all deposits may be kept in one account. A broker must maintain full, complete, and accurate records of all earnest money deposits. Real estate licenses may be revoked or suspended if deposits are not managed properly.

The special escrow account may or may not pay interest, depending on state law. If the account bears interest, some provision must be made in the contract for how the interest earned will be distributed. Often, a check for the interest amount is given to the buyer at closing. On the other hand, the contract may provide for the interest to be paid to the seller as part of the purchase price.

Documenting Cash

With an all-cash contract or one with a very large down payment, it may be necessary to provide the seller with proper documentation showing that the required funds are fully available.

■ DISCLOSURES

Many states have enacted mandatory **disclosure** laws, which help consumers make informed decisions. Some states have instituted procedures for making disclosures and recommended technical experts to ensure that purchasers have accurate information about the purchase of real estate. Disclosure of property conditions may be included as part of a sales contract, or on a separate form. Many states require separate forms for disclosing environmental problems. In addition, disclosure of the licensee's agency relationship is required by most states.

CONVEYANCE OF THE PROPERTY

Specific details regarding the official conveyance of the property to the new owner may include the following:

- The type of deed being provided; the purchaser may be presented with a general warranty deed, a special warranty deed (grant deed), or a bargain and sale deed (all will be discussed in detail in Chapter 8).
- A specific date for the closing and transfer of possession of the property to the purchaser
- The name of the escrow agent, attorney, or title company that will be conducting the closing or settlement (the actual physical process for closing both the loan and the conveyance of the property varies in different parts of the country).
- Provision of evidence that the title has been searched and no problems found. In cases where there is a cloud on the title, minor problems can usually be solved before settlement; more serious problems may delay the closing or negate the entire contract.

Destruction of Premises

In many states, once the sales contract is signed by both parties, the buyer assumes the risk of any damage to the property that may occur before closing the contract. However, laws and court decisions in many states have placed the risk of loss on the seller. A growing number of states have incorporated provisions of the Uniform Vendor and Purchaser Risk Act, which specifically provides that the seller bear any loss that occurs before the title passes or the buyer takes possession.

CONTINGENCIES

Additional conditions that must be satisfied before a sales contract is fully enforceable are called contingencies. A contract may be contingent upon some action being taken, a satisfactory inspection of some sort, attorney approval, or any other consideration important to the purchaser. Chapter 6 focuses on different types of contingencies and how they may be implemented.

SIGNATURES

The dated signatures of all parties will be required. In some states (including Texas), a seller's non-owning spouse will be required to release potential marital or homestead rights. In most cases, each page of the contract will need to be initialed.

ADDENDA AND AMENDMENTS

An amendment is a change or modification to the existing content of a contract. Any time words or provisions are added to or deleted from the body of the contract, the contract is amended. For example, a form contract's provision requiring closing in 90 days might be crossed out and replaced with a 60-day period. Amendments must be initialed or signed by all parties. If agreement is not reached, the original contract will stand. TREC promulgates an amendment for use by licensees.

An addendum contains additional information that is part of the contract/agreement. An addendum must be signed by all parties. TREC promulgates a number of addenda for use by licensees.

The proper use of addenda and amendments will be covered in Chapter 6.

■ DEFAULT AND BREACH REMEDIES

For the purposes of this text, the terms *default* and *breach* will be treated the same. They are essentially a failure to meet an obligation or perform on any promises made in a contract. The term *contract*, as used here, includes any contract that is used in the sale, leasing, and/or closing of real estate.

Remedies   A non-defaulting party may have remedies available, including

- suit for monetary damages,
- rescission of the contract, and
- suit for specific performance.

When there is a breach, first determine the damages. If there are no damages, there is likely no remedy which would have a monetary result. In order to claim damages, there must be actual damages.

■ **FOR EXAMPLE**   A buyer contracts to buy a home, and, 10 days later, the seller does not get the job transfer he thought he was getting. In the meantime, the buyer applied for a loan, had a home inspection, and paid for an appraisal. The only viable remedy is a rescission of the contract if the seller reimburses the out-of-pocket expense the buyer has made and makes him whole. It is unlikely that the seller would prevail in a specific performance suit unless the property was so unique that there would never be an opportunity for the seller to get another offer.

■ **FOR EXAMPLE**   A buyer contracts to buy a 72-unit apartment building in a very tight market. The buyer pays $56,000 per unit and plans to close with an Internal Revenue Code Section 1031 tax deferred exchange, which will save him $86,000 in taxes. Everyone agrees that the closing would take place in six months, because the seller also wants to do a tax-deferred exchange. The seller is unable to find a property to buy, so he wants to cancel the contract to sell. In the meantime, similar properties are now selling for $62,000 a unit. Because of the 1031 rules, the buyer cannot now do the tax-deferred exchange. The damages would be a combination of the increase of price ($72 \times \$6,000 = \$432,000$) plus the taxes ($86,000) = $518,000. This is a good case for damages or specific performance.

Texas does not have an automatic liquidated damages provision (see below). The agent may, however, suggest that the at-risk earnest money be sufficient to balance the market risk of a home seller in the event of default. The promulgated contracts give the majority of market risk to the seller for the time during the option period. To balance the market, offer additional earnest money in an amount which balances the market risk.

The amount generally considered adequate for liquidated damages is 3% of the purchase price, or a little more if the seller moves out of the property prior to closing in anticipation of that closing.

Suit for Specific Performance   If the seller breaches a real estate sales contract, the buyer may sue for specific performance unless the contract specifically states otherwise. In a **suit for specific performance**, the buyer asks the court to force the seller to go through with the sale and transfer the property as previously agreed.

The seller tenders the deed and asks that the buyer be required to pay the agreed price. In anticipation of a buyer planning to default on the contract, the seller is usually advised to proceed towards settlement as scheduled in order to show good faith intent to carry out the terms of the contract.

Curable Breach   Not all breaches result in termination. This concept allows the defaulting party to come into compliance with the contract. With the exception of the termination option (paragraph 23), the One to Four Family Residential Contract (Resale) does not have a "time is of the essence" provision, which may allow extra time for performance.

If the buyer fails to close on the close date without an extension granted in the contract, this is considered a curable breach and closing may take place in a reasonable time.

Anticipatory Breach   The most common example of an anticipatory breach is when the buyer decides to not proceed with the contract. The question then becomes one of loss mitigation on the part of the seller. With this notice in mind, the listing agent should consider returning to marketing efforts demonstrated prior to the current contract. Most agents will mark the listing "active" in the MLS, remove the "pending" sign, and look for a new buyer.

Substantial Compliance   The following example demonstrates the concept of substantial compliance.

■ **FOR EXAMPLE**   The contract calls for the seller to remove all the rocks in the garden. At closing, most of the rocks were moved, but two very small rocks were still there. One might argue that this breach would allow the buyer the remedy of rescission, but likely, substantial compliance would control.

As with all contract issues, the parties should be advised by their agents to use common sense in the resolution of disputes. It is the agent's responsibility to avoid any unnecessary strain on customers/clients. Only when this fails should they be advised to seek legal help.

Liquidated Damages   To avoid a lawsuit if one party breaches the contract, the parties may agree on a certain amount of money that will compensate the non-breaching party. Such money is called **liquidated damages**. If a sales contract specifies that the earnest money deposit is to serve as liquidated damages in case the buyer defaults, the seller will be entitled to keep the deposit if the buyer refuses to perform without good reason. The seller who keeps the deposit as liquidated damages may not sue for any further damages if the contract provides that the deposit is the seller's sole remedy.

The contract may limit the remedies available to the parties. A liquidated damages clause in a real estate purchase contract specifies the amount of money to which the seller is entitled if the buyer breaches the contract.

■ SUMMARY

A real estate contract contains the complete agreement between a buyer and a seller. It includes

- sales price and terms,
- legal description,
- evidence of title, and
- all terms and conditions plus any contingencies.

The process includes offer to purchase, possible counteroffers, and final acceptance.

Sales contracts must be in writing to be enforceable due to the statute of frauds.

In some states, a shorter binder is prepared before an actual contract is written.

During the time between contract acceptance and closing, the buyer has equitable title.

The document includes

- sales price and terms;
- personal and financial information;
- legal description—three methods:
  - metes and bounds—older system, rotates around point of beginning,
  - rectangular survey system—uses meridian and range lines to form townships, with townships divided into sections, and
  - lot and block—based on recorded subdivision plat;
- earnest money deposit; and
- required agency or property disclosures.

Conveyance of the property involves

- type of deed,
- date and place of closing,
- name of closing agent,
- results of title search,
- possible destruction of premises,
- contingencies to be satisfied,
- signatures of all parties, and
- addenda or amendments.

Default and breach of contract provisions that may be included in the contract include the following:

- Rescission
- Suit for money damages
- Suit for specific performance

UNIT 5 REVIEW QUESTIONS

1. In a standard sales contract, several words were crossed out or inserted by the parties. To eliminate future controversy as to whether the changes were made before or after the contract was signed, the usual procedure is to
   a. write a letter to each party listing the changes.
   b. have each party write a letter to the other approving the changes.
   c. redraw the entire contract.
   d. have both parties initial or sign in the margin near each change.

2. A broker uses earnest money placed in the company trust account to pay for the rent owed on the broker's office. Using escrow funds for this purpose is
   a. commingling of funds and is illegal.
   b. legal if the trust account is reimbursed by the end of the calendar month.
   c. legal if the seller gives consent in writing.
   d. conversion of funds and is illegal.

3. A sales contract may include additional details, such as any of the following EXCEPT
   a. a legal description of the land.
   b. a statement of the form of deed to be delivered by the seller.
   c. a history of previous owners of the property.
   d. the kind of title evidence to be provided.

4. An offer to purchase by a potential buyer is considered accepted when the
   a. seller signs the contract.
   b. buyer is notified that the seller has accepted the offer.
   c. seller notifies the listing broker.
   d. seller initials any changes.

5. A buyer makes an offer to purchase certain property listed with a licensee and leaves an escrow deposit with the licensee to show good faith. The broker should
   a. immediately apply the deposit to the listing expenses.
   b. put the deposit in an account, as provided by state law.
   c. give the deposit to the seller when the offer is presented.
   d. put the deposit in the broker's personal checking account.

6. In describing real estate, the system that may use a property's physical features to determine boundaries and measurements is
   a. rectangular survey.
   b. metes and bounds.
   c. government survey.
   d. lot and block.

7. In any township, the number of the section designated as the school section is
   a. 1.
   b. 16.
   c. 25.
   d. 36.

8. The LEAST specific method for identifying real property is
   a. rectangular survey.
   b. metes and bounds.
   c. street address.
   d. lot and block.

9. When buyer default creates a breach of contract, the seller may take advantage of any of the following remedies EXCEPT
   a. rescission of the contract.
   b. place a lis pendens.
   c. sue for damages.
   d. file a suit for specific performance.

10. The law that provides that the seller bear any loss due to destruction of the property before settlement is called
    a. "time is of the essence."
    b. suit for specific performance.
    c. the Uniform Probate Code.
    d. the Uniform Vendor and Purchaser Risk Act.

CHAPTER 6

Contingencies, Addenda, and Amendments

■ **identify** common contingencies included in sales contracts;

■ **state** the purpose for using a loan contingency;

■ **identify** the possible ramifications of an appraisal contingency;

■ **explain** the use of an approval of homeowner or condominium documents contingency;

■ **explain** the types of inspections sometimes required or requested by a buyer;

■ **identify** types of hazardous substances frequently covered in an inspection contingency;

■ **discuss** the benefits and the risks of allowing a sale of property contingency;

■ **describe** an amendment and how and when it is used; and

■ **describe** an addendum and how and when it is used.

■ KEY TERMS

addendum	kick-out clause	short sale
amendment	loan-to-value ratio (LTV)	synthetic stucco
asbestos	marketable title	underground storage tank
carbon monoxide (CO)	mold	(UST)
contingency	radon	walk-through items
home inspection		

■ INTRODUCTION

The sale price is usually the first thing that sellers will look at when presented with a contract, but it is often the other conditions that are included in the offer that lead to the offer's being either accepted or rejected. Sellers have been known to accept a lower offer when other conditions better suited their own plans for the future. In some cases, the decision may revolve around a requested contingency to the contract or around financing versus cash.

■ CONTINGENCIES

Additional conditions that must be satisfied before a sales contract is fully enforceable are called **contingencies**. A contingency includes the following four elements:

1. The actions necessary to satisfy the contingency
2. The time frame within which the actions must be performed
3. How the contingency may be removed
4. Who is responsible for the cost (if applicable)

Many standard form contracts include the following:

■ A loan contingency that protects the buyer's earnest money until a lender commits the loan funds
■ An appraisal contingency to substantiate the purchase price and ensure that the financing described in the contract is feasible
■ A title contingency to ensure that the purchaser receives clear title to the property
■ An approval of homeowners or condominium association documents contingency

Other common contingencies include the following:

■ An inspection contingency may be requested for termites, wood-boring insects, lead-based paint, structural and mechanical systems, sewage facilities, and radon or other toxic materials.
■ A property sale contingency occurs when buyers make the sales contract contingent on the sale of their current home. This protects the buyers from owning two homes at the same time and also helps ensure the availability of cash for the purchase.
■ A third-party financing addendum is used any time there is a new loan of any kind other than seller financing. Under this addendum, the buyer has the burden to inform the seller that the buyer was unable to obtain financing along the terms specified in the addendum. The promulgated form to be used is the Third Party Financing Addendum for Credit Approval.

Loan Contingencies

Because of the difficulty of obtaining financing today, it has become even more important that a sales contract be contingent on the buyer being able to obtain the financing as described in the sales contract. Without a loan contingency, the buyer is at risk of losing the earnest money deposit if unable to provide financing. A preapproval letter from a lender makes for a much stronger contract (see Chapter 7).

The loan contingency is actually a protection for both the buyer and the seller. If the buyer is not able to obtain the financing, the contract is void. The seller is also protected as long as there is a set time limit for the buyer to provide proof of the ability to obtain the described financing. This period should not be for more than a week or two at most. If the buyer cannot fulfill this contingency, the seller has an opportunity to void the contract and put the property back on the market.

In some states, the residential real estate purchase agreement automatically includes a financing contingency as a default provision. As long as both parties initial and complete the purchase agreement, the contingency is binding. A contract with an automatic financing contingency also provides for the contingency to be automatically removed as soon as the buyer secures financing. The risk now shifts from the seller to the buyer. Once the financing contingency is removed, the buyer must complete the sales transaction or be in default. If the original lender fails to come through with the financing offered to the buyer, either due to changes in the lender's capabilities or because the buyer provided incomplete or false information in the loan application, the buyer will now be in default. Some contracts provide that the full earnest money deposit is to be forfeited to the seller if the buyer defaults. Otherwise, the seller may sue the buyer for breach of contract.

IN PRACTICE   A seller needs to review the financing contingency terms carefully. If the financing that is described is not feasible (such as 2% interest with a 100% loan-to-value ratio), the buyer has an easy out when the financing cannot be obtained or when a loan program is no longer available. For the buyer, the financing needs to be described in sufficient detail to be within comfortable means; an acceptable rate of interest and number of points should be included.

An Appraisal Contingency

An appraisal contingency is closely tied to the mortgage contingency. An appraisal that comes in for less than the sales price, will most likely present a problem for the buyer. A lender establishes a **loan-to-value ratio (LTV)** for different loan programs. The LTV is the percentage of the sales price that the lender will allow a buyer to borrow. An LTV of 80% will allow $80,000 to be borrowed on a $100,000 sales price; an LTV of 90% would allow for a $90,000 loan. In earlier years, many lenders offered loans with 97% and even 100% LTV. As a result of the tightened qualifying standards brought on by the economic crisis starting in 2007, anything higher than a 95% LTV is rare. The only exceptions are with FHA loans that use 96.5% LTV and VA loans with 100% LTV.

IN PRACTICE   A house sells for $200,000. The buyer's lender will allow an LTV of 90%, meaning that the lender will loan $180,000. If the house only appraises for $190,000, the lender will still only loan 90% of the $190,000 or $171,000. If the buyer does not have adequate funds to pay the difference in the down payment, the contract will be in jeopardy.

An appraisal contingency in the sales contract should state what happens in the case of a low appraisal. Possible resolutions are

- the contract is automatically declared void,
- the buyer is given a certain amount of time to find a different loan program,
- the buyer shows evidence of additional cash to increase the amount of down payment, and
- the seller agrees to lower the sales price to the appraised amount.

Note that with a VA loan, the buyer has the right to void the contract, regardless of a decrease in sales price.

A Title Contingency

Many form contracts include a paragraph stating that the seller will provide a **marketable title** to the purchaser. The term *marketable* is the key word. When a title search is made by a title and escrow company, certain defects in the title may be found. In some cases, the title company is willing to "insure over the defect" and provide title insurance to the new owner. However, the defect remains in place and can present a problem for any future purchaser of the property. This becomes a legal issue as to whether or not a marketable title is being conveyed and may require consultation with an attorney.

Approval of Homeowners and Condominium Association Documents Contingency

The regulation of homeowners and condominium associations varies according to the state where the property is located, but whenever a condominium unit, or a residence located within a community subject to homeowners association guidelines, is purchased, the purchaser must be made aware of the required obligations and/or restrictions for residents in such developments.

State law may specify the exact forms and documents that must be provided to a potential purchaser, but subjects certain to be covered include

- the amount of fees or dues to be paid monthly, quarterly, or annually;
- any requirements for maintenance upkeep or repairs;
- any restrictions on painting, fencing, or parking; and
- use of common-area facilities such as swimming pool, tennis courts, and picnic or playground areas.

The seller is given a certain time frame to provide the required documents for the purchaser; the purchaser is given a set time to respond with either approval or rejection of the documents. The contingency should also include language that provides that the purchaser's earnest money deposit is to be returned without penalty if the documents are rejected. Because this puts the seller at risk for the duration of the contingency, the time frame given for the purchaser to either approve or reject should be kept short. In some states, failure to provide these condominium or association documents for purchaser to review may give the purchaser legal grounds to void the contract.

IN PRACTICE   A young woman is making her first home purchase. She has selected a two-bedroom condominium unit close to public transportation and featuring numerous amenities that are very attractive to her. She makes an offer to purchase on Tuesday, May 1. According to her state law, she must receive a package of condominium documents within three business days. She then has three business days to either accept or reject the documents. The seller's agent delivers the condo documents to the buyer's agent on Thursday, May 3. The agent is not able to deliver the documents because the purchaser is out of town on business and does not return until Thursday, May 10. The state law specifies that if there is no response from the purchaser within the stated time frame, the contingency may be considered removed and the contract will be in full force. As long as this is agreeable with the purchaser, there is no problem. However, while on the business trip, she was offered a new job with a much higher salary but located in another city, and she no longer wants to buy this property. Now she has a problem.

An Inspection Contingency

The time frame for an inspection contingency is very important. The seller has taken the property off the market to allow the buyer to complete a requested inspection. If problems arise as result of the inspection, it may take additional time to reach a satisfactory resolution for both parties. Generally, a contingency for any type of inspection does not extend more than 10 to 15 days. At the end of the stated period, the purchaser will either sign off that the results of the inspection were satisfactory or give notice to the seller that unless any defects uncovered by the inspection are to be resolved, the contract will become void.

Home Inspection

The most common inspection contingency is for a **home inspection**. A home inspection provides the buyer with the opportunity to learn valuable information about the electrical, plumbing, and heating and cooling systems in the house; the condition of appliances and the roof; and any signs of poor drainage causing water in the basement. The selection of a home inspector is important. Most sellers will not agree to have the home inspection done by anyone other than a licensed, certified inspector. In some cases, a seller may even require that the inspector be a member of the American Society of Home Inspectors (ASHI).

After the home inspection is completed, the purchaser can present the seller with a list of defective items reported by the home inspector. If the seller is unwilling to remedy the problems, the purchaser is free to terminate the contract with full refund of earnest money deposit. In some cases, the seller may agree to correct some of the listed defects, but not others. This becomes a counteroffer to the buyer, who may then either accept the terms provided by the seller or make a further counter. Hopefully, a compromise can be reached and the contract may continue toward settlement. A seller who is unable or does not wish to make the corrections required by the seller may offer a monetary amount of credit to be given at settlement. This needs to be handled carefully, however, because it may affect the terms of the financing being used for the purchase. Many loan programs have a limitation on the amount of monetary credit that a seller may give to a purchaser.

Unless a sales contract specifies that all systems and appliances are to be conveyed in an as-is condition, it is customarily expected that plumbing, electrical, and heating and cooling systems, along with appliances, will be in normal working condition. The list of items that are either defective or in need of repair received from a home inspector often includes items that fall under this category. It can be helpful if the purchaser and the purchaser's agent make separate lists of items needing attention based on the home inspection and **walk-through items** that will need to be brought into normal working condition before settlement.

The cost for a home inspection varies throughout the country and may be either a set fee or based on a percentage of the value of the home. The home inspector is basically a generalist—that is, having a lot of knowledge about the systems and construction of a house, but not being an expert in any one field. For example, if the home inspector notes a possible structural problem, the purchaser would be referred to a structural engineer for consultation.

The Federal Housing Administration (FHA) requires that any potential purchaser planning to obtain an FHA loan for the purchase of property be given the one-page flyer For Your Protection: Get a Home Inspection (see Figure 6.1). Although only required for FHA loans, it is good advice for all purchasers.

Regulatory Inspections

Certain types of inspections may be required by either federal or state law.

Lead-Based Paint   Federal law requires sellers and landlords to provide a disclosure of known lead-based paint hazards for any property built before 1978. Although the law does not require the seller to test for the presence of lead-based paint or to remove it, purchasers, especially those with small children, may require that their contract be contingent on a satisfactory lead-based paint inspection. If lead-based paint is found and the purchaser requires its removal, there are additional regulations for how the removal must be handled. See Figure 4.6 for the disclosure form provided by the Environmental Protection Agency (EPA).

Termites   Many states, especially those in the South, require a mandatory inspection for termites or other wood-destroying insects for all properties being sold. A termite inspection is not usually part of a home inspection but must be contracted for separately. The responsibility for this inspection and any remedial action is usually borne by the seller. Because the seller bears the responsibility for correction of any problems, the purchaser may choose to select the inspector. An inspector should be licensed by either the state's Department of Agriculture or the state agency responsible for regulating termite control within the state. In Texas, inspectors are licensed by the Texas Department of Agriculture. Note that termites can also cause problems in northern states, even Alaska.

Well and Septic   Inspection of well and septic systems is regulated by local jurisdiction and is more common in suburban and rural areas. Specific guidelines generally detail the requirements for approval of these systems. A contingency for a satisfactory well and septic inspection is often mandatory in some areas. If public water and/or waste systems are available, the purchaser may be required to hook up to these lines. A contingency dealing with any potential costs for installation should be prepared to protect the purchaser in such case.

Underground Storage Tanks   State and federal laws impose strict requirements on landowners whose property contains **underground storage tanks (USTs)**. EPA regulations apply to tanks that contain hazardous substances or liquid petroleum products that store at least 10% of their volume underground. Some states have adopted laws that are even more stringent than the federal laws. A contingency requiring inspection or removal of any underground storage tanks by the seller before closing could save the purchaser from a great deal of later expense for detection, removal, and cleanup of surrounding contaminated soil.

FIGURE   6.1

For Your Protection: Get a Home Inspection

CAUTION

U.S. Department of Housing
and Urban Development
Federal Housing Administration (FHA)

OMB Approval No: 2502-0538
(exp. 05/31/2014)

For Your Protection:
Get a Home Inspection

Why a Buyer Needs a Home Inspection

A home inspection gives the buyer more detailed information about the overall condition of the home prior to purchase. In a home inspection, a qualified inspector takes an in-depth, unbiased look at your potential new home to:

- ✔ Evaluate the physical condition: structure, construction, and mechanical systems;
- ✔ Identify items that need to be repaired or replaced; and
- ✔ Estimate the remaining useful life of the major systems, equipment, structure, and finishes.

Appraisals are Different from Home Inspections

An appraisal is different from a home inspection. Appraisals are for lenders; home inspections are for buyers. An appraisal is required to:

- ✔ Estimate the market value of a house;
- ✔ Make sure that the house meets FHA minimum property standards/requirements; and
- ✔ Make sure that the property is marketable.

FHA Does Not Guarantee the Value or Condition of your Potential New Home

If you find problems with your new home after closing, FHA can not give or lend you money for repairs, and FHA can not buy the home back from you. That is why it is so important for you, the buyer, to get an independent home inspection. Ask a qualified home inspector to inspect your potential new home and give you the information you need to make a wise decision.

Radon Gas Testing

The United States Environmental Protection Agency and the Surgeon General of the United States have recommended that all houses should be tested for radon. For more information on radon testing, call the toll-free National Radon Information Line at 1-800-SOS-Radon or 1-800-767-7236. As with a home inspection, if you decide to test for radon, you may do so before signing your contract, or you may do so after signing the contract as long as your contract states the sale of the home depends on your satisfaction with the results of the radon test.

Be an Informed Buyer

It is your responsibility to be an informed buyer. Be sure that what you buy is satisfactory in every respect. You have the right to carefully examine your potential new home with a qualified home inspector. You may arrange to do so before signing your contract, or may do so after signing the contract as long as your contract states that the sale of the home depends on the inspection.

EQUAL HOUSING
OPPORTUNITY

HUD-92564-CN (6/06)

CAUTION

Other Hazardous Substances

Depending on the potential purchaser's personal concerns or requirements, a number of other hazardous substances might cause purchasers to request a contingency for a satisfactory inspection.

Asbestos   A fire-resistant mineral once used extensively as insulation and to strengthen other building materials, **asbestos** was banned from use in 1978. According to the EPA, it is still found in about 20% of the nation's commercial and public buildings, though not as often in residential property except for in floor and ceiling tiles. Removal of asbestos requires state-licensed technicians and specially sealed environments.

Radon   Radon is a colorless, odorless, tasteless, radioactive gas produced by the decay of radioactive substances. Purchasers who are particularly concerned about the potential of cancer due to exposure to radon can make the contract contingent on a satisfactory radon inspection. If testing shows unsatisfactory levels of radon, mitigation can be fairly simple by installing a pipe and a fan to draw the radon up and out of the house.

Carbon Monoxide   Incomplete combustion of burning fuels such as wood, oil, and natural gas causes a by-product of **carbon monoxide (CO)**. Because CO is colorless, odorless, and tasteless, it can be quickly absorbed by the body without warning. Some jurisdictions may mandate the placement of CO detectors, along with required smoke detectors, in residential property. A contract can be contingent on either inspection of existing detectors or their placement in the property for sale.

Mold   The presence of mold can cause serious health problems if not removed. There are no federal requirements for the disclosure of mold, although some states do require such disclosure. **Mold** is primarily a moisture problem that can be corrected by repairing leaks, making changes to landscaping directing water away from the building, and providing adequate ventilation. Some states now require the disclosure of exterior insulation finish systems (EIFS), also called **synthetic stucco**, which does not allow moisture to escape. Purchasers subject to allergies and asthma should consider including a contingency on the disclosure and removal of any existing mold problems.

IN PRACTICE   The question of whether or not to require special inspections for hazardous conditions depends on the needs and concerns of the purchaser. Someone with severe allergies may be concerned about mold; someone with small children may be worried about lead-based paint; someone with a history of lung cancer in the family may be most concerned about possible radon. Since real estate professionals have no way to discern these issues, they should make sure buyers are fully aware of all the options.

A Property Sale Contingency

Except for first-time homebuyers, most people need to sell their present home in order to move to another property. This may be a "move up" wish for a larger home, one in a different neighborhood, or one with additional acreage. Unfortunately, when the overall real estate market is slow, as has been the case for several years, it may take a long time for a property to sell. Most sellers are not willing to have the sale of their property contingent on the buyers selling their home. That sale could be held in a pending position for a long time and possibly never be executed.

As a compromise position, the seller could accept the offer to purchase but make it contingent on the buyer's accepting a **kick-out clause**. In Texas, the buyers agree to a kick-out clause by making the sale contingent on the sale of their current property; the kick-out clause is paragraph B of the Addendum for Sale of Other Property by Buyer. This allows the seller to keep the property on the market with full disclosure in the multiple listing service that there is a contract in place, but other offers are welcome. If a new offer is made, there is a specified time (usually no more than 24 to 72 hours) for the original buyers to remove the home sale contingency and proceed with the contract. In most cases, the original buyers are unable to do so and their contract becomes void, the earnest money deposit is returned, and the new offer moves into place. Occasionally, the buyers have the financial capability to remove the contingency.

In some cases, the contingency may specify that the buyers must list their home with a real estate broker and make it available through the local multiple listing service within a short period. Cautious sellers might even specify a price range for the property to be listed. The listing broker should be able to provide the seller with sales information indicating the probability of the buyer's home being sold within a reasonable time. If the buyers already have a ratified contract on their home, the sellers might make the contract contingent on receiving a copy of that sales agreement and information regarding the prospective buyers of that property. These types of contingencies may be seen as an inappropriate invasion of the buyer's personal business, but the seller may not be willing to take any chances on the contract falling out, especially if the sellers are in the process of purchasing another property. The failure of the first contract can create a domino effect, caus-ing all contracts to become void.

Some sellers may be flexible about a time for closing, but many are not. The sellers may be planning to purchase another home in the area or may be making an offer on a house located in the town or city where they are being transferred. Elder sell-ers may be moving into an assisted-living arrangement and will lose out on their reservation unless their house is sold and settled by a certain time.

IN PRACTICE   The buyers made their contract contingent on the sale of their present property, although they actually have the funds needed to complete the purchase if they redeem a part of their portfolio of stocks and bonds. When notified that the kick-out clause is going into effect, they must act quickly to provide proof that they have the funds available and are willing to remove the home sale contingency.

The offer to purchase from the second set of purchasers should also be contingent on voiding the original contract within a certain time frame.

In a reverse situation, the seller can make the contract contingent on the seller being able to find a new home to purchase. In this case, the buyer needs to be protected by having a specific time for the completion of this new purchase. If the seller is being extremely picky or unrealistic about finding a home of choice, the buyers could be held to a pending contract for a long time, only to have it become void. If the buyers have also put their home on the market in anticipation of making the move, and the buyers' property sells, these buyers could end up with nowhere to live.

Other Types of Contingencies

The variety of types of contingencies is only limited by the wants and needs of either the buyer or the seller. Basically, a contract may be made contingent on anything as long as the three components are met:

- What is it?
- How long is it good for?
- How can it be resolved?

Following are examples of contingencies related to a specific situation:

- On buyer's being allowed to move in prior to settlement (raises questions of liability, maintenance, repairs, and others)
- On seller's renting back until children finish school where presently enrolled
- On seller's providing a property disclosure report to buyer (this is actually mandatory in some states)
- On purchaser's being able to run an internet consultation business from the home
- On verification of legal water rights for proposed use of the property
- On the ability of the land to percolate (necessary for septic fields)
- On removal of trash from the backyard
- On repainting of master bedroom
- On leaving existing washer and dryer in place
- On trimming trees in front yard
- On receiving approval from parents (particularly seen where parents are providing money for down payment or closing)
- On purchasers' getting married (VA loans require borrowers to be married)
- On appraisal of antique jewelry to be sold to provide funds for down payment

A contract can be made contingent on the receipt of further information regarding issues particular to a specific geographic area (e.g., marine clay, sinkholes, earthquake faults, coastal erosion, flood zones, or any other areas of concern to the potential purchaser).

■ AMENDMENT

The written contract is generally considered the entirety of the agreement. Changes to the terms or conditions that are made orally will be considered irrelevant in any later dispute. In order to make any changes to the existing contract, a separate written amendment or addendum must be incorporated into the original contract, as agreed upon and signed by all parties.

An **amendment** is a change or modification to the existing content of a contract. Any time words or provisions are added to or deleted from the body of the contract, the contract has been amended. Once the original contract has been ratified (signed by all parties), any changes need to be addressed in a separate form.

The Amendment to Contract form (see Figure 6.2) promulgated by TREC must be used in connection with any amendment to the contract. The form has eight specific common paragraph points, plus a designated space for "other modifications." The amendment must always reference the original contract, listing the parties involved, the date of ratification, and the legal address of the property. The amendment form may include space at the bottom for the recipient to accept, reject, or counteroffer. The process continues until all parties have reached agreement or the amendment is declared void.

FIGURE 6.2

Amendment to Contract

PROMULGATED BY THE TEXAS REAL ESTATE COMMISSION (TREC) 12-05-11

EQUAL HOUSING OPPORTUNITY

AMENDMENT

TO CONTRACT CONCERNING THE PROPERTY AT

____
(Street Address and City)

Seller and Buyer amend the contract as follows: (check each applicable box)

❑(1) The Sales Price in Paragraph 3 of the contract is:
A. Cash portion of Sales Price payable by Buyer at closing .... $________________
B. Sum of financing described in the contract.. $________________
C. Sales Price (Sum of A and B) .... $________________

❑(2) In addition to any repairs and treatments otherwise required by the contract, Seller, at Seller's expense, shall complete the following repairs and treatments:

❑(3) The date in Paragraph 9 of the contract is changed to ___________________________, 20_______.

❑(4) The amount in Paragraph 12A(1)(b) of the contract is changed to $ ______________________.

❑(5) The cost of lender required repairs and treatment, as itemized on the attached list, will be paid as follows: $ _________________________ by Seller; $ __________________________ by Buyer.

❑(6) Buyer has paid Seller an additional Option Fee of $ __________________ for an extension of the unrestricted right to terminate the contract on or before ___________________________________, 20________. This additional Option Fee ❑ will ❑ will not be credited to the Sales Price.

❑(7) Buyer waives the unrestricted right to terminate the contract for which the Option Fee was paid.

❑(8) The date for Buyer to give written notice to Seller that Buyer cannot obtain Credit Approval as set forth in the Third Party Financing Condition Addendum for Credit Approval is changed to _________________, 20_______.

❑(9) **Other Modifications**: (Insert only factual statements and business details applicable to this sale.)

EXECUTED the ______day of ______________________________, 20_____ . (BROKER: FILL IN THE DATE OF FINAL ACCEPTANCE.)

______________________ Buyer	______________________ Seller
______________________ Buyer	______________________ Seller

This form has been approved by the Texas Real Estate Commission for use with similarly approved or promulgated contract forms. Such approval relates to this form only. TREC forms are intended for use only by trained real estate licensees. No representation is made as to the legal validity or adequacy of any provision in any specific transactions. It is not intended for complex transactions. Texas Real Estate Commission, P.O. Box 12188, Austin, TX 78711-2188, 512-936-3000 (http://www.trec.texas.gov) TREC No. 39-7. This form replaces TREC No. 39-6..

TREC NO. 39-7

The three most common amendments are presented as follows.

Paragraph 2

☐(2) In addition to any repairs and treatments otherwise required by the contract, Seller, at Seller's expense, shall complete the following repairs and treatments:

This is followed by about five typewritten lines in which to record any pertinent information, but if that space is insufficient, then attach an exhibit and so note in the space provided. The quantity and quality of the repairs should be specific enough so that there is no disappointment on the part of either party. For example, if there is peeling paint on the fascia board, it would not be sufficient to write "paint fascia." Instead, write

> *"peeling paint on fascia board on the west side; repair as follows: Scrape all loose paint, sand sufficiently smooth and then (when the temperature is between 55 and 85 degrees Fahrenheit, prime with oil base paint. Clean, scuff and then paint entire west side with Behr paint #S-G 760 Chocolate Coco, semi-gloss paint."*

Here is another example: Instead of writing "put enough insulation in attic to meet code," write:

> *"(1) Remove all debris from attic, then (2) remove existing mineral wool insulation. Prior to proceeding with Step 3, inform buyer that Steps 1 and 2 are complete and allow 48 hours for an inspection. (Note that notification protocol is contained in the contract.) (3) Seal all gaps and install Energy Star-approved insulation barriers around eight recessed "can" lighting fixtures. Install Owens-Corning loose-fill blown-in insulation to a minimum of R-38."*

These two examples are demonstrations of specificity; agents are required to both understand the condition and the fix that will be satisfactory to the customer/client.

Paragraph 3

☐(3) The date in Paragraph 9 of the contract is changed to _____, 20_____.

This clause is self-explanatory but is usually a disappointment to the parties involved. Common reasons for the extension of time to close include

- unresolved repair issues,
- loan underwriter issues,
- contingent home sale closing delay, and
- title defect issues, usually regarding an estate.

Paragraph 6

☐(6) Buyer has paid Seller an additional Option Fee of $ _____ for an extension of the unrestricted right to terminate the contract on or before _____ , 20_____. This additional Option Fee ☐ will ☐ will not be credited to the Sales Price.

This clause is used when the buyer wishes to have extra time, such as for further inspections. After the general home inspection, the report may call for additional inspections or evaluations by specific contractors which may require additional time, especially if the initial option period was short.

■ **FOR EXAMPLE**   A standard form contract has a provision requiring closing in 90 days. If the purchaser wanted settlement to occur within 60 days, this change could be made during the offer and counteroffer period by striking the 90 days and replacing it with 60 days, marking the margin with a cross-hatch for all parties to initial. However, if this change is to be made after all parties have signed off, a separate amendment must be prepared requiring the signature of all parties. If one party is not willing to agree to the amendment, the original contract remains in place.

IN PRACTICE   Settlement is scheduled for May 15 in the sales contract. The sellers want to amend the contract to have settlement on May 30 in order for their oldest child to graduate from high school while still living in the family's present home. In some cases, this would be agreeable to the buyers but not always. Suppose the buyers are scheduled to settle on their present home on May 16. To change the date of settlement on the new property would leave them without a place to live from May 16 to May 30.

■ ADDENDUM

An amendment amends or changes a provision in the original contract, while an **addendum** provides additional material to augment the original contract. The addendum must name the parties involved and include the date of ratification and the legal address of the property.

There are many specified promulgated addendum choices in paragraph 22 of the One to Four Family Residential Contract (Resale) (see Figure 5.1). One or more boxes may be checked when using this paragraph.

Third Party Financing Addendum for Credit Approval

This form is used any time there is a new loan of any kind except seller financing. The buyer has the burden to inform the seller that the buyer was unable to obtain financing along the terms specified in the addendum.

Seller Financing Addendum

In any case where the seller has agreed to provide the financing for the sale, an addendum needs to be prepared outlining all the credit terms, taxes and assessments, method and time of payment, required disclosures, title insurance, and any other information pertinent to local jurisdiction regulations.

The seller has seven days to terminate the contract, even if the buyer does not provide the documentation within the time specified in paragraph A. Paragraph D(1) invites the seller to determine if there will be an alienation clause in the deed of trust. Finally, the seller must decide if he wants to have the burden of collecting, paying, accounting for, and providing an escrow analysis every year.

Addendum for Property Subject to Mandatory Membership in a Property Owners Association

The buyer and the buyer's agent should ensure that they understand each clause in this form. In paragraphs A and B, the actual amount of the fees required should be ascertained in advance of having either party sign a blank check. The bold notice just before the signature lines outlines repairs by the association; it is not unusual for the buyer's agent to prepare a repair request for items that the seller is not able to perform.

Buyer's Temporary Residential Lease

This form encompasses the attributes of a regular lease except that the entire amount of the rent will be collected at closing. Another issue is the holdover rent amount, which most buyers put at two or three times the market rent for the property.

Loan Assumption Addendum

This form specifies whether the seller is released from liability in the note.

Addendum for Sale of Other Property by Buyer

Paragraph E is the "time is of the essence" provision. A seller who accepts this contingency will usually give the buyer between one and three days to remove it and will require an amount necessary to cover liquidated damages (usually about 3% of the selling price).

Addendum for Reservation of Oil, Gas and Other Minerals

This form is used when the seller is reserving part or all of the minerals. Great care must be taken when discussing the use of this form with sellers, and it may be to the sellers' benefit to contact a lawyer.

Addendum for "Back-Up" Contract

An addendum is required whenever there are backup offers on a property. The addendum should state that in the event the primary contract becomes void, the backup contract becomes primary. Attention must be paid to disposition of earnest money, time frame for acceptance, and right of the buyer to terminate.

Note that the option fee and earnest money will be handled as if the contract were moving forward. Also consider what happens if the first contract asks for an extension. There are two effective dates to think about: the one in the contract, which is handled just like any other contract, and the amended effective date, which starts when acceptance notice is given by the seller, at which all time periods in the first contract start.

Addendum for Coastal Area Property

This disclosure requires the buyer to understand the potential boundary issue with reference to the tidal action of waterways.

Environmental Assessment, Threatened or Endangered Species, and Wetlands Addendum

This form gives the buyer, at his own expense, an opportunity to determine if there are any environmental or wetland issues. The burden to remove this contingency rests with the buyer. It cannot be used as an excuse to terminate the contract without a report that indicates that the property is adversely affected by items specified in the form.

Seller's Temporary Residential Lease

This form is used when the seller will occupy the property after the closing. If the buyer is obtaining a Fannie Mae owner-occupied loan, this lease should not extend beyond 60 days, even though it is good for up to 90 days. The deed of trust requires the borrower to occupy the home within 60 days or default. Fannie Mae and other lenders are required to perform quality control (QC) on loans, and they primarily check whether the owner actually occupies the home within 60 days.

Short Sale Addendum

As a result of the economic crisis suffered in this country, many properties have been sold as a **short sale**. Because short sales can be complex and difficult, short-sale addendum forms have been produced by TREC, lenders, multiple-listing services, and REALTOR® organizations that provide standard forms. Freddie Mac provides a short-sale addendum form that is required of all servicers of Freddie Mac loans.

Addendum for Property Located Seaward of the Gulf Intracoastal Waterway

This form is used for waterfront properties and should be read carefully by the buyer. The two primary issues are potential public access over the property and erosion of the property due to tidal action and/or weather.

Addendum for Seller's Disclosure of Information on Lead-based Paint and Lead-based Paint Hazards as Required by Federal Law

Note that paragraphs B, C, and D must be checked and that paragraph F must be signed by the buyer(s), seller(s), and both the listing agent and the selling agent.

Addendum for Property in a Propane Gas System Service Area

This required disclosure was developed to give information to any buyer that is considering buying a property serviced by a propane distribution company. The disclosure must be given to the buyer prior to execution of a binding contract.

■ SUMMARY

Contingencies are additional conditions that must be satisfied before a sales contract is fully enforceable. Three elements are necessary:

■ The actions necessary to satisfy the contingency
■ The time frame within which the actions must be performed
■ How the contingency may be removed

Contingencies are often included in standard form contracts:

■ Mortgage contingency—protects buyer's earnest money
■ Appraisal contingency—substantiates purchase price
■ Title contingency—ensures buyer receives clear title
■ Approval of homeowners or condominium association documents—mandated by state regulations

Other common contingencies include the following:

- Inspection contingency—home, regulatory, or hazard
- Property sale contingency—sale of buyer's home

An amendment is a change to the original contract.

An addendum is additional information that is part of the original contract.

CHAPTER 6 REVIEW QUESTIONS

1. A seller willing to accept a contingency on the purchasers selling their present home would be protected by all of the following *EXCEPT*

   a. requiring the purchaser's property to be entered in the MLS within 24 hours.

   b. having the listing agent prepare a competitive market analysis on the purchaser's home.

   c. including a kick-out clause to allow continued marketing of the seller's home.

   d. leaving the termination date of the contingency open until the projected closing date.

2. On property built before January 1978, the obligation to provide a buyer with a lead-based paint disclosure belongs to the

   a. lender.

   b. seller.

   c. buyer's broker.

   d. listing broker.

3. Including a contingency in a sales contract makes the contract

   a. valid.

   b. void.

   c. voidable.

   d. unenforceable.

4. A contingency that might result in the seller lowering the sales price is a

   a. mortgage contingency.

   b. appraisal contingency.

   c. title contingency.

   d. inspection contingency.

5. A home inspector is considered a generalist. This means that the home inspector

   a. has served in the military.

   b. is an expert in all aspects of home construction.

   c. is knowledgeable about most home systems and construction but is not an expert.

   d. is similar to a general contractor.

6. The main difference between an amendment and an addendum is that an amendment

   a. is a change to existing content in the contract.

   b. is additional material to be added to a contract.

   c. is the same as a contingency.

   d. does not require signatures from all parties.

7. The two most common inspections for a homebuyer are

   a. home inspection and termite.

   b. roof and termite.

   c. home inspection and septic system.

   d. septic and energy.

8. The short sale addendum may be used

   a. if the commission will be less than 6%.

   b. if the seller wishes to avoid capital gains tax.

   c. when the final selling price will be less than the loan amount.

   d. in none of these situations.

9. It is best to allow time between the inspection and the end of the option period because

   a. sellers and agents will not extend option periods.

   b. the buyer will be in breach if she does not complete all repairs prior to closing.

   c. sellers are obligated to repair all health and safety issues prior to closing.

   d. it gives time to negotiate repairs.

10. The contingency most often used for the buyer's protection is the

    a. inspection contingency.

    b. loan contingency.

    c. title contingency.

    d. escrow closing contingency.

CHAPTER 7

Financing Real Estate

■ **LEARNING OBJECTIVES** *When you have completed this chapter, you will be able to*

■ **identify** the basic components of a promissory note;

■ **define** loan origination fee, discount points, and prepayment penalty;

■ **explain** a deed of trust and why lenders prefer it;

■ **explain** the use of a land contract or owner financing;

■ **identify** the two general types of foreclosure proceedings;

■ **identify** the types of institutions in the primary and secondary mortgage markets;

■ **describe** the various types of financing techniques available;

■ **discuss** the significance of private mortgage insurance on conventional loans;

■ **compare** FHA and VA government loans; and

■ **examine** the role of government financing regulations: Truth in Lending, Equal Credit Opportunity, and Real Estate Settlement Procedures Acts.

■ KEY TERMS

acceleration clause	Federal Home Loan Bank (FHLB)	novation
adjustable-rate mortgage (ARM)	Federal Reserve System (the Fed)	package loan
alienation clause	first mortgage or deed of trust	payment cap
amortized loan	foreclosure	prepayment penalty
annual percentage rate (APR)	Freddie Mac	primary mortgage market
assume	Ginnie Mae	private mortgage insurance (PMI)
balloon payment	home equity line of credit (HELOC)	promissory note
beneficiary	home equity loan	purchase-money mortgage (PMM)
buydown	hypothecation	rate cap
certificate of eligibility	impound or escrow account	Regulation Z
certificate of reasonable value (CRV)	in arrears	release deed
computerized loan origination (CLO)	index	reverse mortgage
conforming loan	interest	satisfaction
construction loan	interest-only mortgage	second mortgage or deed of trust
conventional loan	land contract	secondary mortgage market
deed in lieu of foreclosure	lien theory	straight loan
deed of trust	loan origination fee	"subject to"
deficiency judgment	loan-to-value ratio (LTV)	thrifts
discount point	margin	trigger terms
draws	mortgage	trustee
equitable right of redemption	mortgage insurance premium (MIP)	trustor
Fannie Mae	negotiable instrument	Truth in Lending Act (TILA)
Farmer Mac	nonconforming loan	usury

■ INTRODUCTION

Perhaps the most important investment decision most individuals ever make is buying a home. In the United States, relatively few homes are purchased for cash. Most homes are bought with borrowed money, and a huge lending industry has been built to service the financial requirements of homebuyers. It was pointed out in Chapter 6 that a buyer can be protected by making the contract contingent on the buyer's being able to obtain a certain type of financing as described in the contract. If the buyer cannot get funding to purchase the property, there can be no transaction.

Although a typical sales contract only contains a paragraph or two regarding financing, this chapter provides an overall review of financing principles and practice that can be an important asset for licensees who will be preparing the contract and discussing financing options with a client.

■ MORTGAGE LAW

A **mortgage** is a lien or encumbrance on real property. The borrower, or trustor, receives a loan and in return gives a note and deed of trust to the lender. When the loan is paid in full, the lender issues a release of lien. The deed of trust is a voluntary, specific lien. If the debtor defaults, the lender can foreclose on the deed of trust.

In **lien theory** states, the borrower retains both legal and equitable title. The lender simply has a lien on the property as security for the debt. The deed of trust is collateral for the loan. If the borrower defaults, the lender must go through a formal foreclosure proceeding to obtain legal title. The property is offered for sale at public auction, and the funds from the sale are used to pay the balance of the remaining debt. In some states, a defaulting mortgagor may redeem (buy back) the property during a certain period after the sale.

■ SECURITY AND DEBT

Mortgage loans are secured loans. Mortgage loans have two parts: the debt itself and the security for the debt. When a property is mortgaged, the owner must *execute* (sign) two separate instruments—a promissory note stating the amount owed, and a security document, either a mortgage or deed of trust, specifying the collateral used to secure the loan.

Hypothecation

In mortgage lending practice, a borrower is required to pledge specific real property as security (collateral) for the loan. The debtor retains the right of possession and control, while the creditor receives an underlying equitable right in the pledged property. This type of pledging is termed **hypothecation**. The right to foreclose on the pledged property in the event a borrower defaults is contained in a security agreement, such as a mortgage or a deed of trust.

■ PROMISSORY NOTE

The **promissory note**, called the note or financing instrument, is the borrower's personal promise to repay a debt according to agreed terms.

A promissory note executed by a borrower is a contract complete in itself. It generally states the amount of the debt, the time and method of payment, and the rate of interest. When signed by the borrowers, the note becomes a legally enforceable and fully negotiable instrument of debt. When the terms of the note are satisfied, the debt is discharged. If the terms of the note are not met, the lender may choose to sue to collect on the note or to foreclose.

A note is a **negotiable instrument** like a check or bank draft. The lender who holds the note is called the payee and may transfer the right to receive payment by assigning the note to a third party.

IN PRACTICE All notes should be clearly dated. Accurate dates are essential because time is of the essence in every real estate contract. Also, the dates of the notes may be necessary to determine the chronological order of priority rights.

Interest

Interest is a charge for the use of money. A lender charges a percentage in interest on the principal over the time of loan. Payments made at the end of a payment period are called payments **in arrears** and are the general practice.

Usury   Charging interest in excess of the maximum rate allowed by law is called **usury**. To protect consumers from unscrupulous lenders, many states have enacted laws limiting the interest rate that may be charged on loans. In most cases, usury laws do not apply to depository institutions.

Loan Origination Fee

When a mortgage loan is originated, a **loan origination fee** is charged by most lenders to cover the expenses involved in generating the loan. A loan origination fee is not prepaid interest; it is a charge that must be paid to the originator. The typical loan origination fee is 1% of the loan amount, although origination fees may range from one to three points (one point equals 1% of the loan amount).

Discount points are used to increase the lender's yield (rate of return) on its investment. For example, the interest rate that a lender charges for a loan might be less than the yield an investor demands. To make up the difference, the lender charges the borrower discount points. The number of points charged depends on two factors:

- The difference between the loan's stated interest rate and the yield required by the lender
- How long the lender expects it will take the borrower to pay off the loan

A point is 1% of the amount being borrowed; it is not 1% of the purchase price.

For borrowers, one discount point equals 1% of the loan amount and is charged as prepaid interest at the closing. For example, three discount points charged on a $100,000 loan are $3,000 ($100,000 × 3%, or 0.03). If a house sells for $100,000 and the borrower seeks an $80,000 loan, each point would be $800, not $1,000. In some cases, the points in a new acquisition may be paid in cash at closing by the buyer (or by the seller on the buyer's behalf) rather than being financed as part of the total loan amount.

Prepayment Penalty

Most mortgage loans are paid in installments over a long period. As a result, the total interest paid by the borrower may add up to more than the principal amount of the loan. If the borrower repays the loan before the end of the term, the lender collects less than the anticipated interest. For this reason, some mortgage notes contain a prepayment clause that requires the borrower to pay a **prepayment penalty** for any payments made ahead of schedule. Lenders may not charge prepayment penalties on mortgage loans insured or guaranteed by the federal government or on those loans that have been sold to Fannie Mae or Freddie Mac.

■ MORTGAGES OR DEEDS OF TRUST

In some states, lenders may use a three-party instrument called a **deed of trust**. The deed is given as security for the loan to a third party, called the **trustee**. The trustee holds bare title (no right of possession) on behalf of the lender, who is called the **beneficiary**. The deed of trust establishes the actions that the trustee may take if the borrower, the **trustor**, defaults under any of the deed of trust terms (see Figures 7.1 and 7.2 for a comparison of mortgages and deeds of trust).

F I G U R E   7.1

Mortgages

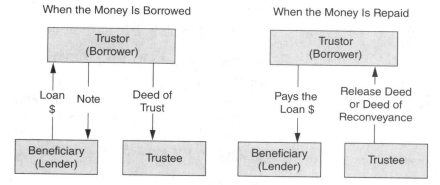

Mortgage —Two Parties

When the Money Is Borrowed

Mortgagor (Borrower) → Note and Mortgage → Mortgagee (Lender)
Mortgagee (Lender) → Loan $ → Mortgagor (Borrower)

When the Money Is Repaid

Mortgagor (Borrower) → Pays the Loan $ → Mortgagee (Lender)
Mortgagee (Lender) → Satisfaction of Mortgage → Mortgagor (Borrower)

F I G U R E   7.2

Deeds of Trust

Deed of Trust—Three Parties

When the Money Is Borrowed

Trustor (Borrower)
Beneficiary (Lender) → Loan $ → Trustor (Borrower)
Trustor (Borrower) → Note → Beneficiary (Lender)
Trustor (Borrower) → Deed of Trust → Trustee

When the Money Is Repaid

Trustor (Borrower) → Pays the Loan $ → Beneficiary (Lender)
Trustee → Release Deed or Deed of Reconveyance → Trustor (Borrower)

In states where the deed of trust is commonly used, foreclosure procedures for default are usually simpler and faster than for mortgage loans. In most cases, the lender chooses the trustee and reserves the right to substitute trustees in the event of death or dismissal.

A mortgage or deed of trust must clearly establish that the property is security for a debt, identify the lender and the borrower, and include an accurate legal description of the property. Both instruments incorporate the terms of the note by reference. They should be signed by all parties who have an interest in the real estate. Common provisions of both instruments are discussed in the following paragraphs.

Duties of the Mortgagor or Trustor

The borrower is required to fulfill certain obligations created by the mortgage or deed of trust. These usually include the following:

- Payment of the debt in accordance with the terms of the note
- Payment of all real estate taxes on the property given as security
- Maintenance of adequate insurance to protect the lender if the property is destroyed or damaged by fire, windstorm, or other hazard
- Maintenance of the property in good repair at all times
- Receipt of lender authorization before making any major alterations on the property

Failure to meet any of these obligations can result in a borrower's default. The loan documents may, however, provide for a grace period (such as 30 days) during which the borrower can meet the obligation and cure the default. If the borrower does not do so, the lender has the right to foreclose the mortgage or deed of trust and collect on the note.

Provisions for Default

The mortgage or deed of trust typically includes an **acceleration clause** to assist the lender in foreclosure. If a borrower defaults, the lender has the right to declare the entire debt due and payable immediately. Without an acceleration clause, the lender would have to sue the borrower every time a payment was overdue.

Assignment of the Mortgage

Without changing the provisions of a contract, a note may be sold to a third party, such as an investor or another mortgage company. The original mortgagee endorses the note to the third party and executes an assignment of mortgage. The assignee becomes the new owner of the debt and security instrument.

Release of the Mortgage Lien or Deed of Trust

When all loan payments have been made and the note has been paid in full, the lender is required to execute a **satisfaction**. Entering this release in the public record shows that the debt has been removed from the property. The release must be executed and recorded by the assignee or mortgagee when the mortgage or deed of trust has been assigned.

When a real estate loan secured by a deed of trust has been completely repaid, the beneficiary must make a written request that the trustee execute and deliver a **release deed** (sometimes called a deed of reconveyance) to the trustor. The release deed should be acknowledged (notarized) and recorded in the public records of the county in which the property is located.

Tax and Insurance Reserves

Many lenders require that borrowers provide a reserve fund to meet future real estate taxes and property insurance premiums. This fund is called an **impound or escrow account**. When the mortgage or deed of trust loan is made, the borrower starts the reserve by depositing funds to cover the amount of unpaid real estate taxes. If a new insurance policy has just been purchased, the insurance premium reserve will be started with the deposit of one-twelfth of the insurance premium liability. The borrower's monthly loan payments will include PITI: principal, interest, taxes, and insurance. Other costs are included, such as flood insurance. Federal regulations limit the total amount of reserves that a lender may require.

Buying "Subject to" or Assuming a Seller's Mortgage or Deed of Trust

When a person purchases real estate that has an outstanding mortgage or deed of trust, the buyer may take the property in one of two ways. The property may be purchased **"subject to"** the mortgage or deed of trust, or the buyer may **assume** the mortgage or deed of trust and agree to pay the debt. Because this technical distinction becomes important if the buyer defaults and the mortgage or deed of

Memory Tip

Recurring Monthly Costs

The basic recurring components of a borrower's monthly loan payment may be remembered as PITI:

- Principal
- Interest
- Taxes
- Insurance

trust is foreclosed, it is very important for the sale contract to accurately describe which method is being used.

When the property is sold "subject to" the mortgage, the buyers are not personally obligated to pay the debt in full. The buyers take title to the real estate knowing that they must make payments on the existing loan. Upon default, the lender forecloses and the property is sold by court order to pay the debt. If the sale does not pay off the entire debt, the purchaser is not liable for the difference; however, the original seller may continue to be liable.

In contrast, a buyer who purchases a property and assumes the seller's debt becomes personally obligated for the payment of the entire debt. If a seller wants to be completely free of the original mortgage loan, the seller(s), the buyer(s), and the lender must execute a **novation** agreement in writing. The novation makes the buyer solely responsible for any default on the loan and the original borrower (seller) is freed of any liability.

Because a loan may not be assumed without lender approval, the lending institution would require the assumer to qualify financially, and many lending institutions charge a transfer fee to cover the costs of changing the records.

Alienation Clause   The lender may want to prevent a future purchaser of the property from being able to assume the loan, particularly if the original interest rate is low. For this reason, most lenders include an **alienation clause** (also called a due-on-sale clause or call clause) in the note. An alienation clause provides that when the property is sold, the lender may either declare the entire debt due immediately or permit the buyer to assume the loan at an interest rate acceptable to the lender.

Recording a Mortgage or Deed of Trust

The mortgage document or deed of trust must be recorded in the recorder's office of the county in which the real estate is located. Recording gives constructive notice to the world of the borrower's obligations. Recording also establishes the lien's priority.

Priority of a Mortgage or Deed of Trust

Priority of mortgages and other liens normally is determined by the order in which they were recorded. A mortgage or deed of trust on land that has no prior mortgage lien is a **first mortgage or deed of trust**. If the owner later executes another loan for additional funds, the new loan becomes a **second mortgage or deed of trust** (or a junior lien) when it is recorded. Second loans represent greater risk to the lender, and they usually have a higher interest rate.

■ PROVISIONS OF LAND CONTRACTS AND OWNER FINANCING

Real estate can be purchased under a **land contract**, also called a contract for deed or an installment contract (see Chapter 3). Under a land contract, the buyer agrees to make a down payment and a monthly loan payment that includes interest and principal. The payment may also include real estate tax and insurance reserves. The seller retains legal title to the property during the contract term, and the buyer is granted equitable title and possession. At the end of the loan term, the seller delivers clear title. The contract usually permits the seller to evict the buyer in the event of default. In that case, the seller may keep any money the buyer has already paid, which is construed as rent.

While land contracts or owner financing can occur with residential or commercial properties, they are more common with unimproved acreage and farmland sales. Sometimes the seller is the primary lender, and at other times, the seller may be in a secondary position. In either case, the sellers would want to secure their interest either by the use of a deed, note and mortgage, deed of trust, or perhaps the use of a contract for deed instrument.

FORECLOSURE

When a borrower defaults on the payments or fails to fulfill any of the other obligations set forth in the mortgage or deed of trust, the lender's rights can be enforced through foreclosure. **Foreclosure** is a legal procedure in which property pledged as security is sold to satisfy the debt. The foreclosure procedure brings the rights of the parties and all junior lienholders to a conclusion. It passes title to either the person holding the mortgage document or deed of trust or to a third party who purchases the property at a foreclosure sale. The purchaser could be the mortgagee. The property is sold free of the foreclosing mortgage and all junior liens.

Methods of Foreclosure

There are two general types of foreclosure proceedings: judicial and non-judicial. The specific provisions and procedures depend on state law.

Judicial Foreclosure   Judicial foreclosure allows the property to be sold by court order after the mortgagee has given sufficient public notice. When a borrower defaults, the lender may accelerate the due date of the remaining principal balance, along with all overdue monthly payments and interest, penalties, and administrative costs. The lender's attorney can then file a suit to foreclose the lien. After presentation of the facts in court, the property is ordered sold. A public sale is advertised and held, and the real estate is sold to the highest bidder.

Nonjudicial Foreclosure   Some states allow nonjudicial foreclosure procedures to be used when the security instrument contains a power-of-sale clause. In nonjudicial foreclosure, no court action is required. In those states that recognize deed of trust loans, the trustee is generally given the power of sale. Some states allow a similar power of sale to be used with a mortgage loan.

To institute a nonjudicial foreclosure, the trustee or mortgagee may be required to record a notice of default at the county recorder's office. The default must be recorded within a designated period to give notice to the public of the intended auction. The notice is generally provided by newspaper advertisements that state the total amount due and the date of the public sale. After selling the property, the trustee or mortgagee may be required to file a copy of a notice of sale or an affidavit of foreclosure.

Deed in Lieu of Foreclosure

As an alternative to foreclosure, a lender may accept a **deed in lieu of foreclosure** from the borrower. This is sometimes called a friendly foreclosure because it is carried out by mutual agreement rather than by lawsuit. The disadvantage of the deed in lieu of foreclosure is to the lender because it does not eliminate junior liens. In a foreclosure action, all junior liens are eliminated. Also, by accepting a deed in lieu of foreclosure, the lender usually loses any rights pertaining to FHA or private mortgage insurance or to VA guarantees. Finally, it should be pointed out that a deed in lieu of foreclosure is still considered an adverse component in the borrower's credit history.

Cure

Most states give defaulting borrowers a chance to redeem their property through the **equitable right of redemption**. If, after default, but before the foreclosure sale, the borrower (or any other person who has an interest in the real estate, such as another creditor) pays the lender the amount in default, plus costs, the debt will be reinstated. In some cases, the person who redeems may be required to repay the accelerated loan in full. If some person other than the mortgagor or trustor redeems the real estate, the borrower becomes responsible to that person for the amount of the redemption.

Deed to Purchaser at Sale

If redemption is not made or if state law does not provide for a redemption period, the successful bidder at the sale receives a deed to the real estate. In Texas, there is generally no statutory right of redemption. An official such as a sheriff, an officer of the court, or a trustee executes this deed to the purchaser to convey whatever title the borrower had.

Deficiency Judgment

The foreclosure sale may not produce enough cash to pay the loan balance in full after deducting expenses and accrued unpaid interest. In this case, the mortgagee may be entitled to a **deficiency judgment** against the borrower for the unpaid balance. Any money that remains from the foreclosure sale after paying the debt and any other liens (such as a second mortgage or a mechanic's lien), expenses, and interest is paid to the borrower.

■ THE REAL ESTATE FINANCING MARKET

The real estate financing market has the following three basic components:

- ■ Government influences, primarily the Federal Reserve System
- ■ Primary mortgage market
- ■ Secondary mortgage market

Under the umbrella of the financial policies set by the Federal Reserve System, the primary mortgage market originates loans that are bought, sold, and traded in the secondary mortgage market.

The Federal Reserve System

The role of the **Federal Reserve System (the Fed)** is to maintain sound credit conditions, help counteract inflationary and deflationary trends, and create a favorable economic climate. The Fed divides the country into 12 federal reserve districts, each served by a federal reserve bank. All nationally chartered banks must join the Fed and purchase stock in its district reserve banks. The Fed regulates the flow of money and interest rates in the marketplace through its member banks by controlling their reserve requirements and discount rates.

The Primary Mortgage Market

The **primary mortgage market** is made up of the lenders that originate mortgage loans. Income on the loan is realized from the following two sources:

■ Finance charges collected at closing, such as loan origination fees and discount points
■ Recurring income, the interest collected during the term of the loan

In addition to the income directly related to loans, some lenders derive income from servicing loans for other mortgage lenders or investors who have purchased the loans. Servicing involves

■ collecting payments (including taxes and insurance),
■ accounting,
■ bookkeeping,
■ preparing insurance and tax records,
■ processing payments of taxes and insurance, and
■ following up on loan payment and delinquency.

Some of the major lenders in the primary market for home mortgages include the following:

■ *Thrifts, savings associations, and commercial banks.* These institutions are called fiduciary lenders because of their fiduciary obligations to protect and preserve their depositors' funds. **Thrifts** is a generic term for the savings associations.
■ *Credit unions.* Credit unions are cooperative organizations whose members place money in savings accounts. In the past, credit unions made only short-term consumer and home improvement loans. Now, they routinely originate first and second mortgage and deed of trust loans.
■ *Mortgage banking companies.* Mortgage banking companies originate mortgage loans with money belonging to insurance companies, pension funds, and individuals, and with funds of their own. They make real estate loans with the intention of selling them to investors and receiving a fee for servicing the loans.
■ *Mortgage brokers.* Mortgage brokers are not lenders. They are intermediaries who bring borrowers and lenders together. Mortgage brokers locate potential borrowers, process preliminary loan applications, and submit the applications to lenders for final approval. They do not service loans once the loans are made.

IN PRACTICE A growing number of consumers apply for mortgage loans via the internet. Many major lenders have websites that offer information to potential borrowers regarding their current loan programs and requirements. In addition, online brokerages link lenders with potential borrowers.

The Secondary Mortgage Market

In addition to the primary mortgage market, where loans are originated, there is a **secondary mortgage market**. The secondary mortgage market helps lenders raise capital to continue making mortgage loans.

In the secondary market, various agencies purchase a number of mortgage loans and assemble them into packages (called *pools*). These agencies purchase the mortgages from banks and savings associations. Securities that represent shares in these pooled mortgages are then sold to investors or other agencies (see Figure 7.3).

Secondary Market and Makeup of Loan Packages

Institution	Secondary Market Function
Fannie Mae	Conventional, VA, FHA loans
Freddie Mac	Mostly conventional loans
Ginnie Mae	Special assistance loans
Federal Home Loan Bank (FHLB)	Conventional loans
Farmer Mac	USDA/RHS loans

Fannie Mae (Federal National Mortgage Association) is a government-sponsored-enterprise (GSE) that purchases blocks or pools of both conventional and government loans (FHA and VA). These blocks or pools of mortgages may then be used as collateral for mortgage-backed securities that are sold on the global market. Since September 2008, Fannie Mae, along with Freddie Mac, has been in conservatorship under the Federal Finance Housing Agency (FHFA).

Freddie Mac (Federal Home Loan Mortgage Corporation) is also a GSE. It provides a secondary market for mortgage loans, primarily conventional loans.

Many lenders use the standardized forms and follow the guidelines issued by Fannie Mae and Freddie Mac for lenders that wish to sell mortgages in the agencies' secondary mortgage market. The standardized documents include loan applications, credit reports, and appraisal forms.

Ginnie Mae (Government National Mortgage Association) is a division of the U.S. Department of Housing and Urban Development (HUD). Ginnie Mae administers special-assistance programs and guarantees mortgage-backed securities using FHA and VA loans as collateral.

Federal Home Loan Bank (FHLB) is a GSE that purchases loans from its member savings associations (thrifts).

Farmer Mac (Federal Agricultural Mortgage Corporation) provides a secondary market for loans originated by the U.S. Department of Agriculture Rural Housing Service and the Farm Credit System.

■ FINANCING TECHNIQUES

Real estate financing comes in a wide variety of forms. While the payment plans described in the following sections are commonly called mortgages, they are really loans secured by either a mortgage or a deed of trust.

A **straight loan** (also called a term loan) essentially divides the loan into two amounts to be paid off separately. The borrower makes periodic payments of interest only, followed by the payment of the principal in full at the end of the term. Straight loans were once the only form of mortgage available. Today, they are generally used for home improvement and second mortgages rather than for residential first mortgage loans.

An **interest-only mortgage** is a mortgage that requires the payment of interest only for a stated period with the principal balance due at the end of the term. In the past, interest-only mortgages were used primarily for short-term financing. They became popular for a short time in the early years of the 2000 decade but due to the economic crisis starting in 2007, interest-only loans are very rare today.

A **balloon payment** is required when the periodic payments are not enough to fully amortize the loan by the time the final payment is due, resulting in the final payment being much larger than the others. It is a partially amortized loan because some of the principal is still owed at the end of the term.

Each payment in an **amortized loan** partially pays off both principal and interest. Most mortgage and deed in trust loans are amortized loans. The word *amortize* means to kill off. The loan is paid off in equal payments over a term of years (15 and 30 being the most common). Each payment is applied first to the interest owed; the balance of the payment is then applied to the principal amount. As a result, while each payment remains the same, the portion applied to repayment of the principal grows and the interest due declines as the unpaid balance of the loan is reduced. At the end of the term, the full amount of the principal and all interest due is reduced to zero.

IN PRACTICE Financial calculators can accurately perform most standard mortgage lending calculations, and most commercial lenders provide mortgage calculators on their websites. Nonetheless, it's valuable to understand how the calculations are performed. A mortgage interest rate factor chart indicates the amount of monthly payment per $1,000 of the loan, depending on the term and interest rate. This factor is multiplied by the number of thousands of the amount borrowed (see Figure 7.4).

Adjustable-rate mortgages (ARMs) generally originate at one rate of interest, then fluctuate up or down during the loan term, based on an economic indicator. The loan payment changes when there is a change in the interest rate. Details of how and when the interest rate will change must be included in the ARM note. Common components of an ARM include the following:

■ The **index** is an economic indicator that is used to adjust the interest rate in the loan.
■ The interest rate is the index rate plus a premium, called the **margin**. The margin represents the lender's cost of doing business.
■ **Rate caps** limit the amount the interest rate may change. Most ARMs have two types of rate caps. A periodic rate cap limits the amount the rate may increase per adjustment period. A life-of-the-loan rate cap limits the amount the rate may increase over the entire life of the loan.
■ The mortgagor may be protected from unaffordable individual payments by a payment cap. The **payment cap** sets a maximum amount for payments.
■ The adjustment establishes how often the rate may be changed (monthly, quarterly, or annually).
■ Lenders may offer a conversion option that permits the mortgagor to convert from an adjustable-rate to a fixed-rate loan at certain intervals during the life of the mortgage.

A **growing-equity mortgage** uses a fixed interest rate, but payments of principal are increased according to an index or a schedule. The total payment increases, and the loan is paid off more quickly.

A **reverse mortgage** allows people 62 or older to borrow money against the equity they have built in their home. Reverse mortgages are the opposite of conventional mortgages in that the homeowner's equity diminishes as the loan amount increases. The money may be used for any purpose and may be received in a lump sum, fixed monthly payments, an open line of credit, or other options. The borrower is charged a fixed rate of interest and no payments are due until the property is sold or the borrower defaults, moves, or dies. The FHA home equity conversion mortgage (HECM) is the most common reverse mortgage.

FIGURE 7.4

Mortgage Factor Chart

How To Use This Chart

To use this chart, start by finding the appropriate interest rate. Then follow that row over to the column for the appropriate loan term. This number is the *interest rate factor* required each month to amortize a $1,000 loan.

To calculate the principal and interest (PI) payment, multiply the interest-rate factor by the number of 1,000s in the total loan. For example, if the interest rate is 4% for a term of 30 years, the interest-rate factor is 4.78. If the total loan is $100,000, the loan contains 100 $1,000s. Therefore, 100 × 4.78 = $478 PI only.

To estimate a mortgage loan amount using the amortization chart, divide the PI payment by the appropriate interest-rate factor. Using the same facts as in the first example, the amount is calculated in this way:

$478 ÷ 4.78 = $100 $1,000s or $100,000

Rate	Term 10 Years	Term 15 Years	Term 20 Years	Term 25 Years	Term 30 Years
3	9.66	6.91	5.55	4.74	4.22
3⅛	9.71	6.97	5.61	4.81	4.28
3¼	9.77	7.03	5.67	4.87	4.35
3⅜	9.83	7.09	5.74	4.94	4.42
3½	9.89	7.15	5.80	5.01	4.49
3⅝	9.95	7.21	5.86	5.07	4.56
3¾	10.01	7.27	5.93	5.14	4.63
3⅞	10.07	7.33	5.99	5.21	4.70
4	10.13	7.40	6.06	5.28	4.78
4⅛	10.19	7.46	6.13	5.35	4.85
4¼	10.25	7.53	6.20	5.42	4.92
4⅜	10.31	7.59	6.26	5.49	5.00
4½	10.37	7.65	6.33	5.56	5.07
4⅝	10.43	7.72	6.40	5.63	5.15
4¾	10.49	7.78	6.47	5.71	5.22
4⅞	10.55	7.85	6.54	5.78	5.30
5	10.61	7.91	6.60	5.85	5.37
5⅛	10.67	7.98	6.67	5.92	5.45
5¼	10.73	8.04	6.74	6.00	5.53
5⅜	10.80	8.11	6.81	6.07	5.60
5½	10.86	8.18	6.88	6.15	5.68
5⅝	10.92	8.24	6.95	6.22	5.76
5¾	10.98	8.31	7.03	6.30	5.84
5⅞	11.04	8.38	7.10	6.37	5.92
6	11.10	8.44	7.16	6.44	6.00
6⅛	11.16	8.51	7.24	6.52	6.08
6¼	11.23	8.57	7.31	6.60	6.16
6⅜	11.29	8.64	7.38	6.67	6.24
6½	11.35	8.71	7.46	6.75	6.32
6⅝	11.42	8.78	7.53	6.83	6.40
6¾	11.48	8.85	7.60	6.91	6.49
6⅞	11.55	8.92	7.68	6.99	6.57
7	11.61	8.98	7.75	7.06	6.65
7⅛	11.68	9.06	7.83	7.15	6.74
7¼	11.74	9.12	7.90	7.22	6.82
7⅜	11.81	9.20	7.98	7.31	6.91
7½	11.87	9.27	8.05	7.38	6.99
7⅝	11.94	9.34	8.13	7.47	7.08
7¾	12.00	9.41	8.20	7.55	7.16
7⅞	12.07	9.48	8.29	7.64	7.25
8	12.14	9.56	8.37	7.72	7.34

Other Financing Techniques

Because borrowers often have different needs, a variety of other financing techniques have been created. A few of those most applicable to residential home mortgages are:

A **purchase-money mortgage (PMM)** is created when the seller agrees to finance all or part of the purchase price and consists of a first or junior lien. PMM is often used when the buyer does not qualify for a typical lender loan. The buyer/borrower executes a note and mortgage at the time of purchase; the seller records the mortgage against the property. Payments are made to the seller, according to the terms of the note; if the buyer stops making payments, the seller has recourse to foreclose on the property.

■ **FOR EXAMPLE** A man wants to buy a farm for $200,000. He has a $40,000 down payment and agrees to assume an existing mortgage of $80,000. Because the buyer might not qualify for a new mortgage under the circumstances, the owner agrees to finance a purchase-money second mortgage in the amount of $80,000. At the closing, the buyer will execute a mortgage and note in favor of the owner, who will convey title to the buyer.

A **package loan** includes real and personal property. This type of loan is popular with developers and purchasers of furnished condominiums. Package loans usually include furniture, drapes, the kitchen range, refrigerator, dishwasher, washer, dryer, food freezer, and other appliances as part of the sales price of the home.

A **construction loan** is made to finance the construction of improvements on real estate such as homes, apartments, and office buildings. The lender commits to the full amount of the loan but disburses the funds in payments during construction. These payments are also called **draws**. Draws are made to the general contractor or the owner for that part of the construction work that has been completed since the previous payment. Before each payment, the lender inspects the work. The general contractor must provide the lender with adequate waivers that release all mechanics' lien rights for the work covered by the payment.

Construction loans are generally short-term or interim financing. The borrower pays interest only on the monies that have actually been disbursed. The borrower is expected to arrange for a permanent loan, also called an end loan or take-out loan, which will repay the construction financing lender when the work is completed.

A **buydown** is a way to temporarily (or permanently) lower the interest rate on a mortgage or deed of trust loan. A lump sum is paid in cash to the lender at the closing. The payment offsets (and so reduces) the interest rate and monthly payments during the mortgage's first few years. Typical buydown arrangements reduce the interest rate by 1% to 2% over the first one to two years of the loan term. After that, the rate rises. In a permanent buydown, a larger up-front payment reduces the effective interest rate for the life of the loan.

Home equity loans are a source of funds using the equity built up in a home. The original mortgage loan remains in place; the home equity loan is junior to the original lien. It is an alternative to refinancing and can be used for almost any purpose.

A home equity loan can be taken out as a fixed loan amount or as an equity line of credit. With the **home equity line of credit (HELOC)**, the lender extends a line of credit that the borrower can use at will.

■ LOAN PROGRAMS

Mortgage loans are generally classified based on their **loan-to-value ratio (LTV)**. The LTV is the ratio of debt to value of the property. Value is the sales price or the appraisal value, whichever is less. The lower the ratio of debt to value, the higher the down payment by the borrower. For the lender, the higher down payment means a more secure loan, which minimizes the lender's risk.

IN PRACTICE   If a property has an appraised value of $200,000, secured by an $180,000 loan, the LTV is $180,000 ÷ $200,000 = 90%. An LTV of 95% on a $100,000 loan allows $95,000 to be borrowed.

Conforming Loans

Conventional loans are viewed as the most secure loans because their loan-to-value ratios are often lowest. Traditionally, the ratio is 80% of the value of the property or less because the borrower makes a down payment of at least 20%.

The secondary mortgage market has a significant impact on borrower qualifications, standards for the collateral, and documentation procedures followed by lenders. Loans must meet strict criteria to be sold to Fannie Mae and Freddie Mac. Lenders still can be flexible in their lending decisions, but they may not be able to sell unusual loans in the secondary market.

To qualify for a conventional loan under Fannie Mae guidelines, the borrower's monthly housing expenses, including PITI (principal, interest, taxes, and insurance), must not exceed 28% of total monthly gross income. Also, the borrower's total monthly obligations, including housing costs plus other regular monthly payments, must not exceed 36% of total monthly gross income with 80% LTV loans. Loans that meet these criteria are called **conforming loans** and are eligible to be sold in the secondary market.

IN PRACTICE   The Federal Housing Finance Agency (FHFA) publishes the maximum loan limits for loans sold to Fannie Mae and Freddie Mac. In 2013, the maximum loan limit for a single-family home ranged from $417,000 to $721,050 in high-cost areas. Specific loan limits are established for each county (or equivalent).

Loans that do not meet the Fannie Mae/Freddie Mac guidelines are called **nonconforming loans**. Although there is a market for these loans, they often remain held in the lender's investment portfolio.

■ **FOR EXAMPLE**   Following is the qualifying math for a $160,000 loan at 7.5% interest for 30 years with payments of $1,200 per month in principal and interest:

Combined Monthly Gross Income: $8,000

Monthly Housing Expenses:

Principal and Interest	1,200
Property Taxes	400
Hazard Insurance	50
PMI Insurance	90
Homeowners Association Dues	+ 30
Total Housing Expense	$1,770

$1,770 ÷ 8,000 = 22%

Debt Expense:

Installment Payments	$200
Revolving Charges	80
Auto Loan	250
Child Care	300
Other	+ 200
Total Debt Expense	$1,030
Plus Housing	+ $1,770
Grand Total	$2,800

$2,800 ÷ 8,000 = 35%

These borrowers will qualify for this loan under conventional loan guidelines of 28% and 36%.

Private Mortgage Insurance

One way a borrower can obtain a conventional mortgage loan with a lower down payment is by obtaining **private mortgage insurance (PMI)**. In a PMI program, the buyer purchases an insurance policy that provides the lender with funds in the event that the borrower defaults on the loan.

PMI protects the top portion of a loan, usually 20% to 30%, against borrower default. The borrower pays a monthly premium or fee that may be financed within the loan. Because only a portion of the loan is insured, once the loan is repaid to a certain level, the lender may agree to allow the borrower to terminate the PMI coverage.

IN PRACTICE   On loans originating after July 1999, federal law requires that PMI automatically terminate if a borrower has accumulated at least 22% equity in the home and is current on mortgage payments. The 22% of equity is based on the purchase price of the home, not on any appreciation of the property. Once the original loan has been reduced to 80% LTV, the borrower can request removal of the PMI, but the lender will require an appraisal.

FHA-Insured Loans

The Federal Housing Administration (FHA), which operates under HUD, insures lenders against loss from borrower default.

The most popular FHA program is Title II, Section 203(b), fixed-interest-rate loans for 10 to 30 years on one- to four-family residences. Rates are competitive with other types of loans, even though they are high-LTV loans. Under this program, the borrower is eligible for approximately 96.5% financing for one- to four-unit structures. Certain requirements must be met before the FHA will insure the loans. These requirements include the following:

■ The borrower must pay a down payment of at least 3.5% of the purchase price.

■ The borrower is charged a **mortgage insurance premium (MIP)** for all FHA loans. The up-front premium is charged at closing and can be financed into the mortgage loan. The borrower is also responsible for paying an annual premium that is charged monthly. The up-front premium is charged on all FHA loans except those for the purchase of a condominium.

■ The mortgaged real estate must be appraised by an approved FHA appraiser.

■ The FHA sets maximum mortgage limits for various regions of the country.

■ The borrower must meet standard FHA credit qualifications.

Financing for manufactured homes (factory-built housing) is also available along with special programs such as the Good Neighbor Program that assists police officers, fire fighters, teachers, and emergency medical technicians (EMTs).

A qualified buyer may assume an existing FHA-insured loan. For loans originating after December 1, 1989, assumptions are only permitted with complete buyer qualification.

Discount Points   The lender of an FHA-insured loan may charge discount points in addition to a loan origination fee. The payment of points is a matter of negotiation between the seller and the buyer. If the seller pays more than 6% of the costs normally paid by the buyer (such as discount points, the loan origination fee, the mortgage insurance premium, buydown fees, prepaid items, and impound or escrow amounts), the lender will treat the payments as a reduction in sales price and recalculate the mortgage amount accordingly.

VA-Guaranteed Loans

The Department of Veterans Affairs (VA) is authorized to guarantee loans to purchase or construct homes for eligible veterans and their spouses (including unremarried spouses of veterans whose deaths were service-related). The VA also guarantees loans to purchase manufactured homes and lots on which to place them. A veteran who meets any of the following time-in-service criteria is eligible for a VA loan:

■ 90 days of active service for veterans of World War II, the Korean War, the Vietnam conflict, and the Persian Gulf War

■ A minimum of 181 days of active service during interconflict periods between July 26, 1947, and September 6, 1980

■ Two full years of service during any peacetime period since 1980 for enlisted and since 1981 for officers

■ Six or more years of continuous duty as a reservist in the Army, Navy, Air Force, Marine Corps, or Coast Guard, or as a member of the Army or Air National Guard

The VA assists veterans in financing the purchase of homes with little or no down payments at market interest rates. The VA issues rules and regulations that set forth the qualifications, limitations, and conditions under which a loan may be guaranteed and requires that the owner must live on the property.

There is no VA dollar limit on the amount of the loan a veteran can obtain; this limit is determined by the lender and the qualification of the buyer. The VA limits the amount of the loan it will guarantee.

IN PRACTICE The VA loan guarantee is tied to the current conforming loan limit for Fannie Mae and Freddie Mac. Typically, lenders will loan four times the guarantee (e.g., a conforming loan of $417,000 ÷ 4 = $104,250 VA guarantee).

To determine what portion of a mortgage loan the VA will guarantee, the veteran must apply for a **certificate of eligibility** that sets forth the maximum guarantee to which the veteran is entitled. For individuals with full eligibility, no down payment is required for a loan up to the maximum guarantee limit.

The VA also issues a **certificate of reasonable value (CRV)** for the property being purchased, which is the property's current market value based on a VA-approved appraisal. If the purchase price is greater than the amount cited in the CRV, the veteran may pay the difference in cash but only with VA approval.

The VA borrower pays a loan origination fee to the lender, as well as a funding fee (2% to 3%, depending on the down payment amount) to the VA. With no down payment, the funding fee depends on whether it is first-time use (2.15%) or a subsequent use (3.3%). The funding fee drops with down payments of 5% or more. Reservists and National Guard veterans pay higher funding fees. Reasonable discount points may be charged on a VA-guaranteed loan, and either the veteran or the seller may pay them.

Assumption Rules For loans made on or after March 1, 1988, the VA must approve the buyer and the assumption agreement. The original veteran borrower remains personally liable for the repayment of the loan unless the VA approves a release of liability. The release of liability will be issued by the VA only if

- the buyer assumes all the veteran's liabilities on the loan, and
- the VA or the lender approves both the buyer and the assumption agreement.

Releases are also possible if veterans use their own entitlement in assuming another veteran's loan.

Agricultural Loan Programs

The Farm Service Agency (FSA) is a federal agency of the Department of Agriculture. The FSA offers programs to help families purchase or operate family farms. Through the Rural Housing Service (RHS), it also provides loans to help families purchase or improve single-family homes in rural areas (generally areas with populations of fewer than 10,000 people).

The Farm Credit System (Farm Credit) provides loans to farmers, ranchers, rural homeowners, agricultural cooperatives, rural utility systems, and agribusinesses. Unlike commercial banks, Farm Credit System banks and associations do not take deposits. Instead, loanable funds are raised through the system-wide sale of bonds and notes in the nation's capital markets.

Farmer Mac Farmer Mac (Federal Agricultural Mortgage Corporation, or FAMC) was created to improve the availability of long-term credit at stable interest rates to America's farmers, ranchers, and rural homeowners, businesses, and communities. Farmer Mac pools or bundles agricultural loans from lenders for sale as mortgage-backed securities.

■ FINANCING LEGISLATION

The federal government regulates the lending practices of mortgage lenders through the Truth in Lending Act (TILA), the Equal Credit Opportunity Act, and the Real Estate Settlement Procedures Act (RESPA).

Both TILA and RESPA will change as of August 1, 2015. To find out more about the changes, visit www.consumerfinance.gov/regulatory-implementation/tila-respa/.

Truth in Lending Act and Regulation Z

The federal **Truth in Lending Act (TILA)** requires that credit institutions inform borrowers of the true cost of obtaining credit. Under TILA, a consumer must be fully informed of all finance charges and the true interest rate before a transaction is completed. The finance charge disclosure or truth-in-lending (TIL) statement must include any loan fees, finder's fees, service charges and points, as well as interest. In the case of a mortgage loan made to finance the purchase of a dwelling, the lender must compute and disclose the **annual percentage rate (APR)**, which includes the total amount of money being paid to the lender: interest, discount points, and loan fees. The only accurate way to compare different loan programs is to compare the APR for each. TILA provides for a three-day right of rescission for many types of loans but not for home mortgages.

Regulation Z of TILA provides strict regulation of real estate advertisements (in all media, including newspapers, flyers, signs, billboards, websites, radio or television ads, and direct mailings) that refer to mortgage financing terms.

Specific credit terms, such as down payment, monthly payment, dollar amount of the finance charge, or term of the loan, are called **trigger terms**. These terms may not be advertised unless the advertisement includes the following information:

■ Cash price
■ Required down payment
■ Number, amounts, and due dates of all payments
■ Annual percentage rate (APR)

Penalties   The penalty for violation of Regulation Z is $10,000 for each day the violation continues. In addition, a creditor may be liable to a consumer for twice the amount of the finance charge. Willful violation is a misdemeanor punishable by a fine of up to $5,000, one year's imprisonment, or both.

Equal Credit Opportunity Act

The federal Equal Credit Opportunity Act (ECOA) prohibits lenders and others who grant or arrange credit to consumers from discriminating against credit applicants on the basis of

■ race,
■ color,
■ religion,
■ national origin,
■ sex,
■ marital status,
■ age (provided the applicant is of legal age), or
■ dependence on public assistance.

Furthermore, lenders and other creditors must inform all rejected credit applicants of the principal reasons for the denial or termination of credit. The notice must be provided in writing within 30 days. The federal ECOA also provides that a borrower is entitled to a copy of the appraisal report if the borrower paid for the appraisal.

Real Estate Settlement Procedures Act

The federal Real Estate Settlement Procedures Act (RESPA) applies to any residential real estate transaction involving a new first mortgage loan. RESPA is designed to ensure that the buyer and the seller are both fully informed of all settlement costs. RESPA regulations will be covered in detail in Chapter 9.

■ COMPUTERIZED LOAN ORIGINATION (CLO)

A **computerized loan origination (CLO)** system is an electronic network for handling loan applications through remote computer terminals linked to lenders' computers. Automated underwriting systems like Freddie Mac's Loan Prospector and Fannie Mae's Desktop Underwriter reduce approval time to minutes.

Credit Scoring

Lenders today generally require a tri-merge credit report from the three major credit reporting agencies: Equifax, Experian, and TransUnion. If the credit scores are different, the lender usually takes the middle score. The higher the FICO score, the less risk to the lender in making the loan.

■ SUMMARY

In a mortgage, the mortgagor (owner) borrows money from the mortgagee (lender), and the real estate is used as security for the debt.

The term *mortgage* refers to any financing instrument by which real estate is used as security for a debt. The mortgage can take the form of either a mortgage lien or a deed of trust. In either case, a promissory note is attached. A mortgage is a two-party agreement between a borrower and a lender. A deed of trust is a three-party agreement that transfers title from the trustor (property owner) to a trustee, who holds it on behalf of a borrower (lender).

The characteristics of both mortgage documents are similar, with the exception of the foreclosure procedures for each.

■ A mortgage document is executed by the borrower and recorded in the county in which the property is located.

■ When a loan is paid in full, a conveyance clause requires the lender to execute a release of lien (release or discharge) that is recorded to clear title (a deed of reconveyance with a deed of trust).

■ If the borrower defaults, the lender can accelerate the due date of the remaining principal balance and all other payments and costs.

■ The trustor transfers legal title to the beneficiary or trustee but retains equitable title and has the right to possession and use of the mortgaged property.

An impound (escrow) account may be required to create a reserve fund to ensure that future tax, property insurance, and other payments are made.

When property with an outstanding mortgage or deed of trust is assumed, the new owner may take title as follows:

■ "Subject to" existing mortgage—the new owner makes payments on existing loans but is not personally liable if the property is sold on default.
■ Assuming the existing mortgage or deed of trust—the new owner takes personal responsibility for existing loans.

An alienation clause (due-on-sale clause) in a loan document will, at the lender's discretion, prevent future purchasers of the property from assuming the loan.

A novation agreement may be used to release the seller from any future liability on loans secured by the real estate.

The Federal Reserve System (the Fed) consists of 12 federal reserve district banks.

The primary mortgage market consists of lenders that earn income from

■ finance charges collected at loan closing, including loan origination fees, and discount points;
■ recurring income—interest collected during the term of loan;
■ funds generated by the sale of loans to the secondary mortgage market; and
■ fees for loan servicing for other mortgage lenders or investors who have purchased the loans.

The primary mortgage market lenders include the following:

■ Depository institutions (thrifts, savings associations, and commercial banks)
■ Credit unions
■ Mortgage bankers
■ Mortgage brokers
■ Private lenders

The secondary mortgage market, where loans are bought and sold after being funded, does the following:

■ Provides additional funds to lenders to make more loans, with lenders often retaining servicing functions for a fee (seller/servicers)
■ Purchases mortgage loans through agencies, assembles them into packages called pools, and sells them as securities

Secondary market players are as follows:

■ Fannie Mae creates mortgage-backed securities using pools of conventional, FHA, and VA loans.
■ Freddie Mac purchases mortgages, pools them, and sells as securities on the open market.
■ Ginnie Mae is a division of the Department of Housing and Urban Development (HUD) that administers special-assistance programs and guarantees mortgage-backed securities based on FHA and VA loans.
■ The Federal Home Loan Bank purchases loans from member banks.
■ Farmer Mac purchases agriculture/rural loans.

The following are types of financing:

■ Straight loan (term loan or interest-only loan)—periodic payments of interest only for the life of the loan, with payment of principal in full at the end of the loan term
■ Balloon payment (partially amortized) loan—periodic payments of interest and principal are not great enough to pay down entire amount borrowed by the end of the loan term, resulting in a larger final payment
■ Amortized (fully amortized) loan—equal periodic payments of interest and principal, resulting in complete payment of amount borrowed over the term of the loan
■ Adjustable-rate mortgage (ARM)—lower initial rate of interest that may change over the life of the loan, based on a specified index, usually tied to U.S. Treasury securities
■ Growing equity (rapid payoff) mortgage—fixed interest rate, but payments of principal are increased according to an index or schedule so that the loan is paid off more quickly
■ Reverse mortgage—payments made by the lender to the borrower at regular intervals (such as monthly), in a lump sum, or as a line of credit to be drawn against, allowing the borrower to remain in the home while receiving income

Other types of loans include the following:

■ A purchase-money mortgage is a note and mortgage created at the time of purchase.
■ The package loan includes all personal property and appliances, as well as real estate.
■ Construction loans finance the construction of property improvements.
■ A buydown is a payment made at closing to reduce the interest rate on the loan.
■ A home equity loan (home equity line of credit, or HELOC) is junior to the original lien.

Conventional loans are the most secure loans. Note the following:

■ The loan-to-value ratio (LTV) is often lowest for these loans—traditionally 80%—meaning the down payment is 20%.
■ Conforming loans meet all the requirements of the secondary market, set by Fannie Mae and Freddie Mac, for conforming loans, including the following:
— The borrower's monthly housing expenses, including PITI, should be no more than 28% of total monthly gross income.
— The borrower's total monthly obligations, including housing costs and other regular monthly payments, must not exceed 36% of the total monthly gross income.
■ Nonconforming loans do not meet conforming guidelines; may be retained in the lender's investment portfolio.
■ Private mortgage insurance (PMI) required for LTVs higher than 80% (down payments of less than 20%). Federal law requires PMI to automatically terminate if the borrower has accumulated 22% equity in the home (based on purchase price) and is current on mortgage payments.

FHA-insured loans are backed by the Federal Housing Administration (FHA), which is part of HUD. FHA does not make loans but insures loans made by an FHA-approved lending institution.

FHA mortgage insurance premium (MIP) has an up-front fee along with monthly installments. The premium can be financed within the loan.

VA-guaranteed loans are backed by the Department of Veterans Affairs and are available to eligible veterans and spouses.

The Rural Housing Service (RHS) is part of the Department of Agriculture and has the following programs to help families purchase or operate family farms:

- Farm Credit System (Farm Credit)
- Farmer Mac (formerly Federal Agricultural Mortgage Corporation), which purchases farm loans

The Truth in Lending Act, Regulation Z of the Federal Trade Commission (FTC), requires that when a loan is secured by a residence, lenders inform borrowers of the true cost of obtaining credit, within the following rules:

- The borrower has a three-day right of rescission (not on mortgage loans).
- Advertising is strictly regulated.
- There is a $10,000 penalty for each day the violation continues.

The Equal Credit Opportunity Act (ECOA) prohibits discrimination in granting or arranging credit on the basis of race, color, religion, national origin, sex, marital status, age (as long as the applicant is not a minor), or dependence on public assistance.

The Real Estate Settlement Procedures Act ensures that buyers and sellers are fully informed of all costs of settlement.

Computerized loan origination (CLO) is an electronic network for handling loan applications.

Automated underwriting (loan processing) programs include Fannie Mae's Desktop Underwriter and Freddie Mac's Loan Prospector.

Credit scoring has become an important part of the loan application evaluation process.

CHAPTER 7 REVIEW QUESTIONS

1. A prospective buyer needs to borrow money to buy a house. The buyer applies for and obtains a real estate loan from a mortgage company. Then the buyer signs a note and a mortgage. In this example, the buyer is called the
   a. mortgagor.
   b. beneficiary.
   c. mortgagee.
   d. vendor.

2. Which clause would give a lender the right to have all future installments become due upon default?
   a. Escalation
   b. Defeasance
   c. Alienation
   d. Acceleration

3. Which of the following is NOT a participant in the secondary market?
   a. Fannie Mae
   b. Ginnie Mae
   c. Credit union
   d. Freddie Mac

4. If buyers seek a mortgage on a single-family house, they would be LEAST likely to obtain the mortgage from a
   a. mutual savings bank.
   b. life insurance company.
   c. credit union.
   d. commercial bank.

5. The primary activity of Freddie Mac is to
   a. guarantee mortgages with the full faith and credit of the federal government.
   b. buy and pool blocks of conventional mortgages.
   c. act in tandem with Ginnie Mae to provide special assistance in times of tight money.
   d. buy and sell VA and FHA mortgages.

6. Which characteristic of a fixed-rate home loan that is amortized according to the original payment schedule is TRUE?
   a. The amount of interest to be paid is predetermined.
   b. The loan cannot be sold in the secondary market.
   c. The monthly payment amount will fluctuate each month.
   d. The interest rate change may be based on an index.

7. Funds for Federal Housing Administration (FHA) loans are usually provided by
   a. the FHA.
   b. the Federal Reserve.
   c. approved lenders.
   d. the seller.

8. A home is purchased using a fixed-rate, fully amortized mortgage loan. Which statement regarding this mortgage is TRUE?
   a. A balloon payment will be made at the end of the loan.
   b. Each principal and interest mortgage payment amount is the same.
   c. Each mortgage payment reduces the principal by the same amount.
   d. The principal amount in each payment is greater than the interest amount.

9. The federal Equal Credit Opportunity Act allows lenders to discriminate against potential borrowers on the basis of
   a. race.
   b. sex.
   c. age.
   d. amount of income.

10. Which law requires that all advertising that references mortgage financing terms contain certain disclosures?
    a. Equal Credit Opportunity Act
    b. Fair Housing Act
    c. Community Reinvestment Act
    d. Truth in Lending Act (Regulation Z)

CHAPTER 8

Conveyance of Title

■ KEY TERMS

abstract of title	general warranty deed	quitclaim deed
acknowledgment	grantee	reconveyance deed
actual notice	granting clause	recording
adverse possession	grantor	special warranty deed
attorney's opinion of title	habendum clause	suit to quiet title
bargain and sale deed	heir	testate
certificate of title	holographic will	testator
chain of title	intestate	title
cloud on the title	involuntary alienation	title insurance
codicil	marketable title	title search
constructive notice	nuncupative will	transfer tax
deed	power of attorney	trustee's deed
deed of trust	priority	voluntary alienation
devise	probate	will

■ INTRODUCTION

Transfer of title is an aspect of the real estate transaction generally handled by lawyers and title companies, rarely by the licensee. Nonetheless, as with other legal aspects of the transaction, a licensee who is aware of the fundamentals of deeds and title issues will know what kind of questions to ask. An informed licensee will also know when to direct clients to other real estate professionals to avoid potential title problems.

■ TITLE

The term *title* has two functions. **Title** to real estate means the right to or ownership of the land; it represents the owner's bundle of legal rights (see Chapter 2). Title also serves as evidence of that ownership. A person who holds the title, if challenged in court, would be able to recover or retain ownership or possession of a parcel of real estate. Title is just a way of referring to ownership; it is not an actual printed document.

Real estate may be transferred voluntarily by sale or gift. Alternatively, it may be transferred involuntarily by operation of law. Real estate may be transferred while the owner lives or by will or descent after the owner dies.

■ VOLUNTARY ALIENATION

- A *grantor* conveys property to a grantee.
- A *grantee* receives property from a grantor.
- A *deed* is the instrument that conveys property from a grantor to a grantee.

Voluntary alienation is the legal term for the voluntary transfer of title. The owner may voluntarily transfer title by either making a gift or selling the property. To transfer during their lifetime, owners must use some form of document to show the conveyance.

A **deed** is the written instrument by which an owner of real estate intentionally conveys the right, title, or interest in the parcel of real estate to someone else. The statute of frauds requires that all deeds be in writing. The owner who transfers the title is called the **grantor**, and the person who acquires the title is called the **grantee**. A deed is executed (or signed) by the grantor. To be able to execute a valid deed, the grantor must have legal capacity (see Figure 8.1).

FIGURE 8.1

Remembering Legal Terminology: "OR" Versus "EE"

Throughout this book, people are called *grantors* and *grantees*, *trustors* and *trustees*, *mortgagors* and *mortgagees*, and so forth. This chart provides a guide for remembering the terminology.

Product	Person Giving the Product	Person Receiving the Product
Devise	Devisor	Devisee
Deed	Grantor	Grantee
Legacy	Legator	Legatee
Lease	Lessor	Lessee
Mortgage	Mortgagee	Mortgagor
Offer	Offeror	Offeree
Option	Optionor	Optionee
Sublease	Sublessor	Sublessee
Trust	Trustor	Trustee

Requirements for a Valid Deed

Although formal requirements vary, most states require that a valid deed contain the following elements:

- Grantor who has the legal competency to execute (sign) the deed
- Grantee named with reasonable certainty to be identified
- Statement of consideration
- Granting clause (words of conveyance)
- Habendum clause (to define ownership taken by the grantee)
- Accurate legal description of the property conveyed
- Any relevant exceptions or reservations
- Signature of the grantor, which must be acknowledged (notorization)
- Delivery of the deed and acceptance by the grantee to pass title

A deed also may include a description of any limitations on the conveyance of a full fee simple estate and a statement of any exceptions and reservations that affect title to the property.

Grantor   A grantor must be of lawful age, usually at least 18 years old. A deed executed by a minor is generally voidable.

A grantor also must be of sound mind. Generally, any grantor who can understand the action is viewed as mentally capable of executing a valid deed. A deed executed by someone who was mentally impaired at the time is voidable, but it is not void. If, however, the grantor has been judged legally incompetent, the deed will be void. Real estate owned by someone who is legally incompetent can be conveyed only with a court's approval.

The grantor's name must be spelled correctly and consistently throughout the deed. If the grantor's name has changed since the title was acquired, as when a person's name changes with marriage, both names should be shown (for example, "Mary Smith, formerly Mary Jones").

Grantee   To be valid, a deed must name a grantee. The grantee must be specifically named so that the person to whom the property is being conveyed can be readily identified from the deed itself.

■ **FOR EXAMPLE**   Olive wanted to convey Whiteacre to her nephew, Jack Jackson. In the deed, Olive wrote the following words of conveyance: "I, Olive Burbank, hereby convey to Jack all my interest in Whiteacre." The only problem was that Olive also had a son named Jack, a cousin Jack, and a neighbor Jack. The grantee's identity could not be discerned from the deed itself. Olive should have conveyed Whiteacre "to my nephew, Jack Jackson."

If more than one grantee is involved, the granting clause should specify their rights in the property. For example, the clause might state that the grantees will take title as joint tenants or tenants in common. This is especially important when specific wording is necessary to create a joint tenancy.

Consideration   A valid deed must contain a clause acknowledging that the grantor has received consideration. Generally, the amount of consideration is stated in dollars. When a deed conveys real estate as a gift to a relative, love and affection may be sufficient consideration. In most states, it is customary to recite a nominal consideration, such as "$10 and other good and valuable consideration."

Granting Clause (Words of Conveyance)   A deed must contain a **granting clause** that states the grantor's intention to convey the property. Depending on the type of deed and the obligations agreed to by the grantor, the wording would be similar to one of the following:

■   "I, JKL, convey and warrant . . ."
■   "I, JKL, remise, release, alienate, and convey . . ."
■   "I, JKL, grant, bargain, and sell . . ."
■   "I, JKL, remise, release, and quitclaim . . ."

A deed that conveys the grantor's entire fee simple interest usually contains wording such as "to ABC and to her heirs and assigns forever." If less than the grantor's complete interest is conveyed, such as a life estate, the wording must indicate this limitation—for example, "to ABC for the duration of her natural life."

Habendum Clause   When it is necessary to define or explain the ownership to be enjoyed by the grantee, a **habendum clause** may follow the granting clause. The habendum clause begins with the words "to have and to hold." Its provisions must agree with those stated in the granting clause. For example, if a grantor conveys a time-share interest or an interest less than fee simple absolute, the habendum clause would specify the owner's rights as well as how those rights are limited (a specific time frame or certain prohibited activities, for example).

Legal Description of Real Estate   To be valid, a deed must contain an accurate legal description of the real estate conveyed. Land is considered adequately described if a professional surveyor can locate the property using the description.

Exceptions and Reservations   A valid deed must specifically note any encumbrances, reservations, or limitations that affect the title being conveyed. This might include such things as restrictions and easements that run with the land. In addition to citing existing encumbrances, a grantor may reserve some right in the land, such as an easement, for the grantor's use. A grantor may also place certain restrictions on a grantee's use of the property. Developers often restrict the number of houses that may be built on each lot in a subdivision. Such private restrictions must be stated in the deed or contained in a previously recorded document, such as the subdivider's master deed, that is expressly referred to in the deed. Many of these deed restrictions have time limits and often include renewal clauses.

Signature of Grantor   To be valid, a deed must be signed by all grantors named in the deed. Some states also require witnesses to or notarization of the grantor's signature.

Most states permit a power of attorney (written specific authority) to sign legal documents for a grantor (a power of attorney is not necessarily an attorney-at-law). The person having **power of attorney** has written authority to execute and sign one or more legal instruments for another person. Usually, the power of attorney must be recorded in the county where the property is located.

In some states, a grantor's spouse is required to sign any deed of conveyance to waive any marital or homestead rights. This requirement varies according to state law and depends on the manner in which title to real estate is held. In Texas, any conveyance of community property requires the signature of both spouses.

Many states still require a seal (or simply the word seal) to be written or printed after an individual grantor's signature. The corporate seal may be required of a corporate grantor.

Acknowledgment   An **acknowledgment** is a formal declaration under oath that the person who signs a written document does so voluntarily and that the signature is genuine. The declaration is made before a registered notary public or an authorized public officer, such as a judge, justice of the peace, or some other person, as prescribed by state law. An acknowledgment usually states that the person signing the deed or other document is known to the officer or has produced sufficient identification to prevent a forgery. After verifying the person's information, the notary public will sign and stamp the form, which allows the person to be able to record the document, completely satisfying the instrument.

An acknowledgment is not essential to the validity of the deed unless it is required by state statute. In Texas, acknowledgment is not required for validity. However, a deed that is not acknowledged is not a completely satisfactory instrument. In most states (including Texas), an unacknowledged deed is not eligible for recording.

Delivery and Acceptance   A title is not considered transferred until the deed is actually delivered to and accepted by the grantee. The grantor may deliver the deed to the grantee either personally or through a third party.

> Transfer of title requires both delivery and acceptance of the deed.

Title is said to pass only when a deed is delivered and accepted. The effective date of the transfer of title from the grantor to the grantee is the date of delivery of the deed itself. Delivery and acceptance are usually presumed if the deed has been examined and registered by the county clerk.

Execution of Corporate Deeds

The laws governing a corporation's right to convey real estate vary from state to state. However, two basic rules must be followed:

- A corporation can convey real estate only by authority granted in its bylaws or on a proper resolution passed by its board of directors. If all or a substantial portion of a corporation's real estate is being conveyed, a resolution authorizing the sale usually must be secured from the shareholders.
- Deeds to real estate can only be signed by an authorized officer.

Types of Deeds

A deed can take several forms, depending on the extent of the grantor's promises to the grantee. Regardless of any guarantees the deed offers, the grantee will want additional assurance that the grantor has the right to offer what the deed conveys. To obtain this protection, grantees commonly seek evidence of title.

The most common deeds are the following:

- General warranty deed
- Special warranty deed
- Bargain and sale deed
- Quitclaim deed

A **general warranty deed** provides the greatest protection to the buyer because the grantor is legally bound by certain covenants (promises) or warranties. In most states, the warranties are implied by the use of certain words specified by statute. In some states, the grantor's warranties are expressly written into the deed itself. Each state law should be examined, but some of the specific words include convey and warrant or warrant generally. The basic warranties are as follows:

> **General Warranty Deed**
>
> Five covenants:
> - Covenant of seisin
> - Covenant against encumbrances
> - Covenant of quiet enjoyment
> - Covenant of further assurance
> - Covenant of warranty forever

- *Covenant of seisin.* Grantors warrant that they own the property and have the right to convey title to it. (The term *seisin* simply means possession.) The grantee may recover damages up to the full purchase price if this covenant is broken.
- *Covenant against encumbrances.* The grantor warrants that the property is free from liens or encumbrances, except for any specifically stated in the deed. Encumbrances generally include mortgages, mechanics' liens, and easements. If this covenant is breached, the grantee may sue for the cost of removing the encumbrances.
- *Covenant of quiet enjoyment.* The grantor guarantees that the grantee's title will be good against third parties who might bring court actions to establish superior title to the property. If the grantee's title is found to be inferior, the grantor is liable for damages.
- *Covenant of further assurance.* The grantor promises to obtain and deliver any instrument needed to make the title good. For example, if the grantor's spouse has failed to sign away dower rights, the grantor must deliver a quit-claim deed to clear the title.
- *Covenant of warranty forever.* The grantor promises to compensate the grantee for the loss sustained if the title fails at any time in the future.

These covenants in a general warranty deed are not limited to matters that occurred during the time the grantor owned the property; they extend back to its origins. The grantor defends the title against both herself and all those who previously held title.

A **special warranty deed** contains two basic warranties:

> **Special Warranty Deed**
>
> Two warranties:
> - Warranty that grantor received title
> - Warranty that property was unencumbered by grantor

- That the grantor received title
- That the property was not encumbered during the time the grantor held title, except as otherwise noted in the deed

In effect, grantors defend the title against themselves. The granting clause generally contains these words: "Grantor remises, releases, alienates, and conveys." The grantor may include additional warranties, but they must be specifically stated in the deed. In areas where a special warranty deed is more commonly used, the purchase of title insurance is viewed as providing adequate protection to the grantee.

A special warranty deed may be used by fiduciaries such as trustees, executors, and corporations. A special warranty deed is appropriate for fiduciaries because they lack the authority to warrant against acts of predecessors in title (former owners). A fiduciary may hold title for a limited time without having a personal interest in the proceeds. Sometimes a special warranty deed is used by a grantor who has acquired title at a tax sale.

A **bargain and sale deed** contains no express warranties against encumbrances. However, it does imply that the grantor holds title and possession of the property. The granting clause usually states a person's name or name of an entity and the words *grants and releases* or *grants, bargains, and sells*. Because the warranty is not specifically stated, the grantee has little legal recourse if title defects appear later. In some areas, this deed is used in foreclosures and tax sales. The buyer should purchase, or the seller should provide, title insurance for protection.

A covenant against encumbrances initiated by the grantor may be added to a standard bargain and sale deed to create a bargain and sale deed with covenant against the grantor's acts. This deed is closely equivalent to a special warranty deed. Warranties used in general warranty deeds may be inserted in a bargain and sale deed to give the grantee similar protection.

A **quitclaim deed** provides the grantee with the least protection of any deed. It carries no covenants or warranties and generally conveys only whatever interest the grantor may have when the deed is delivered. If the grantor has no interest, the grantee will acquire nothing. Nor will the grantee acquire any right of warranty claim against the grantor. A quitclaim deed can convey title as effectively as a warranty deed if the grantor has good title when the deed is delivered, but it provides none of the guarantees of a warranty deed. Through a quitclaim deed, the grantor only "remises, releases, and quitclaims" the grantor's interest in the property, if any.

Usually, a quitclaim deed is the only type of deed that may be used to convey less than a fee simple estate. This is because a quitclaim deed conveys only the grantor's right, title, or interest.

A quitclaim deed is frequently used to cure a defect, called a **cloud on the title**. For example, if the name of the grantee is misspelled on a warranty deed filed in the public record, a quitclaim deed with the correct spelling may be executed to the grantee to perfect the title.

A quitclaim deed is also used when a grantor allegedly inherits property but is not certain that the decedent's title was valid. A warranty deed in such an instance could carry obligations of warranty, while a quitclaim deed would convey only the grantor's interest, whatever it may be.

Another distinction between a grant deed and a quitclaim deed is after-acquired title. In the grant deed, if the grantor does not have the title described in the deed instrument, but subsequently acquires it, then it automatically transfers to the grantee. The quitclaim deed not only has no warranties, but it does not convey after-acquired title, which is the main distinction of this deed form.

A **deed of trust** (or deed in trust, in some states) is the means by which a trustor conveys real estate to a trustee for the benefit of the trustor. The real estate is held by the trustee to fulfill the purpose of the trust (see Figure 8.2). This was also discussed in Chapter 7.

Bargain and Sale Deed

No express warranties:
- Implication that grantor holds title and possession

Quitclaim Deed

No express or implied covenants or warranties:
- Used primarily to convey less than fee simple or to cure a title defect

FIGURE 8.2

Trust Deeds

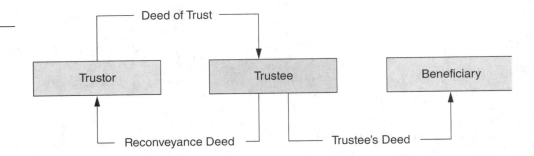

Reconveyance Deed
■ Conveyance from trustee back to trustor

Trustee's Deed
■ Conveyance from trustee to third party

A **reconveyance deed** is used by a trustee to return title to the trustor. For example, when a loan secured by a deed of trust has been fully paid, the beneficiary notifies the trustee. The trustee then reconveys the property to the trustor. As with any document of title, a reconveyance deed should be recorded to prevent title problems in the future.

A deed executed by a trustee is a **trustee's deed**. It is used when a trustee conveys real estate held in the trust to anyone other than the trustor. The trustee's deed must state that the trustee is executing the instrument in accordance with the powers and authority granted by the trust instrument.

Deed Executed Pursuant to a Court Order   Executors' and administrators' deeds, masters' deeds, sheriffs' deeds, and many other types are all deeds executed pursuant to a court order. These deeds are established by state statute and are used to convey title to property that is transferred by court order or by will. The form of such a deed must conform to the laws of the state in which the property is located.

One common characteristic of deeds executed pursuant to court order is that the full consideration is usually stated in the deed. Instead of "$10 and other valuable consideration," for example, the deed would list the actual sales price.

Transfer Tax Stamps

Texas does not have a transfer tax, but many states have enacted laws providing for a state **transfer tax** (also called a grantor's tax in some states) on conveyances of real estate. In these states, the tax is usually payable when the deed is recorded. In some states, the taxpayer purchases stamps from the recorder of the county in which the deed is recorded. The stamps must be affixed to deeds and conveyances before the documents can be recorded. In other states, the taxpayer simply pays the clerk of court or county recorder the appropriate transfer tax amount in accordance with state and local law.

The transfer tax may be paid by either the seller or the buyer, or split between them, depending on local custom or agreement in the sales contract. The actual tax rate varies and may be imposed at the state, county, or city level. For example, the rate might be calculated as $1.10 for every $1,000 of the sales price, as $0.26 for every $500, or as a simple percentage.

IN PRACTICE   A state has a transfer tax of $1.50 for each $500 (or fraction of $500) of the sales price of any parcel of real estate. The transfer tax is paid by the seller. To calculate the transfer tax due in the sale of a $300,000 house, use the following formula:

$$(value \div unit) \times rate\ per\ unit = tax$$

In this example:

$$\$300,000 \div \$500 = 600\ taxable\ units$$

$$600 \times \$1.50 = \$900$$

The seller in this transaction must pay a transfer tax of $900 to the state.

In many states, a transfer declaration form (or transfer statement or affidavit of real property value) must be signed by both the buyer and the seller or their agents. The transfer declaration states

- the full sales price of the property;
- the property's legal description;
- the type of improvement;
- the address, date, and type of deed; and
- whether the transfer is between relatives or in accordance with a court order.

Certain deeds may be exempted from the tax, such as the following:

- Gifts of real estate
- Deeds not made in connection with a sale (such as a change in the form of co-ownership)
- Conveyances to, from, or between government bodies
- Deeds by charitable, religious, or educational institutions
- Deeds securing debts or releasing property as security for a debt
- Partitions
- Tax deeds
- Deeds pursuant to mergers of corporations
- Deeds from subsidiary to parent corporations for cancellations of stock

■ INVOLUNTARY ALIENATION

Title to property may be transferred without the owner's consent by **involuntary alienation** (see Figure 8.3). Involuntary transfers are usually carried out by operation of law, such as by condemnation or a sale to satisfy delinquent tax or mortgage liens. When a person dies **intestate** (with no will), the title to the real estate passes to the state by the state's power of escheat because there are no heirs. Land may be acquired through the process of accretion or actually lost through erosion. Other acts of nature, such as earthquakes, hurricanes, sinkholes, and mudslides, may create or eliminate a landowner's holdings.

F I G U R E   8.3

Involuntary Alienation

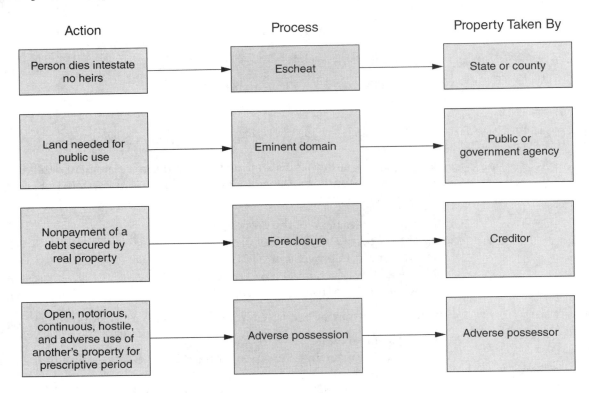

Transfer by Adverse Possession

Adverse possession is another means of involuntary transfer. An individual who makes a claim to a certain property, takes possession of it and, most important, uses it, may take title away from an owner who fails to use or inspect the property for a period of years. The law recognizes that the use of land is an important function of its ownership.

Usually the possession by the claimant must be all of the following:

- Open (obvious to anyone who looks)
- Notorious (known by others)
- Continuous (uninterrupted)
- Hostile (without the true owner's consent)
- Adverse (to the true owner's possession)

The necessary period of uninterrupted possession is a matter of state law. The statutory periods range from as few as 5 years in some states to as many as 30 years in others. Texas has four different time periods, which are 3, 5, 10, or 25 years. Which time period applies depends on the circumstances by which the adverse possessor came into possession.

In order to establish title by adverse possession, there must be proof of nonpermissive use that is actual, open, notorious, exclusive, and adverse for the statutorily prescribed period. To claim title, the adverse possessor normally files an action in court to receive undisputed title.

There is often some confusion between obtaining the right to property by way of an easement by prescription versus adverse possession. The number of years required in order to claim either varies from state to state. The prescriptive period in Texas is 10 years.

IN PRACTICE   The right of adverse possession is a statutory right. State requirements must be followed carefully to ensure the successful transfer of title. The parties to a transaction that might involve adverse possession should seek legal counsel.

■ CONVEYANCE OF A DECEDENT'S PROPERTY

A person who dies **testate** has prepared a will indicating how the deceased's property will be disposed of. In contrast, when a person dies **intestate** (without a will), real estate and personal property pass to the decedent's heirs according to the state's statute of descent and distribution. In effect, the state makes a will for an intestate decedent.

Legally, when a person dies, ownership of real estate immediately passes either to the heirs by descent or to the persons named in the will. Before these individuals can take full title and possession of the property, the estate must go through a judicial process called probate, and all claims against the estate must be satisfied.

Transfer of Title by Will

A **will** is made by an owner to convey title to real or personal property after the owner's death. This differs from a deed, which must be delivered during the lifetime of the grantor and which conveys a present interest in property. While the **testator**, the person who makes a will, is alive, any property included in the will can still be conveyed by the owner. The parties named in a will have no rights or interests as long as the party who made the will is alive; they acquire interest or title only after the owner's death.

Only property owned by the testator at the time of the testator's death may be transferred by will. The gift of real property by will is called a **devise**, and a person who receives real property by will is called a devisee. The other two gifts by will are a bequest, which is a gift of personal property, and a legacy, which is a gift of money.

For title to pass to the devisees, state laws require that on the death of a testator, the will must be filed with the court and probated. Probate is a legal procedure for verifying the validity of a will and accounting for the decedent's assets. The process can take several months to complete. Probate is the formal judicial process.

A will cannot supersede the state laws of dower and curtesy, which were enacted to protect the inheritance rights of a surviving spouse. When a will does not provide a spouse with the minimum statutory inheritance, the spouse may demand it from the estate (see Chapter 4).

Legal Requirements for Making a Will   A will must be executed and prepared according to the laws of the state in which the real estate is located. Only a valid and probated will can effectively convey title to real estate.

A testator must have legal capacity to make a will. There are no rigid tests to determine legal capacity. Usually, a person must be of legal age and of sound mind. Legal age varies from state to state. To demonstrate sound mind, the testator must have sufficient mental capacity to understand the nature and extent of the property the testator owns. Testators must understand the identity of their natural heirs and that the property will go to those persons named in the will. The drawing of a will must be a voluntary act, free of any undue influence by other people.

In most states, a written will must be signed by its testator before two or more witnesses, who must also sign the document. The witnesses should not be individuals who are named as devisees in the will. Some states do not permit real property to be conveyed by **nuncupative** (oral) **wills** or **holographic** (handwritten) **wills**.

A testator may alter a will any time. Any modification, amendment, or addition to a previously executed will is contained in a separate document called a **codicil**.

Transfer of Title by Descent

Under a state's statute of descent and distribution, the primary **heirs** of the deceased are the surviving spouse and close blood relatives (such as children, parents, brothers, sisters, aunts, uncles, and, in some cases, first and second cousins). The right to inherit under laws of descent varies from state to state, and intestate property is distributed according to the laws of the state in which the property is located.

Probate Proceedings

Probate is a formal judicial process that

- proves or confirms the validity of a will,
- determines the precise assets of the deceased person, and
- identifies the people to whom the assets are to pass.

The purpose of probate is to see that the assets are distributed correctly. All assets must be accounted for, and the decedent's debts must be satisfied before any property is distributed to the heirs or devisee. In addition, estate taxes must be paid before any distribution. The laws of each state govern the probate proceedings and the functions of the individuals appointed to administer the decedent's affairs.

Assets that are distributed through probate are those that do not otherwise distribute themselves. For example, property held in joint tenancy or tenancy by the entirety passes immediately. Probate proceedings take place in the county in which the decedent resided. If the decedent owned real estate in another county, probate would occur in that county as well.

The person who has possession of the will—normally the person designated in the will as executor—presents it for filing with the court. The court is responsible for determining whether the will meets the statutory requirements for its form and execution. If the will was modified or if more than one will exists, the court will decide how these documents should be probated.

The court must rule on a challenge if a will is contested. Once the will is upheld, the assets can be distributed according to its provisions. Probate courts distribute assets according to statute only when no other reasonable alternative exists.

When a person dies intestate, the court determines who inherits the assets by reviewing proof from relatives of the decedent and their entitlement under the statute of descent and distribution. Once the heirs have been determined, the court appoints an administrator or personal representative to administer the affairs of the estate—the role usually taken by an executor.

IN PRACTICE   A broker entering into a listing agreement with the executor or administrator of an estate in probate should be aware that the amount of commission is approved by the court and that the commission is payable only from the proceeds of the sale. The broker will not be able to collect a commission unless the court approves the sale.

■ PUBLIC RECORDS

Public records are just that—records that are open to the public—which means that anyone interested in a particular property can review the records to learn about the documents, claims, and other details that affect its ownership. A prospective buyer, for example, needs to be sure that the seller can convey title to the property. If the property is subject to any liens or other encumbrances, a prospective buyer or lender needs to know. An attorney or title company typically performs a search of the public records to ensure that good title is being conveyed. Nonetheless, it is important for a real estate licensee to understand what is in the public record and what the searchers are likely to find.

Public records contain detailed information about each parcel of real estate in a city or county. These records are crucial in establishing ownership, giving notice of encumbrances, and establishing priority of liens. They protect the interests of real estate owners, taxing bodies, creditors, and the public. The real estate recording system includes written documents that affect title, such as deeds and mortgages. Public records regarding taxes, judgments, probate, and marriage also may offer important information about the title to a particular property.

Public records are maintained by

- recorders of deeds,
- county clerks,
- county treasurers,
- city clerks,
- collectors, and
- clerks of court.

IN PRACTICE   Prospective buyers rarely search public records for evidence of title or encumbrances themselves. Instead, title companies, attorneys, and lenders conduct the searches.

Recording

In most states, written documents that affect land must be recorded in the county where the land is located.

Recording is the act of placing documents in the public record. The specific rules for recording documents are a matter of state law. Although the details may vary, all recording acts essentially provide that any written document that affects any estate, right, title, or interest in land must be recorded in the county (or, in some states, the town) where the land is located to serve as public notice. This way, anyone interested in the title to a parcel of property will know where to look to discover the various interests of all other parties. Recording acts also generally give legal priority to those interests recorded first—the *first in time, first in right* or *first come, first served* principle.

An unrecorded deed has priority over a subsequent recorded instrument if it was known to the subsequent party. The concept of recording is to impart "constructive" knowledge, which only controls if the subsequent recording parties had actual notice of its existence.

To be eligible for recording, a document must be drawn and executed according to the recording acts of the state in which the real estate is located. For example, a state may require that the parties' names be typed below their signatures or that the document be acknowledged before a notary public. In some states, the document must be witnessed. Others require that the name of the person who prepared the document appear on it. States may have specific rules about the size of documents and the color and quality of paper they are printed on. Electronic recording—using computers or fax machines, for example—is permitted in a growing number of localities. Some states require a certificate of real estate value and the payment of current property taxes due for recording.

Notice

Anyone with an interest in a parcel of real estate can take certain steps, called giving notice, to ensure that the interest is available to the public. The two basic types of notice are constructive notice and actual notice.

Constructive notice is the legal presumption that information may be obtained by an individual through due diligence. Properly recording documents in the public record serves as constructive notice to the world of an individual's rights or interest, as does the physical possession of a property. Because the information or evidence is readily available to the world, a prospective purchaser or lender is responsible for discovering the interest.

Actual notice means not only that the information is available but also that someone has been given the information and actually knows it. An individual who has searched the public records and inspected the property has actual notice, also called direct knowledge. If it can be proved that an individual has had actual notice of information, that person cannot use a lack of constructive notice (such as an unrecorded deed) to justify a claim.

Priority

Priority refers to the order of when documents or liens were recorded. Many complicated situations can affect the priority of rights in a parcel of real estate—who recorded first, which party was in possession first, or who had actual or constructive notice. How the courts rule in any situation depends, of course, on the specific facts of the case. These are strictly legal questions that should be referred to the parties' attorneys.

■ **FOR EXAMPLE** Buyer A purchased a property from seller B and received a deed. A did not record the deed but took possession of the property in June. In November, B sold the same property to buyer C who received a deed, which C promptly recorded. C never inspected the property to determine whether someone was in possession of it. By taking possession of the property, A has the superior right to the property even though A did not record the deed.

Unrecorded Documents

Certain types of liens are not recorded. Real estate taxes and special assessments are liens on specific parcels of real estate and are not usually recorded until sometime after the taxes or assessments are past due. Inheritance taxes and franchise taxes are statutory liens and are placed against all real estate owned by a decedent at the time of death or by a corporation at the time the franchise taxes became a lien. Like real estate taxes, they are not recorded.

Notice of these liens must be gained from sources other than the recorder's office. Evidence of the payment of real estate taxes, special assessments, municipal utilities, and other taxes can be gathered from paid tax receipts and letters from municipalities. Creative measures are often required to get information about off–the-record liens.

Chain of Title

Chain of title is the record of a property's ownership. Beginning with the earliest owner, a title may pass to many individuals. Each owner is linked to the next so that a chain is formed. An unbroken chain of title can be traced through linking conveyances from the present owner back to the earliest recorded owner. Chain of title does not include liens and encumbrances or any other document not directly related to ownership.

If ownership cannot be traced through an unbroken chain, a gap or cloud in the chain of title is said to exist. In these cases, the cloud on the title makes it necessary to establish ownership by a court action called a **suit to quiet title**. For example, a suit might be required when a grantor acquired title under one name and conveyed it under another name. Or there may be a forged deed in the chain, after which no subsequent grantee acquired legal title.

Title Search and Abstract of Title

A **title search** is an examination of all of the public records to determine whether any defects exist in the chain of title. The records of the conveyances of ownership are examined, beginning with the present owner. Then the title is traced backward to its origin (or 40 to 60 years or some definite period, depending on state statute). The time beyond which the title must be searched is limited in states that have adopted the Marketable Title Act. This law extinguishes certain interests and cures certain defects arising before the root of the title—the conveyance that establishes the source of the chain of title.

Other public records are examined to identify wills, judicial proceedings, and other encumbrances that may affect title. These include a variety of taxes, special assessments, and other recorded liens.

An **abstract of title** is a summary report of what the title search found in the public record. A person who prepares this report is called an abstractor. The abstractor searches all the public records and then summarizes the various events and proceedings that affected the title throughout its history. The report begins with the original grant (or root) and then provides a chronological list of recorded instruments. All recorded liens and encumbrances are included, along with their current status. A list of all of the public records examined is also provided as evidence of the scope of the search.

IN PRACTICE   An abstract of title is a condensed history of those items that can be found in public records. It does not reveal such items as encroachments or forgeries or any interests or conveyances that have not been recorded.

Marketable Title

Under the terms of the typical real estate sales contract, the seller is required to deliver **marketable title** to the buyer at the closing. To be marketable, a title must

- disclose no serious defects and not depend on doubtful questions of law or fact to prove its validity;
- not expose a purchaser to the hazard of litigation or threaten the quiet enjoyment of the property; and
- convince a reasonably well-informed and prudent purchaser, acting on business principles and with knowledge of the facts and their legal significance, that the purchaser could sell or mortgage the property at a later time.

Although a title that does not meet these requirements still can be transferred, it contains certain defects that may limit or restrict its ownership. A buyer cannot be forced to accept a conveyance that is materially different from the one bargained for in the sales contract. However, questions of marketable title must be raised by a buyer before acceptance of the deed. Once a buyer has accepted a deed with unmarketable title, the only available legal recourse is to sue the seller under any covenants of warranty contained in the deed.

In some states, a preliminary title search is conducted as soon as an offer to purchase has been accepted. In fact, it may be customary to include a contingency in the sales contract that gives the buyer the right to review and approve the title report before proceeding with the purchase. A preliminary title report also benefits the seller by giving the seller an early opportunity to cure title defects.

■ PROOF OF OWNERSHIP

Proof of ownership is evidence that title is marketable. A deed by itself is not considered sufficient evidence of ownership. Even though a warranty deed conveys the grantor's interest, it contains no proof of the condition of the grantor's title at the time of the conveyance. The grantee needs some assurance that ownership is actually being acquired and that the title is marketable. A certificate of title, title insurance, or a Torrens certificate is commonly used to prove ownership.

Certificate of Title

A **certificate of title** is a statement of opinion of the title's status on the date the certificate is issued. A certificate of title is not a guarantee of ownership. Rather, it certifies the condition of the title based on an examination of the public records—a title search. The certificate may be prepared by a title company, licensed abstractor, or attorney. An owner, mortgage lender, or buyer may request the certificate.

Although a certificate of title is used as evidence of ownership, it is not perfect. Unrecorded liens or rights of parties in possession cannot be discovered by a search of the public records. Hidden defects, such as transfers involving forged documents, incorrect marital information, incompetent parties, minors, or fraud, cannot be detected. A certificate offers no defense against these defects because they are unknown. The person who prepares the certificate is liable only for negligence in preparing the certificate.

An abstract and **attorney's opinion of title** are used in some areas of the country as evidence of title. It is an opinion of the status of the title based on a review of the abstract. Similar to a certificate of title, the opinion of title does not protect against defects that cannot be discovered from the public records. Many buyers purchase title insurance to defend the title from these defects.

Title Insurance

Title insurance is a contract under which the policyholder is protected from losses arising from defects in the title. A title insurance company determines whether the title is insurable, based on a review of the public records. If so, a policy is issued. Unlike other insurance policies that insure against future losses, title insurance protects the insured from an event that occurred before the policy was issued. Title insurance is considered the best defense of title: the title insurance company will defend any lawsuit based on an insurable defect and pay claims if the title proves to be defective.

After examining the public records, the title company usually issues what may be called a preliminary report of title or a commitment to issue a title policy. This describes the terms of policy that will be issued and includes

- the name of the insured party,
- the legal description of the real estate,
- the estate or interest covered,
- conditions and stipulations under which the policy is issued, and
- a schedule of all exceptions, including encumbrances and defects found in the public records and any known unrecorded defects.

The premium for the policy is paid once, at closing. The maximum loss for which the company may be liable cannot exceed the face amount of the policy (unless the amount of coverage has been extended by use of an inflation rider).

Coverage   Exactly which defects the title company will defend depends on the type of policy (see Figure 8.4). A standard coverage policy normally insures the title as it is known from the public records. In addition, the standard policy insures against such hidden defects as forged documents, conveyances by incompetent grantors, incorrect marital statements, and improperly delivered deeds.

FIGURE 8.4

Owner's Title Insurance Policy

Standard Coverage	Extended Coverage	Not Covered by Either Policy
Defects found in public records Forged documents Incompetent grantors Incorrect marital statements Improperly delivered deeds	Standard coverage plus defects discoverable through the following: ■ Property inspection, including unrecorded rights of persons in possession ■ Examination of survey ■ Unrecorded liens not known by policyholder	Defects and liens listed in policy Defects known to buyer Changes in land use brought about by zoning ordinances

Extended coverage as provided by an American Land Title Association (ALTA) policy includes the protections of a standard policy plus additional protections. An extended policy protects the homeowner against defects that may be discovered by inspection of the property: rights of parties in possession, examination of a survey, and certain unrecorded liens.

Title insurance does not offer guaranteed protection against all defects. A title company will not insure a bad title or offer protection against defects that clearly appear in a title search. The policy generally names certain uninsurable losses, called exclusions. These exclusions include zoning ordinances, restrictive covenants, easements, certain water rights, and current taxes and special assessments.

Types of Policies   The different types of policies depend on who is named as the insured. An owner's policy is issued for the benefit of the owner (new buyer) and the owner's heirs or devisees. A lender's policy is issued for the benefit of the mortgage company. The amount of the coverage depends on the amount of the mortgage loan.

■ SUMMARY

Title is ownership, or the right to ownership, of land and evidence of that ownership.

Voluntary alienation is the voluntary transfer of title to real estate by gift or sale, using some form of deed.

- Grantor (person who transfers title) must be of legal age and legally competent to execute (sign) a deed. A deed executed by a minor is voidable.
  — If the grantor has been declared incompetent by a judge, the deed is void.
  — All names the grantor has used should be provided.
- Grantee must be identifiable with sufficient certainty.
- Consideration (payment) of some form must be stated.
- Granting clause (words of conveyance) must be used.
- Habendum clause must define ownership interest taken by the grantee; it specifies limits on ownership, such as with a time-share.
- Legal description of the property conveyed is essential.
- Exceptions or reservations of any relevance must be included.
- Signature of the grantor(s) must be acknowledged by a notary public or other official authorized by the state in which the property is located.
- Delivery of the deed and acceptance by the grantee are necessary.

Types of deeds include the following:

- General warranty deed provides the greatest protection to the grantee and includes
  — covenant of seisin—warrants the grantor has the right to convey title;
  — covenant against encumbrances—warrants the property is free from liens or encumbrances, unless expressly stated;
  — covenant of quiet enjoyment—makes the grantor liable for damages if the grantee's title is found to be inferior;
  — covenant of further assurance—the grantor's promise to obtain any other document necessary to convey good title; and
  — covenant of warranty forever—the grantor's promise to compensate the grantee if title fails at any future time.
- Special warranty deed includes the warranties that the grantor received title and that the property was not encumbered during the time the grantor held title, except as otherwise noted.
- Bargain and sale deed implies that the grantor holds title and possession of the property, and there are no express warranties against encumbrances.

■ Quitclaim deed provides the least protection of any deed, carries no covenants or warranties, and conveys only whatever interest the grantor may have when the deed is delivered.

Transfer tax stamps may be required to be affixed to deeds and conveyances before being recorded, with the tax rate depending on state, county, and city requirements.

Involuntary alienation (transfer) of title to property is usually by operation of law.

■ Escheat—property taken by state when the deceased has no heirs
■ Eminent domain—property taken by public or government agency
■ Foreclosure—property taken by creditor for nonpayment of debt secured by real property
■ Adverse possession—property seizure occurring when someone who is not the lawful owner takes possession of property for the length of time specified by state law, and usually in a way that is open, notorious, continuous, hostile, and adverse.

Transfer of title by will occurs when the deceased dies testate, leaving a will prepared as required by state law. The following statements are true:

■ Wills take effect only after death and can be changed by codicil or revoked while the testator is still alive.
■ Devise is a gift of real property by will to the devisee.
■ Bequest is a gift of personal property.
■ Legacy is a gift of money.
■ To pass title to property on death, the will must be filed with the court and probated.
■ Wills cannot supersede state laws protecting inheritance rights of the surviving wife (dower) or husband (curtesy).

Transfer of title under a state's statute of descent and distribution occurs when a person dies intestate (without a will). Probate proceedings must have an administrator appointed, and laws of the state where the real property is located govern property distribution.

Public records are typically searched by title companies that provide title insurance to prospective purchasers based on the findings of the title search.

Constructive notice of a document is assumed when due diligence (such as a search of public records and inspection of the property) would reveal its existence. Actual notice means that an individual has direct knowledge of documents in the public records and facts revealed by an inspection of the property.

Unrecorded documents that may affect title, such as a tax lien, may not be recorded immediately, yet are still given priority by law and require a search of tax records and other sources.

Chain of title is a record of property ownership, but it does not include liens and other encumbrances:

■ A gap in the chain or other dispute of ownership creates a cloud on the title.
■ A cloud on title is resolved by suit to quiet title.

An abstract of title, prepared by an abstractor or an attorney, is a summary report of what the title search reveals. It includes all recorded liens and encumbrances and lists records searched, but it does not indicate forgeries and interests that are unrecorded or could be discovered by property inspection.

A marketable title is one that must

- not have serious defects, nor rely on doubtful questions of law or fact to prove its validity;
- not expose the purchaser to litigation nor threaten quiet enjoyment of property; and
- convince a reasonably well-informed and prudent purchaser that the property could be sold or mortgaged at a later time.

Proof of ownership may be established by certificate of title, but it will not reveal unrecorded liens or rights of parties in possession.

Title insurance, issued as an owner's or mortgagee's (lender) policy under which the insured is protected from losses arising from defects in title, insures against hidden defects and identifies exclusions that include readily apparent title defects, zoning, and others.

CHAPTER 8 REVIEW QUESTIONS

1. The grantee receives greatest protection with what type of deed?
   a. Quitclaim
   b. General warranty
   c. Bargain and sale with covenant
   d. Executor's

2. Under the covenant of quiet enjoyment, the grantor
   a. promises to obtain and deliver any instrument needed to make the title good.
   b. guarantees to compensate the grantee if the title fails in the future.
   c. warrants that he is the owner and has the right to convey title to the property.
   d. ensures that the title will be good against the title claims of third parties.

3. Which type of deed merely implies but does NOT specifically warrant that the grantor holds good title to the property?
   a. Special warranty
   b. Bargain and sale
   c. Quitclaim
   d. Trust deed

4. Eminent domain and escheat are two examples of
   a. voluntary alienation.
   b. adverse possession.
   c. transfers of title by descent.
   d. involuntary alienation.

5. A person who has died without a will has died
   a. testate.
   b. in valid conveyance.
   c. intestate.
   d. under the acknowledgment clause.

6. Generally, a probate proceeding involving real property takes place
   a. only in the county in which the property is located.
   b. only in the county in which the decedent resided.
   c. in both the county where the decedent resided and the county in which the property is located.
   d. in the county in which the executor or the beneficiary resides.

7. Chain of title is MOST accurately defined as
   a. a summary or history of all documents and legal proceedings affecting a specific parcel of land.
   b. a report of the contents of the public record regarding a particular property.
   c. an instrument or document that protects the insured parties (subject to specific exceptions) against defects in the examination of the record and hidden risks such as forgeries, undisclosed heirs, errors in the public records, and so forth.
   d. a record of a property's ownership.

8. A sells a portion of property to B. B promptly records the deed in the appropriate county office. If A tries to sell the same portion of property to C, which statement is TRUE?
   a. C has been given constructive notice of the prior sale because B promptly recorded the deed.
   b. C has been given actual notice of the prior sale because B promptly recorded the deed.
   c. Because C's purchase of the property is the more recent, it will have priority over B's interest, regardless of when B recorded the deed.
   d. Because C purchased the property from its rightful owner, C is presumed by law to be aware of B's prior interest.

9. Which of the following are traditionally covered by a standard title insurance policy?

a. Unrecorded rights of persons in possession
b. Improperly delivered deeds
c. Changes in land use due to zoning ordinances
d. Unrecorded liens not known to the policyholder

10. The mortgagee received a title insurance policy on the property a buyer is pledging as security for the mortgage loan. Which of the following is *TRUE*?

a. The policy is issued for the benefit of the buyer.
b. The policy guarantees that the buyer's equity will be protected.
c. The amount of coverage is commensurate with the loan amount.
d. The amount of coverage increases as the borrower's equity increases.

CHAPTER 9

Transaction Process and Closing

■ **LEARNING OBJECTIVES** *When you have completed this chapter, you will be able to*

- ■ **describe** the steps involved in the transaction process from contract to closing;

- ■ **prepare** a list of tasks to be done in preparation for closing by the closing agent;

- ■ **list** the tasks to be done by the buyer and the seller before closing;

- ■ **describe** a face-to-face closing, including where it might be held, individuals who attend, and any special considerations;

- ■ **identify** the items to be deposited by the seller and by the buyer in an escrow closing;

- ■ **discuss** the impact of the Taxpayer Relief Act and the Mortgage Disclosure Improvement Act on closings;

- ■ **identify** the practices that are prohibited by the Real Estate Settlement Procedures Act;

- ■ **define** the disclosures required by the Real Estate Settlement Procedures Act; and

- ■ **identify** items that are typically prorated at closing.

■ KEY TERMS

affidavit of title	depreciation	ownership and use tests
appraisal	escrow or impound account	preapproval letter
assets	escrow closing	prorations
bring down	exchange	Real Estate Settlement Procedures Act (RESPA)
closing	face-to-face closing	sales comparison approach
closing agent	flood insurance	
computerized loan origination (CLO)	Good Faith Estimate (GFE)	Settlement Statement (HUD-1)
controlled business arrangement (CBA)	home inspection	tri-merge credit report
cost approach	income approach	underwriter
credit	kickback	walk-through
credit report	liabilities	zero tolerance
credit score	market value	
debit	net worth	

■ INTRODUCTION

The preparation of the sales contract, along with any contingencies, amendments, or addenda, has been covered in earlier chapters. Once the contract has been ratified with the signatures of all parties, the transaction process begins. This period between the ratification and the settlement, or closing, can take anywhere from a few weeks to a few months, depending on the complexity of the contract or on the personal wishes of the parties involved. In most cases, the closing involves both a closing on the loan and the conveyance of title to the property.

■ TRANSACTION PROCESS

The Contract

After the offer to purchase and any subsequent contingencies or changes have been agreed upon and signatures have been received from all parties, the offer becomes a contract. Signed copies are returned to both buyer and seller and the process begins.

The earnest money deposit that was received, along with the offer to purchase, must now be deposited by either the listing broker or the selling broker, according to state law. Unless otherwise agreed by the parties to the contract, the TREC 20-12 or another TREC-promulgated contract form is used and the broker or salesperson is never the escrow agent for the earnest money. Under those contractual documents, the buyer, not the licensee, is required to deposit the money with the escrow agent (usually a title company) after the contract is formed and executed by both seller and buyer. A broker maintaining a trust account must retain for four years a documentary record of each deposit or withdrawal from the account.

In some cases, the earnest money deposit (EMD) may earn interest. The financing contingency protects the purchaser from losing the earnest money in case the contract falls through due to an inability to obtain financing.

A copy of the contract is sent to the closing agent or title company, as stated in the contract, so that title work can be started.

■ LOAN APPROVAL

A **preapproval letter** from the lender stating that the borrower is approved for a real estate loan up to a specified amount may have been submitted along with the original offer to purchase. In any case, now that a specific property has been selected, the borrower is ready to make a formal loan application. See Figure 9.1 for the Uniform Residential Loan Application form used by most lenders. The application form lists all **assets** and **liabilities** of the borrower in order to determine the applicant's **net worth**.

The lender must provide the borrower with a **Good Faith Estimate (GFE)** of all closing costs involved in obtaining and settling on a mortgage loan within three days of application. Another GFE will be presented at closing and may only differ slightly from the first one. The lender must also provide the borrower with a truth-in-lending (TIL) disclosure statement of all of the costs of credit, including the annual percentage rate (APR).

Credit Report   The loan officer orders a **credit report** (if one is not already on file) and an appraisal. A processor opens a case file that will carry all documentation and reports from this point until closing. In addition to the credit report, verifications of income, employment, and deposits are usually required.

In most cases, a **tri-merge credit report** containing credit information and credit scores from all three major credit reporting agencies is ordered. When the scores are different, the middle one is usually used. An assessment of the information is made to determine the prospective borrower's financial ability and attitude toward meeting financial obligations. The **credit score** (often called the FICO score after the company that originated the scoring system) is based on the borrower's history of payment (35%), the amount owed (30%), the length of credit history (15%), and new credit (10%), as well as other factors, such as the number of credit cards, percentage of credit used, or maxed-out cards (10%). An acceptable credit score may vary depending on the loan program being applied for or the amount of down payment.

An application for a commercial or industrial loan requires much more information than that for a residence. A Dun and Bradstreet, Inc. report, as well as audited financial and profit-and-loss statements for both current and previous years, may be required.

Appraisal   Most lenders have an established loan-to-value ratio (LTV) established for each of their loan programs. An **appraisal** is needed to ensure that the property being used as collateral for the loan is adequate for a recovery of their investment in case of default. If the appraisal is less than the sales price, the LTV may not be met, and the contract may have to be renegotiated.

Lenders can choose an appraiser from either a rotating roster or from a preapproved list. The Federal Housing Finance Agency has issued appraisal standards to improve the quality and consistency of appraisals for mortgages to be sold to Fannie Mae and Freddie Mac. See Figure 9.2 for the Uniform Residential Appraisal Report that is required for most loans.

FIGURE 9.1

Uniform Residential Loan Application

Uniform Residential Loan Application

This application is designed to be completed by the applicant(s) with the Lender's assistance. Applicants should complete this form as "Borrower" or "Co-Borrower," as applicable. Co-Borrower information must also be provided (and the appropriate box checked) when ☐ the income or assets of a person other than the Borrower (including the Borrower's spouse) will be used as a basis for loan qualification or ☐ the income or assets of the Borrower's spouse or other person who has community property rights pursuant to state law will not be used as a basis for loan qualification, but his or her liabilities must be considered because the spouse or other person has community property rights pursuant to applicable law and Borrower resides in a community property state, the security property is located in a community property state, or the Borrower is relying on other property located in a community property state as a basis for repayment of the loan.

If this is an application for joint credit, Borrower and Co-Borrower each agree that we intend to apply for joint credit (sign below):

Borrower _____   Co-Borrower _____

I. TYPE OF MORTGAGE AND TERMS OF LOAN

Mortgage Applied for:	☐ VA ☐ FHA	☐ Conventional ☐ USDA/Rural Housing Service	☐ Other (explain):	Agency Case Number	Lender Case Number

Amount $	Interest Rate %	No. of Months	Amortization Type:	☐ Fixed Rate ☐ GPM	☐ Other (explain): ☐ ARM (type):

II. PROPERTY INFORMATION AND PURPOSE OF LOAN

Subject Property Address (street, city, state & ZIP)	No. of Units

Legal Description of Subject Property (attach description if necessary)	Year Built

Purpose of Loan	☐ Purchase ☐ Construction ☐ Refinance ☐ Construction-Permanent	☐ Other (explain):	Property will be: ☐ Primary Residence ☐ Secondary Residence ☐ Investment

Complete this line if construction or construction-permanent loan.

Year Lot Acquired	Original Cost $	Amount Existing Liens $	(a) Present Value of Lot $	(b) Cost of Improvements $	Total (a + b) $

Complete this line if this is a refinance loan.

Year Acquired	Original Cost $	Amount Existing Liens $	Purpose of Refinance	Describe Improvements ☐ made ☐ to be made Cost: $

Title will be held in what Name(s)	Manner in which Title will be held	Estate will be held in: ☐ Fee Simple ☐ Leasehold (show expiration date)

Source of Down Payment, Settlement Charges, and/or Subordinate Financing (explain)

III. BORROWER INFORMATION

Borrower	**Co-Borrower**
Borrower's Name (include Jr. or Sr. if applicable)	Co-Borrower's Name (include Jr. or Sr. if applicable)

Social Security Number	Home Phone (incl. area code)	DOB (mm/dd/yyyy)	Yrs. School	Social Security Number	Home Phone (incl. area code)	DOB (mm/dd/yyyy)	Yrs. School

☐ Married ☐ Unmarried (include ☐ Separated single, divorced, widowed)	Dependents (not listed by Co-Borrower) no. ages	☐ Married ☐ Unmarried (include ☐ Separated single, divorced, widowed)	Dependents (not listed by Borrower) no. ages

Present Address (street, city, state, ZIP) ☐ Own ☐ Rent ____No. Yrs.	Present Address (street, city, state, ZIP) ☐ Own ☐ Rent ____No. Yrs.

Mailing Address, if different from Present Address	Mailing Address, if different from Present Address

If residing at present address for less than two years, complete the following:

Former Address (street, city, state, ZIP) ☐ Own ☐ Rent ____No. Yrs.	Former Address (street, city, state, ZIP) ☐ Own ☐ Rent ____No. Yrs.

IV. EMPLOYMENT INFORMATION

Borrower	**Co-Borrower**
Name & Address of Employer ☐ Self Employed	Yrs. on this job	Name & Address of Employer ☐ Self Employed	Yrs. on this job
	Yrs. employed in this line of work/profession		Yrs. employed in this line of work/profession
Position/Title/Type of Business	Business Phone (incl. area code)	Position/Title/Type of Business	Business Phone (incl. area code)

If employed in current position for less than two years or if currently employed in more than one position, complete the following:

F I G U R E   9.1

Uniform Residential Loan Application (Continued)

Borrower			IV. EMPLOYMENT INFORMATION (cont'd)	Co-Borrower		
Name & Address of Employer	☐ Self Employed	Dates (from – to)	Name & Address of Employer	☐ Self Employed	Dates (from – to)	
		Monthly Income $			Monthly Income $	
Position/Title/Type of Business		Business Phone (incl. area code)	Position/Title/Type of Business		Business Phone (incl. area code)	
Name & Address of Employer	☐ Self Employed	Dates (from – to)	Name & Address of Employer	☐ Self Employed	Dates (from – to)	
		Monthly Income $			Monthly Income $	
Position/Title/Type of Business		Business Phone (incl. area code)	Position/Title/Type of Business		Business Phone (incl. area code)	

V. MONTHLY INCOME AND COMBINED HOUSING EXPENSE INFORMATION

Gross Monthly Income	Borrower	Co-Borrower	Total	Combined Monthly Housing Expense	Present	Proposed
Base Empl. Income*	$	$	$	Rent	$	
Overtime				First Mortgage (P&I)		$
Bonuses				Other Financing (P&I)		
Commissions				Hazard Insurance		
Dividends/Interest				Real Estate Taxes		
Net Rental Income				Mortgage Insurance		
Other (before completing, see the notice in "describe other income," below)				Homeowner Assn. Dues		
				Other:		
Total	$	$	$	Total	$	$

*   Self Employed Borrower(s) may be required to provide additional documentation such as tax returns and financial statements.

Describe Other Income   *Notice:* **Alimony, child support, or separate maintenance income need not be revealed if the Borrower (B) or Co-Borrower (C) does not choose to have it considered for repaying this loan.**

B/C		Monthly Amount
		$

VI. ASSETS AND LIABILITIES

This Statement and any applicable supporting schedules may be completed jointly by both married and unmarried Co-Borrowers if their assets and liabilities are sufficiently joined so that the Statement can be meaningfully and fairly presented on a combined basis; otherwise, separate Statements and Schedules are required. If the Co-Borrower section was completed about a non-applicant spouse or other person, this Statement and supporting schedules must be completed about that spouse or other person also.

Completed ☐ Jointly ☐ Not Jointly

ASSETS	Cash or Market Value	Liabilities and Pledged Assets. List the creditor's name, address, and account number for all outstanding debts, including automobile loans, revolving charge accounts, real estate loans, alimony, child support, stock pledges, etc. Use continuation sheet, if necessary. Indicate by (*) those liabilities, which will be satisfied upon sale of real estate owned or upon refinancing of the subject property.		
Description				
Cash deposit toward purchase held by:	$			
List checking and savings accounts below		LIABILITIES	Monthly Payment & Months Left to Pay	Unpaid Balance
Name and address of Bank, S&L, or Credit Union		Name and address of Company	$ Payment/Months	$
Acct. no.	$	Acct. no.		
Name and address of Bank, S&L, or Credit Union		Name and address of Company	$ Payment/Months	$
Acct. no.	$	Acct. no.		
Name and address of Bank, S&L, or Credit Union		Name and address of Company	$ Payment/Months	$
Acct. no.	$	Acct. no.		

FIGURE 9.1

Uniform Residential Loan Application (Continued)

VI. ASSETS AND LIABILITIES (cont'd)

Name and address of Bank, S&L, or Credit Union		Name and address of Company	$ Payment/Months	$
Acct. no.	$	Acct. no.		
Stocks & Bonds (Company name/ number & description)	$	Name and address of Company	$ Payment/Months	$
		Acct. no.		
Life insurance net cash value	$	Name and address of Company	$ Payment/Months	$
Face amount: $				
Subtotal Liquid Assets	$			
Real estate owned (enter market value from schedule of real estate owned)	$			
Vested interest in retirement fund	$			
Net worth of business(es) owned (attach financial statement)	$	Acct. no.		
Automobiles owned (make and year)	$	Alimony/Child Support/Separate Maintenance Payments Owed to:	$	
Other Assets (itemize)	$	Job-Related Expense (child care, union dues, etc.)	$	
		Total Monthly Payments	$	
Total Assets a.	$	Net Worth (a minus b) ▶ $	**Total Liabilities b.**	$

Schedule of Real Estate Owned (If additional properties are owned, use continuation sheet.)

Property Address (enter S if sold, PS if pending sale or R if rental being held for income) ▼	Type of Property	Present Market Value	Amount of Mortgages & Liens	Gross Rental Income	Mortgage Payments	Insurance, Maintenance, Taxes & Misc.	Net Rental Income
		$	$	$	$	$	$
Totals		$	$	$	$	$	$

List any additional names under which credit has previously been received and indicate appropriate creditor name(s) and account number(s):

Alternate Name	Creditor Name	Account Number

VII. DETAILS OF TRANSACTION

a.	Purchase price	$
b.	Alterations, improvements, repairs	
c.	Land (if acquired separately)	
d.	Refinance (incl. debts to be paid off)	
e.	Estimated prepaid items	
f.	Estimated closing costs	
g.	PMI, MIP, Funding Fee	
h.	Discount (if Borrower will pay)	
i.	Total costs (add items a through h)	

VIII. DECLARATIONS

If you answer "Yes" to any questions a through i, please use continuation sheet for explanation.

	Borrower		Co-Borrower	
	Yes	No	Yes	No
a. Are there any outstanding judgments against you?	☐	☐	☐	☐
b. Have you been declared bankrupt within the past 7 years?	☐	☐	☐	☐
c. Have you had property foreclosed upon or given title or deed in lieu thereof in the last 7 years?	☐	☐	☐	☐
d. Are you a party to a lawsuit?	☐	☐	☐	☐
e. Have you directly or indirectly been obligated on any loan which resulted in foreclosure, transfer of title in lieu of foreclosure, or judgment?	☐	☐	☐	☐

(This would include such loans as home mortgage loans, SBA loans, home improvement loans, educational loans, manufactured (mobile) home loans, any mortgage, financial obligation, bond, or loan guarantee. If "Yes," provide details, including date, name, and address of Lender, FHA or VA case number, if any, and reasons for the action.)

FIGURE 9.1

Uniform Residential Loan Application (Continued)

VII. DETAILS OF TRANSACTION		VIII. DECLARATIONS				
		If you answer "Yes" to any questions a through i, please use continuation sheet for explanation.	Borrower Yes	Borrower No	Co-Borrower Yes	Co-Borrower No
j.	Subordinate financing	f. Are you presently delinquent or in default on any Federal debt or any other loan, mortgage, financial obligation, bond, or loan guarantee?	☐ ·	☐	☐	☐
k.	Borrower's closing costs paid by Seller	g. Are you obligated to pay alimony, child support, or separate maintenance?	☐	☐	☐	☐
		h. Is any part of the down payment borrowed?	☐	☐	☐	☐
l.	Other Credits (explain)	i. Are you a co-maker or endorser on a note?	☐	☐	☐	☐
m.	Loan amount (exclude PMI, MIP, Funding Fee financed)	--				
		j. Are you a U.S. citizen?	☐	☐	☐	☐
n.	PMI, MIP, Funding Fee financed	k. Are you a permanent resident alien?	☐	☐	☐	☐
o.	Loan amount (add m & n)	l. **Do you intend to occupy the property as your primary residence?**	☐	☐	☐	☐
		If Yes," complete question m below.				
p.	Cash from/to Borrower (subtract j, k, l & o from i)	m. Have you had an ownership interest in a property in the last three years?	☐	☐	☐	☐
		(1) What type of property did you own—principal residence (PR), second home (SH), or investment property (IP)?	_____		_____	
		(2) How did you hold title to the home— by yourself (S), jointly with your spouse (SP), or jointly with another person (O)?	_____		_____	

IX. ACKNOWLEDGEMENT AND AGREEMENT

Each of the undersigned specifically represents to Lender and to Lender's actual or potential agents, brokers, processors, attorneys, insurers, servicers, successors and assigns and agrees and acknowledges that: (1) the information provided in this application is true and correct as of the date set forth opposite my signature and that any intentional or negligent misrepresentation of this information contained in this application may result in civil liability, including monetary damages, to any person who may suffer any loss due to reliance upon any misrepresentation that I have made on this application, and/or in criminal penalties including, but not limited to, fine or imprisonment or both under the provisions of Title 18, United States Code, Sec. 1001, et seq.; (2) the loan requested pursuant to this application (the "Loan") will be secured by a mortgage or deed of trust on the property described in this application; (3) the property will not be used for any illegal or prohibited purpose or use; (4) all statements made in this application are made for the purpose of obtaining a residential mortgage loan; (5) the property will be occupied as indicated in this application; (6) the Lender, its servicers, successors or assigns may retain the original and/or an electronic record of this application, whether or not the Loan is approved; (7) the Lender and its agents, brokers, insurers, servicers, successors, and assigns may continuously rely on the information contained in the application, and I am obligated to amend and/or supplement the information provided in this application if any of the material facts that I have represented herein should change prior to closing of the Loan; (8) in the event that my payments on the Loan become delinquent, the Lender, its servicers, successors or assigns may, in addition to any other rights and remedies that it may have relating to such delinquency, report my name and account information to one or more consumer reporting agencies; (9) ownership of the Loan and/or administration of the Loan account may be transferred with such notice as may be required by law; (10) neither Lender nor its agents, brokers, insurers, servicers, successors or assigns has made any representation or warranty, express or implied, to me regarding the property or the condition or value of the property; and (11) my transmission of this application as an "electronic record" containing my "electronic signature," as those terms are defined in applicable federal and/or state laws (excluding audio and video recordings), or my facsimile transmission of this application containing a facsimile of my signature, shall be as effective, enforceable and valid as if a paper version of this application were delivered containing my original written signature.

Acknowledgement. Each of the undersigned hereby acknowledges that any owner of the Loan, its servicers, successors and assigns, may verify or reverify any information contained in this application or obtain any information or data relating to the Loan, for any legitimate business purpose through any source, including a source named in this application or a consumer reporting agency.

Borrower's Signature X	Date	Co-Borrower's Signature X	Date

X. INFORMATION FOR GOVERNMENT MONITORING PURPOSES

The following information is requested by the Federal Government for certain types of loans related to a dwelling in order to monitor the lender's compliance with equal credit opportunity, fair housing and home mortgage disclosure laws. You are not required to furnish this information, but are encouraged to do so. The law provides that a lender may not discriminate either on the basis of this information, or on whether you choose to furnish it. If you furnish the information, please provide both ethnicity and race. For race, you may check more than one designation. If you do not furnish ethnicity, race, or sex, under Federal regulations, this lender is required to note the information on the basis of visual observation and surname if you have made this application in person. If you do not wish to furnish the information, please check the box below. (Lender must review the above material to assure that the disclosures satisfy all requirements to which the lender is subject under applicable state law for the particular type of loan applied for.)

BORROWER ☐ I do not wish to furnish this information			**CO-BORROWER** ☐ I do not wish to furnish this information		
Ethnicity: ☐ Hispanic or Latino	☐ Not Hispanic or Latino		**Ethnicity:** ☐ Hispanic or Latino	☐ Not Hispanic or Latino	
Race: ☐ American Indian or Alaska Native ☐ Native Hawaiian or Other Pacific Islander	☐ Asian ☐ White	☐ Black or African American	**Race:** ☐ American Indian or Alaska Native ☐ Native Hawaiian or Other Pacific Islander	☐ Asian ☐ White	☐ Black or African American
Sex: ☐ Female ☐ Male			**Sex:** ☐ Female ☐ Male		

To be Completed by Loan Originator:
This information was provided:
☐ In a face-to-face interview
☐ In a telephone interview
☐ By the applicant and submitted by fax or mail
☐ By the applicant and submitted via e-mail or the Internet

Loan Originator's Signature X		Date
Loan Originator's Name (print or type)	Loan Originator Identifier	Loan Originator's Phone Number (including area code)
Loan Origination Company's Name	Loan Origination Company Identifier	Loan Origination Company's Address

FIGURE 9.1

Uniform Residential Loan Application (Continued)

CONTINUATION SHEET/RESIDENTIAL LOAN APPLICATION		
Use this continuation sheet if you need more space to complete the Residential Loan Application. Mark **B** f or Borrower or **C** for Co-Borrower.	Borrower:	Agency Case Number:
	Co-Borrower:	Lender Case Number:

I/We fully understand that it is a Federal crime punishable by fine or imprisonment, or both, to knowingly make any false statements concerning any of the above facts as applicable under the provisions of Title 18, United States Code, Section 1001, et seq.

Borrower's Signature	Date	Co-Borrower's Signature	Date
X		X	

F I G U R E 9.2

Uniform Residential Appraisal Report

Uniform Residential Appraisal Report   File

The purpose of this summary appraisal report is to provide the lender/client with an accurate, and adequately supported, opinion of the market value of the subject property.

SUBJECT

Property Address	City	State Zip Code
Borrower	Owner of Public Record	County
Legal Description		

Assessor's Parcel #   Tax Year   R.E. Taxes $

Neighborhood Name   Map Reference   Census Tract

Occupant ☐ Owner ☐ Tenant ☐ Vacant   Special Assessments $ ☐ PUD HOA $ ☐ per year ☐ per month

Property Rights Appraised ☐ Fee Simple ☐ Leasehold ☐ Other (describe)

Assignment Type ☐ Purchase Transaction ☐ Refinance Transaction ☐ Other (describe)

Lender/Client   Address

Is the subject property currently offered for sale or has it been offered for sale in the twelve months prior to the effective date of this appraisal? ☐ Yes ☐ No

Report data source(s) used, offering price(s), and date(s).

CONTRACT

I ☐ did ☐ did not analyze the contract for sale for the subject purchase transaction. Explain the results of the analysis of the contract for sale or why the analysis was not performed.

Contract Price $ Date of Contract   Is the property seller the owner of public record? ☐ Yes ☐ No Data Source(s)

Is there any financial assistance (loan charges, sale concessions, gift or downpayment assistance, etc.) to be paid by any party on behalf of the borrower? ☐ Yes ☐ No

If Yes, report the total dollar amount and describe the items to be paid.

Note: Race and the racial composition of the neighborhood are not appraisal factors.

NEIGHBORHOOD

Neighborhood Characteristics	One-Unit Housing Trends	One-Unit Housing		Present Land Use %	
Location ☐ Urban ☐ Suburban ☐ Rural	Property Values ☐ Increasing ☐ Stable ☐ Declining	PRICE	AGE	One-Unit	%
Built-Up ☐ Over 75% ☐ 25–75% ☐ Under 25%	Demand/Supply ☐ Shortage ☐ In Balance ☐ Over Supply	$ (000)	(yrs)	2-4 Unit	%
Growth ☐ Rapid ☐ Stable ☐ Slow	Marketing Time ☐ Under 3 mths ☐ 3–6 mths ☐ Over 6 mths	Low		Multi-Family	%
Neighborhood Boundaries		High		Commercial	%
		Pred.		Other	%

Neighborhood Description

Market Conditions (including support for the above conclusions)

SITE

Dimensions   Area   Shape   View

Specific Zoning Classification   Zoning Description

Zoning Compliance ☐ Legal ☐ Legal Nonconforming (Grandfathered Use) ☐ No Zoning ☐ Illegal (describe)

Is the highest and best use of the subject property as improved (or as proposed per plans and specifications) the present use? ☐ Yes ☐ No If No, describe

Utilities	Public	Other (describe)		Public	Other (describe)	Off-site Improvements—Type	Public	Private
Electricity	☐	☐	Water	☐	☐	Street	☐	☐
Gas	☐	☐	Sanitary Sewer	☐	☐	Alley	☐	☐

FEMA Special Flood Hazard Area ☐ Yes ☐ No FEMA Flood Zone   FEMA Map #   FEMA Map Date

Are the utilities and off-site improvements typical for the market area? ☐ Yes ☐ No If No, describe

Are there any adverse site conditions or external factors (easements, encroachments, environmental conditions, land uses, etc.)? ☐ Yes ☐ No If Yes, describe

IMPROVEMENTS

General Description	Foundation	Exterior Description materials/condition	Interior materials/condition
Units ☐ One ☐ One with Accessory Unit	☐ Concrete Slab ☐ Crawl Space	Foundation Walls	Floors
# of Stories	☐ Full Basement ☐ Partial Basement	Exterior Walls	Walls
Type ☐ Det. ☐ Att. ☐ S-Det./End Unit	Basement Area sq. ft.	Roof Surface	Trim/Finish
☐ Existing ☐ Proposed ☐ Under Const.	Basement Finish %	Gutters & Downspouts	Bath Floor
Design (Style)	☐ Outside Entry/Exit ☐ Sump Pump	Window Type	Bath Wainscot
Year Built	Evidence of ☐ Infestation	Storm Sash/Insulated	Car Storage ☐ None
Effective Age (Yrs)	☐ Dampness ☐ Settlement	Screens	☐ Driveway # of Cars
Attic ☐ None	Heating ☐ FWA ☐ HWBB ☐ Radiant	Amenities ☐ Woodstove(s) #	Driveway Surface
☐ Drop Stair ☐ Stairs	☐ Other Fuel	☐ Fireplace(s) # ☐ Fence	☐ Garage # of Cars
☐ Floor ☐ Scuttle	Cooling ☐ Central Air Conditioning	☐ Patio/Deck ☐ Porch	☐ Carport # of Cars
☐ Finished ☐ Heated	☐ Individual ☐ Other	☐ Pool ☐ Other	☐ Att. ☐ Det. ☐ Built-in

Appliances ☐ Refrigerator ☐ Range/Oven ☐ Dishwasher ☐ Disposal ☐ Microwave ☐ Washer/Dryer ☐ Other (describe)

Finished area **above** grade contains: Rooms   Bedrooms   Bath(s)   Square Feet of Gross Living Area Above Grade

Additional features (special energy efficient items, etc.).

Describe the condition of the property (including needed repairs, deterioration, renovations, remodeling, etc.).

Are there any physical deficiencies or adverse conditions that affect the livability, soundness, or structural integrity of the property? ☐ Yes ☐ No If Yes, describe

Does the property generally conform to the neighborhood (functional utility, style, condition, use, construction, etc.)? ☐ Yes ☐ No If No, describe

Freddie Mac Form 70 March 2005   Page 1 of 6   Fannie Mae Form 1004 March 2005

FIGURE 9.2

Uniform Residential Appraisal Report (Continued)

Uniform Residential Appraisal Report

File #

SALES COMPARISON APPROACH

There are comparable properties currently offered for sale in the subject neighborhood ranging in price from $ to $.

There are comparable sales in the subject neighborhood within the past twelve months ranging in sale price from $ to $.

FEATURE	SUBJECT	COMPARABLE SALE # 1		COMPARABLE SALE # 2		COMPARABLE SALE # 3	
Address							
Proximity to Subject							
Sale Price	$		$		$		$
Sale Price/Gross Liv. Area	$ sq. ft.	$ sq. ft.		$ sq. ft.		$ sq. ft.	
Data Source(s)							
Verification Source(s)							
VALUE ADJUSTMENTS	DESCRIPTION	DESCRIPTION	+(-) $ Adjustment	DESCRIPTION	+(-) $ Adjustment	DESCRIPTION	+(-) $ Adjustment
Sale or Financing Concessions							
Date of Sale/Time							
Location							
Leasehold/Fee Simple							
Site							
View							
Design (Style)							
Quality of Construction							
Actual Age							
Condition							
Above Grade Room Count	Total Bdrms. Baths	Total Bdrms. Baths		Total Bdrms. Baths		Total Bdrms. Baths	
Gross Living Area	sq. ft.	sq. ft.		sq. ft.		sq. ft.	
Basement & Finished Rooms Below Grade							
Functional Utility							
Heating/Cooling							
Energy Efficient Items							
Garage/Carport							
Porch/Patio/Deck							
Net Adjustment (Total)		☐ + ☐ -	$	☐ + ☐ -	$	☐ + ☐ -	$
Adjusted Sale Price of Comparables		Net Adj. % Gross Adj. %	$	Net Adj. % Gross Adj. %	$	Net Adj. % Gross Adj. %	$

I ☐ did ☐ did not research the sale or transfer history of the subject property and comparable sales. If not, explain

My research ☐ did ☐ did not reveal any prior sales or transfers of the subject property for the three years prior to the effective date of this appraisal.

Data source(s)

My research ☐ did ☐ did not reveal any prior sales or transfers of the comparable sales for the year prior to the date of sale of the comparable sale.

Data source(s)

Report the results of the research and analysis of the prior sale or transfer history of the subject property and comparable sales (report additional prior sales on page 3).

ITEM	SUBJECT	COMPARABLE SALE # 1	COMPARABLE SALE # 2	COMPARABLE SALE # 3
Date of Prior Sale/Transfer				
Price of Prior Sale/Transfer				
Data Source(s)				
Effective Date of Data Source(s)				

Analysis of prior sale or transfer history of the subject property and comparable sales

Summary of Sales Comparison Approach

Indicated Value by Sales Comparison Approach $

RECONCILIATION

Indicated Value by: Sales Comparison Approach $ Cost Approach (if developed) $ Income Approach (if developed) $

This appraisal is made ☐ "as is", ☐ subject to completion per plans and specifications on the basis of a hypothetical condition that the improvements have been completed, ☐ subject to the following repairs or alterations on the basis of a hypothetical condition that the repairs or alterations have been completed, or ☐ subject to the following required inspection based on the extraordinary assumption that the condition or deficiency does not require alteration or repair:

Based on a complete visual inspection of the interior and exterior areas of the subject property, defined scope of work, statement of assumptions and limiting conditions, and appraiser's certification, my (our) opinion of the market value, as defined, of the real property that is the subject of this report is $, as of , which is the date of inspection and the effective date of this appraisal.

Freddie Mac Form 70 March 2005 Page 2 of 6 Fannie Mae Form 1004 March 2005

FIGURE 9.2

Uniform Residential Appraisal Report (Continued)

Uniform Residential Appraisal Report

File #

ADDITIONAL COMMENTS

COST APPROACH TO VALUE (not required by Fannie Mae)

Provide adequate information for the lender/client to replicate the below cost figures and calculations.

Support for the opinion of site value (summary of comparable land sales or other methods for estimating site value)

ESTIMATED ☐ REPRODUCTION OR ☐ REPLACEMENT COST NEW   OPINION OF SITE VALUE .... = $

Source of cost data   Dwelling   Sq. Ft. @ $ .... =$

Quality rating from cost service   Effective date of cost data   Sq. Ft. @ $ .... =$

Comments on Cost Approach (gross living area calculations, depreciation, etc.)   Garage/Carport   Sq. Ft. @ $ .... =$

Total Estimate of Cost-New   .... = $

Less   Physical   Functional   External

Depreciation   =$(   )

Depreciated Cost of Improvements...=$

"As-is" Value of Site Improvements...=$

Estimated Remaining Economic Life (HUD and VA only)   Years   Indicated Value By Cost Approach .... =$

INCOME APPROACH TO VALUE (not required by Fannie Mae)

Estimated Monthly Market Rent $ X Gross Rent Multiplier   = $ Indicated Value by Income Approach

Summary of Income Approach (including support for market rent and GRM)

PROJECT INFORMATION FOR PUDs (if applicable)

Is the developer/builder in control of the Homeowners' Association (HOA)? ☐ Yes ☐ No   Unit type(s) ☐ Detached ☐ Attached

Provide the following information for PUDs ONLY if the developer/builder is in control of the HOA and the subject property is an attached dwelling unit.

Legal name of project

Total number of phases   Total number of units   Total number of units sold

Total number of units rented   Total number of units for sale   Data source(s)

Was the project created by the conversion of an existing building(s) into a PUD? ☐ Yes ☐ No   If Yes, date of conversion

Does the project contain any multi-dwelling units? ☐ Yes ☐ No   Data source(s)

Are the units, common elements, and recreation facilities complete? ☐ Yes ☐ No   If No, describe the status of completion.

Are the common elements leased to or by the Homeowners' Association? ☐ Yes ☐ No   If Yes, describe the rental terms and options.

Describe common elements and recreational facilities

F I G U R E   9.2

Uniform Residential Appraisal Report (Continued)

Uniform Residential Appraisal Report File #

This report form is designed to report an appraisal of a one-unit property or a one-unit property with an accessory unit; including a unit in a planned unit development (PUD). This report form is not designed to report an appraisal of a manufactured home or a unit in a condominium or cooperative project.

This appraisal report is subject to the following scope of work, intended use, intended user, definition of market value, statement of assumptions and limiting conditions, and certifications. Modifications, additions, or deletions to the intended use, intended user, definition of market value, or assumptions and limiting conditions are not permitted. The appraiser may expand the scope of work to include any additional research or analysis necessary based on the complexity of this appraisal assignment. Modifications or deletions to the certifications are also not permitted. However, additional certifications that do not constitute material alterations to this appraisal report, such as those required by law or those related to the appraiser's continuing education or membership in an appraisal organization, are permitted.

SCOPE OF WORK: The scope of work for this appraisal is defined by the complexity of this appraisal assignment and the reporting requirements of this appraisal report form, including the following definition of market value, statement of assumptions and limiting conditions, and certifications. The appraiser must, at a minimum: (1) perform a complete visual inspection of the interior and exterior areas of the subject property, (2) inspect the neighborhood, (3) inspect each of the comparable sales from at least the street, (4) research, verify, and analyze data from reliable public and/or private sources, and (5) report his or her analysis, opinions, and conclusions in this appraisal report.

INTENDED USE: The intended use of this appraisal report is for the lender/client to evaluate the property that is the subject of this appraisal for a mortgage finance transaction.

INTENDED USER: The intended user of this appraisal report is the lender/client.

DEFINITION OF MARKET VALUE: The most probable price which a property should bring in a competitive and open market under all conditions requisite to a fair sale, the buyer and seller, each acting prudently, knowledgeably and assuming the price is not affected by undue stimulus. Implicit in this definition is the consummation of a sale as of a specified date and the passing of title from seller to buyer under conditions whereby: (1) buyer and seller are typically motivated; (2) both parties are well informed or well advised, and each acting in what he or she considers his or her own best interest; (3) a reasonable time is allowed for exposure in the open market; (4) payment is made in terms of cash in U. S. dollars or in terms of financial arrangements comparable thereto; and (5) the price represents the normal consideration for the property sold unaffected by special or creative financing or sales concessions* granted by anyone associated with the sale.

*Adjustments to the comparables must be made for special or creative financing or sales concessions. No adjustments are necessary for those costs which are normally paid by sellers as a result of tradition or law in a market area; these costs are readily identifiable since the seller pays these costs in virtually all sales transactions. Special or creative financing adjustments can be made to the comparable property by comparisons to financing terms offered by a third party institutional lender that is not already involved in the property or transaction. Any adjustment should not be calculated on a mechanical dollar for dollar cost of the financing or concession but the dollar amount of any adjustment should approximate the market's reaction to the financing or concessions based on the appraiser's judgment.

STATEMENT OF ASSUMPTIONS AND LIMITING CONDITIONS: The appraiser's certification in this report is subject to the following assumptions and limiting conditions:

1. The appraiser will not be responsible for matters of a legal nature that affect either the property being appraised or the title to it, except for information that he or she became aware of during the research involved in performing this appraisal. The appraiser assumes that the title is good and marketable and will not render any opinions about the title.

2. The appraiser has provided a sketch in this appraisal report to show the approximate dimensions of the improvements. The sketch is included only to assist the reader in visualizing the property and understanding the appraiser's determination of its size.

3. The appraiser has examined the available flood maps that are provided by the Federal Emergency Management Agency (or other data sources) and has noted in this appraisal report whether any portion of the subject site is located in an identified Special Flood Hazard Area. Because the appraiser is not a surveyor, he or she makes no guarantees, express or implied, regarding this determination.

4. The appraiser will not give testimony or appear in court because he or she made an appraisal of the property in question, unless specific arrangements to do so have been made beforehand, or as otherwise required by law.

5. The appraiser has noted in this appraisal report any adverse conditions (such as needed repairs, deterioration, the presence of hazardous wastes, toxic substances, etc.) observed during the inspection of the subject property or that he or she became aware of during the research involved in performing this appraisal. Unless otherwise stated in this appraisal report, the appraiser has no knowledge of any hidden or unapparent physical deficiencies or adverse conditions of the property (such as, but not limited to, needed repairs, deterioration, the presence of hazardous wastes, toxic substances, adverse environmental conditions, etc.) that would make the property less valuable, and has assumed that there are no such conditions and makes no guarantees or warranties, express or implied. The appraiser will not be responsible for any such conditions that do exist or for any engineering or testing that might be required to discover whether such conditions exist. Because the appraiser is not an expert in the field of environmental hazards, this appraisal report must not be considered as an environmental assessment of the property.

6. The appraiser has based his or her appraisal report and valuation conclusion for an appraisal that is subject to satisfactory completion, repairs, or alterations on the assumption that the completion, repairs, or alterations of the subject property will be performed in a professional manner.

FIGURE 9.2

Uniform Residential Appraisal Report (Continued)

Uniform Residential Appraisal Report
File #

APPRAISER'S CERTIFICATION: The Appraiser certifies and agrees that:

1. I have, at a minimum, developed and reported this appraisal in accordance with the scope of work requirements stated in this appraisal report.

2. I performed a complete visual inspection of the interior and exterior areas of the subject property. I reported the condition of the improvements in factual, specific terms. I identified and reported the physical deficiencies that could affect the livability, soundness, or structural integrity of the property.

3. I performed this appraisal in accordance with the requirements of the Uniform Standards of Professional Appraisal Practice that were adopted and promulgated by the Appraisal Standards Board of The Appraisal Foundation and that were in place at the time this appraisal report was prepared.

4. I developed my opinion of the market value of the real property that is the subject of this report based on the sales comparison approach to value. I have adequate comparable market data to develop a reliable sales comparison approach for this appraisal assignment. I further certify that I considered the cost and income approaches to value but did not develop them, unless otherwise indicated in this report.

5. I researched, verified, analyzed, and reported on any current agreement for sale for the subject property, any offering for sale of the subject property in the twelve months prior to the effective date of this appraisal, and the prior sales of the subject property for a minimum of three years prior to the effective date of this appraisal, unless otherwise indicated in this report.

6. I researched, verified, analyzed, and reported on the prior sales of the comparable sales for a minimum of one year prior to the date of sale of the comparable sale, unless otherwise indicated in this report.

7. I selected and used comparable sales that are locationally, physically, and functionally the most similar to the subject property.

8. I have not used comparable sales that were the result of combining a land sale with the contract purchase price of a home that has been built or will be built on the land.

9. I have reported adjustments to the comparable sales that reflect the market's reaction to the differences between the subject property and the comparable sales.

10. I verified, from a disinterested source, all information in this report that was provided by parties who have a financial interest in the sale or financing of the subject property.

11. I have knowledge and experience in appraising this type of property in this market area.

12. I am aware of, and have access to, the necessary and appropriate public and private data sources, such as multiple listing services, tax assessment records, public land records and other such data sources for the area in which the property is located.

13. I obtained the information, estimates, and opinions furnished by other parties and expressed in this appraisal report from reliable sources that I believe to be true and correct.

14. I have taken into consideration the factors that have an impact on value with respect to the subject neighborhood, subject property, and the proximity of the subject property to adverse influences in the development of my opinion of market value. I have noted in this appraisal report any adverse conditions (such as, but not limited to, needed repairs, deterioration, the presence of hazardous wastes, toxic substances, adverse environmental conditions, etc.) observed during the inspection of the subject property or that I became aware of during the research involved in performing this appraisal. I have considered these adverse conditions in my analysis of the property value, and have reported on the effect of the conditions on the value and marketability of the subject property.

15. I have not knowingly withheld any significant information from this appraisal report and, to the best of my knowledge, all statements and information in this appraisal report are true and correct.

16. I stated in this appraisal report my own personal, unbiased, and professional analysis, opinions, and conclusions, which are subject only to the assumptions and limiting conditions in this appraisal report.

17. I have no present or prospective interest in the property that is the subject of this report, and I have no present or prospective personal interest or bias with respect to the participants in the transaction. I did not base, either partially or completely, my analysis and/or opinion of market value in this appraisal report on the race, color, religion, sex, age, marital status, handicap, familial status, or national origin of either the prospective owners or occupants of the subject property or of the present owners or occupants of the properties in the vicinity of the subject property or on any other basis prohibited by law.

18. My employment and/or compensation for performing this appraisal or any future or anticipated appraisals was not conditioned on any agreement or understanding, written or otherwise, that I would report (or present analysis supporting) a predetermined specific value, a predetermined minimum value, a range or direction in value, a value that favors the cause of any party, or the attainment of a specific result or occurrence of a specific subsequent event (such as approval of a pending mortgage loan application).

19. I personally prepared all conclusions and opinions about the real estate that were set forth in this appraisal report. If I relied on significant real property appraisal assistance from any individual or individuals in the performance of this appraisal or the preparation of this appraisal report, I have named such individual(s) and disclosed the specific tasks performed in this appraisal report. I certify that any individual so named is qualified to perform the tasks. I have not authorized anyone to make a change to any item in this appraisal report; therefore, any change made to this appraisal is unauthorized and I will take no responsibility for it.

20. I identified the lender/client in this appraisal report who is the individual, organization, or agent for the organization that ordered and will receive this appraisal report.

Freddie Mac Form 70   March 2005   Page 5 of 6   Fannie Mae Form 1004   March 2005

F I G U R E   9.2

Uniform Residential Appraisal Report (Continued)

Uniform Residential Appraisal Report   File

21. The lender/client may disclose or distribute this appraisal report to: the borrower; another lender at the request of the borrower; the mortgagee or its successors and assigns; mortgage insurers; government sponsored enterprises; other secondary market participants; data collection or reporting services; professional appraisal organizations; any department, agency, or instrumentality of the United States; and any state, the District of Columbia, or other jurisdictions; without having to obtain the appraiser's or supervisory appraiser's (if applicable) consent. Such consent must be obtained before this appraisal report may be disclosed or distributed to any other party (including, but not limited to, the public through advertising, public relations, news, sales, or other media).

22. I am aware that any disclosure or distribution of this appraisal report by me or the lender/client may be subject to certain laws and regulations. Further, I am also subject to the provisions of the Uniform Standards of Professional Appraisal Practice that pertain to disclosure or distribution by me.

23. The borrower, another lender at the request of the borrower, the mortgagee or its successors and assigns, mortgage insurers, government sponsored enterprises, and other secondary market participants may rely on this appraisal report as part of any mortgage finance transaction that involves any one or more of these parties.

24. If this appraisal report was transmitted as an "electronic record" containing my "electronic signature," as those terms are defined in applicable federal and/or state laws (excluding audio and video recordings), or a facsimile transmission of this appraisal report containing a copy or representation of my signature, the appraisal report shall be as effective, enforceable and valid as if a paper version of this appraisal report were delivered containing my original hand written signature.

25. Any intentional or negligent misrepresentation(s) contained in this appraisal report may result in civil liability and/or criminal penalties including, but not limited to, fine or imprisonment or both under the provisions of Title 18, United States Code, Section 1001, et seq., or similar state laws.

SUPERVISORY APPRAISER'S CERTIFICATION: The Supervisory Appraiser certifies and agrees that:

1. I directly supervised the appraiser for this appraisal assignment, have read the appraisal report, and agree with the appraiser's analysis, opinions, statements, conclusions, and the appraiser's certification.

2. I accept full responsibility for the contents of this appraisal report including, but not limited to, the appraiser's analysis, opinions, statements, conclusions, and the appraiser's certification.

3. The appraiser identified in this appraisal report is either a sub-contractor or an employee of the supervisory appraiser (or the appraisal firm), is qualified to perform this appraisal, and is acceptable to perform this appraisal under the applicable state law.

4. This appraisal report complies with the Uniform Standards of Professional Appraisal Practice that were adopted and promulgated by the Appraisal Standards Board of The Appraisal Foundation and that were in place at the time this appraisal report was prepared.

5. If this appraisal report was transmitted as an "electronic record" containing my "electronic signature," as those terms are defined in applicable federal and/or state laws (excluding audio and video recordings), or a facsimile transmission of this appraisal report containing a copy or representation of my signature, the appraisal report shall be as effective, enforceable and valid as if a paper version of this appraisal report were delivered containing my original hand written signature.

APPRAISER

Signature_____
Name _____
Company Name _____
Company Address_____
_____
Telephone Number _____
Email Address_____
Date of Signature and Report_____
Effective Date of Appraisal _____
State Certification #_____
or State License # _____
or Other (describe) _____ State # _____
State _____
Expiration Date of Certification or License _____

ADDRESS OF PROPERTY APPRAISED

_____
_____

APPRAISED VALUE OF SUBJECT PROPERTY $ _____

LENDER/CLIENT

Name _____
Company Name _____
Company Address_____
_____
Email Address_____

SUPERVISORY APPRAISER (ONLY IF REQUIRED)

Signature _____
Name_____
Company Name _____
Company Address_____
_____
Telephone Number _____
Email Address_____
Date of Signature _____
State Certification #_____
or State License # _____
State _____
Expiration Date of Certification or License _____

SUBJECT PROPERTY

☐ Did not inspect subject property
☐ Did inspect exterior of subject property from street
   Date of Inspection _____
☐ Did inspect interior and exterior of subject property
   Date of Inspection _____

COMPARABLE SALES

☐ Did not inspect exterior of comparable sales from street
☐ Did inspect exterior of comparable sales from street
   Date of Inspection _____

An appraisal to determine the **market value** of a residential property is usually based on a **sales comparison approach** in which the subject property is evaluated in comparison with other similar properties in the same locale that have recently sold. Adjustments are made to reflect what those properties would have sold for if they exactly matched the subject property. See Figure 9.3 for an illustration of the sales comparison approach to value.

FIGURE 9.3

Sales Comparison Approach to Value

	Subject Property	Comparable Properties		
		A	**B**	**C**
Sales Price		**$260,000**	**$252,000**	**$265,000**
Financing concessions	none	none	none	none
Date of sale		current	current	current
Location	good	same	poorer +6,500	same
Age	6 years	same	same	same
Size of lot	60' × 135'	same	same	larger −5,000
Landscaping	good	same	same	same
Construction				
Style				
No. of rooms				
No. of bedrooms	brick	same	same	same
No. of baths	ranch	same	same	same
Sq. ft. of living	6	same	same	same
space	3	same	poorer +500	same
Other space	1½	same	same	better −500
(basement)	1,500	same	same	better −1,000
Condition—exterior	full basement	same	same	same
Condition—interior	average	better −1,500	poorer +1,000	better −1,500
Garage	good	same	same	better −500
Other	2-car attached	same	same	same
improvements	none	none	none	none
Net adjustments		−1,500	+8,000	−8,500
Adjusted value		$258,500	$260,000	$256,500

Note that the value of a feature that is present in the subject but not in the comparable property is *added* to the sales price of the comparable. Likewise, the value of a feature that is present in the comparable but not in the subject property is *subtracted*. A good way to remember this is CBS CPA: CBS stands for "comp better subtract" and CPA stands for "comp poorer add." The adjusted sales prices of the comparables represent the probable range of value of the subject property. From this range, a single market value estimate can be selected.

For a unique property such as a church, the appraiser could use the **cost approach**, which is based on the current replacement cost of the improvements less **depreciation**, which is calculated over the anticipated life of the property. The **income approach** is used to measure the present worth of a property's income stream with the rate of return required by the investor.

Clear Title   Another part of the loan approval process is receiving notification of clear title to the property. As discussed in Chapter 8, a search of title records is made, and any defects called a cloud on the title must be resolved to the satisfaction of the lender, as well as the buyer. The lender will also require a title insurance policy in an amount adequate to protect the lender's investment.

Homeowners Insurance   The lender requires the borrowers to produce proof of homeowners insurance that will cover any loss because of physical hazards or liability. Due to the number of natural disasters, such as Hurricane Katrina, tornadoes, and earthquakes, obtaining homeowners insurance has become more complicated than in previous years, and it needs to be addressed earlier in the process. **Flood insurance** is required for any property within Federal Emergency Management Agency (FEMA) declared flood zones.

Underwriting   After the loan package is complete, it is submitted to an **underwriter** who will approve, reject, or return the package to processing with contingency requirements that must be met before resubmission for approval. Once the loan has been approved by the underwriter, the package is sent to the lender's closing department, where the various loan documents are prepared and sent to the closing agent, and the **escrow or impound account** for the collection of property taxes and insurance is set up.

Final Approval   An approved loan commitment is now communicated to all parties involved in the transaction, obligating the lender to issue the loan under the agreed terms and conditions. This commitment is only good for a fairly short period. Any delay in settlement might result in a required resubmission.

■ INSPECTIONS

A contract often includes a contingency on the purchaser receiving a satisfactory report on one or more types of inspections (see Chapter 6). In many parts of the country, the seller is responsible for providing a satisfactory report regarding termites or other wood-boring insects. The seller is usually also responsible for making any repairs that are needed.

The most common inspection required by the buyer is a **home inspection**, which is highly recommended for all purchasers, but especially for first-time homebuyers. Other typical inspections include those for the presence of hazardous substances such as lead-based paint or radon.

A time frame should be established for completion of the inspection in order for the contingency to be removed as soon as possible. After receiving a report from the inspector, the purchaser can either remove the contingency or prepare a list of requested items for repair or replacement to be submitted to the seller on an addendum form. A time frame during which the seller must respond should be included. The seller may agree to comply with the entire list, but in many cases, will agree to certain items while refusing others. This then becomes a counteroffer and is returned to the buyer for acceptance, rejection, or further counter.

The agreed repairs and/or replacements must be completed before the final walk-through inspection or the seller may be at risk of default. In a case where the required repair or replacement must occur after closing, the seller should be able to provide proof that the work is scheduled and paid for.

■ TITLE WORK

As previously mentioned, the lender will require proof of clear title before granting final approval of the loan. During the time the loan has been in process and the necessary inspections and repairs/replacements are taking place, the closing attorney or the title company has been conducting the necessary title work.

The chain of title showing ownership has been searched for at least a period of 60 years. Public records have been searched and an abstract of title prepared. The sales contract is usually contingent on the purchaser's receiving marketable title to the property. This means that any defects found must be resolved so that the purchaser will not have any problem selling the property in the future. As long as the contract is contingent on the buyer's receiving clear title, the seller is obligated to take whatever steps are necessary to correct the problem.

A title insurance policy will be required by the lender to cover the amount of the loan. For an additional fee, the purchaser can buy an owner's policy that covers the full value of the property. Title insurance is a one-time charge and protects against any claims made to the property in the future (for more information on the conveyance of title, see Chapter 8).

■ PREPARATION FOR CLOSING

The selection of an attorney, escrow agent, or title company agent to handle the closing of the loan and the conveyance of title was noted on the original contract of sale, along with a projected date for settlement. Hopefully, there has been good communication between the lender, the closing agent, the buyer and seller, and their respective agents throughout the transaction process. At this point, the exact date, time, and place for **closing** should be determined with notice given to all parties. In a case where one of the principals to the transaction is unable to attend, it may be possible to have a power-of-attorney prepared that gives the right for another person to sign on his behalf. This is to be avoided unless absolutely necessary and may not be satisfactory to a lender. The closing agent, the buyer, and the seller all have special duties to perform as the settlement date approaches.

Closing Agent   The **closing agent** must prepare the deed and the Settlement Statement (HUD-1) (see Figure 9.4). A closing, or settlement, statement is an accounting of the parties' debits and credits. A **debit** is a charge—an amount that a party owes and must pay at closing. A **credit** is an amount entered in a person's favor—an amount that has already been paid, an amount being reimbursed, or an amount the buyer promises to pay in the form of a loan.

The loan documents are prepared by the lender but will need to be reviewed. Additional information that will be needed for the HUD-1 includes the following:

- The final pay-off figure for any existing loan, effective date of closing, the unpaid amount of principal, the interest due through the date of payment, the fee for issuing the certificate of satisfaction or release deed, credits (if any) for tax and insurance reserves, and the amount of any prepayment penalties. The same procedure is followed for any other liens that must be released.

- The exact balance of the loan as of the closing date, if the buyer will assume the seller's existing mortgage loan. Usually, the lender is required to provide the buyer with a mortgage reduction certificate, which certifies the amount owed on the mortgage loan, the interest rate, and the date and amount of the last interest payment.

- Proration of property taxes and condominium or homeowners association fees

- Any credits or other adjustments made between buyer and seller

FIGURE 9.4

Settlement Statement (HUD-1)

OMB Approval No. 2502-0265

A. Settlement Statement (HUD-1)

B. Type of Loan

1. ☐ FHA	2. ☐ RHS	3. ☐ Conv. Unins.	6. File Number:	7. Loan Number:	8. Mortgage Insurance Case Number:
4. ☐ VA	5. ☐ Conv. Ins.				

C. Note: This form is furnished to give you a statement of actual settlement costs. Amounts paid to and by the settlement agent are shown. Items marked "(p.o.c.)" were paid outside the closing; they are shown here for informational purposes and are not included in the totals.

D. Name & Address of Borrower:	E. Name & Address of Seller:	F. Name & Address of Lender:
G. Property Location:	H. Settlement Agent:	I. Settlement Date:
	Place of Settlement:	

J. Summary of Borrower's Transaction		K. Summary of Seller's Transaction	
100. Gross Amount Due from Borrower		**400. Gross Amount Due to Seller**	
101. Contract sales price		401. Contract sales price	
102. Personal property		402. Personal property	
103. Settlement charges to borrower (line 1400)		403.	
104.		404.	
105.		405.	
Adjustment for items paid by seller in advance		**Adjustment for items paid by seller in advance**	
106. City/town taxes to		406. City/town taxes to	
107. County taxes to		407. County taxes to	
108. Assessments to		408. Assessments to	
109.		409.	
110.		410.	
111.		411.	
112.		412.	
120. Gross Amount Due from Borrower		**420. Gross Amount Due to Seller**	
200. Amount Paid by or in Behalf of Borrower		**500. Reductions In Amount Due to seller**	
201. Deposit or earnest money		501. Excess deposit (see instructions)	
202. Principal amount of new loan(s)		502. Settlement charges to seller (line 1400)	
203. Existing loan(s) taken subject to		503. Existing loan(s) taken subject to	
204.		504. Payoff of first mortgage loan	
205.		505. Payoff of second mortgage loan	
206.		506.	
207.		507.	
208.		508.	
209.		509.	
Adjustments for items unpaid by seller		**Adjustments for items unpaid by seller**	
210. City/town taxes to		510. City/town taxes to	
211. County taxes to		511. County taxes to	
212. Assessments to		512. Assessments to	
213.		513.	
214.		514.	
215.		515.	
216.		516.	
217.		517.	
218.		518.	
219.		519.	
220. Total Paid by/for Borrower		**520. Total Reduction Amount Due Seller**	
300. Cash at Settlement from/to Borrower		**600. Cash at Settlement to/from Seller**	
301. Gross amount due from borrower (line 120)		601. Gross amount due to seller (line 420)	
302. Less amounts paid by/for borrower (line 220)	( )	602. Less reductions in amounts due seller (line 520)	( )
303. Cash ☐ From ☐ To Borrower		**603. Cash** ☐ To ☐ From Seller	

The Public Reporting Burden for this collection of information is estimated at 35 minutes per response for collecting, reviewing, and reporting the data. This agency may not collect this information, and you are not required to complete this form, unless it displays a currently valid OMB control number. No confidentiality is assured; this disclosure is mandatory. This is designed to provide the parties to a RESPA covered transaction with information during the settlement process.

FIGURE 9.4

Settlement Statement (HUD-1) (Continued)

L. Settlement Charges			Paid From Borrower's Funds at Settlement	Paid From Seller's Funds at Settlement
700. Total Real Estate Broker Fees				
Division of commission (line 700) as follows :				
701. $ to				
702. $ to				
703. Commission paid at settlement				
704.				
800. Items Payable in Connection with Loan				
801. Our origination charge	$	(from GFE #1)		
802. Your credit or charge (points) for the specific interest rate chosen	$	(from GFE #2)		
803. Your adjusted origination charges		(from GFE #A)		
804. Appraisal fee to		(from GFE #3)		
805. Credit report to		(from GFE #3)		
806. Tax service to		(from GFE #3)		
807. Flood certification to		(from GFE #3)		
808.				
809.				
810.				
811.				
900. Items Required by Lender to be Paid in Advance				
901. Daily interest charges from to @ $ /day		(from GFE #10)		
902. Mortgage insurance premium for months to		(from GFE #3)		
903. Homeowner's insurance for years to		(from GFE #11)		
904.				
1000. Reserves Deposited with Lender				
1001. Initial deposit for your escrow account		(from GFE #9)		
1002. Homeowner's insurance months @ $ per month $				
1003. Mortgage insurance months @ $ per month $				
1004. Property Taxes months @ $ per month $				
1005. months @ $ per month $				
1006. months @ $ per month $				
1007. Aggregate Adjustment -$				
1100. Title Charges				
1101. Title services and lender's title insurance		(from GFE #4)		
1102. Settlement or closing fee	$			
1103. Owner's title insurance		(from GFE #5)		
1104. Lender's title insurance	$			
1105. Lender's title policy limit $				
1106. Owner's title policy limit $				
1107. Agent's portion of the total title insurance premium to	$			
1108. Underwriter's portion of the total title insurance premium to	$			
1109.				
1110.				
1111.				
1200. Government Recording and Transfer Charges				
1201. Government recording charges		(from GFE #7)		
1202. Deed $ Mortgage $ Release $				
1203. Transfer taxes		(from GFE #8)		
1204. City/County tax/stamps Deed $ Mortgage $				
1205. State tax/stamps Deed $ Mortgage $				
1206.				
1300. Additional Settlement Charges				
1301. Required services that you can shop for		(from GFE #6)		
1302.	$			
1303.	$			
1304.				
1305.				
1400. Total Settlement Charges (enter on lines 103, Section J and 502, Section K)				

FIGURE 9.4

Settlement Statement (HUD-1) (Continued)

Comparison of Good Faith Estimate (GFE) and HUD-1 Chargges			Good Faith Estimate	HUD-1
Charges That Cannot Increase	HUD-1 Line Number			
Our origination charge	# 801			
Your credit or charge (points) for the specific interest rate chosen	# 802			
Your adjusted origination charges	# 803			
Transfer taxes	# 1203			

Charges That In Total Cannot Increase More Than 10%		Good Faith Estimate	HUD-1
Government recording charges	# 1201		
	#		
	#		
	#		
	#		
	#		
	#		
	#		
Total			
Increase between GFE and HUD-1 Charges		$ or %	

Charges That Can Change		Good Faith Estimate	HUD-1
Initial deposit for your escrow account	# 1001		
Daily interest charges $ /day	# 901		
Homeowner's insurance	# 903		
	#		
	#		
	#		

Loan Terms

Your initial loan amount is	$
Your loan term is	years
Your initial interest rate is	%
Your initial monthly amount owed for principal, interest, and any mortgage insurance is	$ includes ☐ Principal ☐ Interest ☐ Mortgage Insurance
Can your interest rate rise?	☐ No ☐ Yes, it can rise to a maximum of %. The first change will be on and can change again every after . Every change date, your interest rate can increase or decrease by %. Over the life of the loan, your interest rate is guaranteed to never be **lower** than % or **higher** than %.
Even if you make payments on time, can your loan balance rise?	☐ No ☐ Yes, it can rise to a maximum of $
Even if you make payments on time, can your monthly amount owed for principal, interest, and mortgage insurance rise?	☐ No ☐ Yes, the first increase can be on and the monthly amount owed can rise to $. The maximum it can ever rise to is $
Does your loan have a prepayment penalty?	☐ No ☐ Yes, your maximum prepayment penalty is $
Does your loan have a balloon payment?	☐ No ☐ Yes, you have a balloon payment of $ due in years on .
Total monthly amount owed including escrow account payments	☐ You do not have a monthly escrow payment for items, such as property taxes and homeowner's insurance. You must pay these items directly yourself. ☐ You have an additional monthly escrow payment of $ that results in a total initial monthly amount owed of $. This includes principal, interest, any mortagage insurance and any items checked below: ☐ Property taxes ☐ Homeowner's insurance ☐ Flood insurance ☐ ☐ ☐

Note: If you have any questions about the Settlement Charges and Loan Terms listed on this form, please contact your lender.

The closing agent examines the title commitment or the abstract that was issued several days or weeks before the closing. Because liens may have been filed during the interval, two searches of the public record are often made. The first search shows the status of the seller's title on that date. The second search, called a **bring down**, is made after the closing and before any new documents are filed.

Buyer The buyer has many tasks to complete in the last few days before closing:

- Arrangements must be made for transferring utilities to the buyer's name. If the buyer is new to an area, a deposit may be required from the utility company.
- A change of address needs to be filed, along with transfer of cable or television systems.
- The buyer conducts a **walk-through**, or final inspection, to verify that all necessary repairs have been made, that the property has been well maintained, and that all systems and fixtures are in substantially the same condition that they were in at the time the contract was finalized. The walk-through should be done shortly before closing. Any problems uncovered will be handled at the settlement table.
- The Good Faith Estimate and HUD-1 should be reviewed if possible (they are not always available prior to closing).
- Obtain a cashier's check or certified funds to bring to closing. (Note that banks may not be open after 4:00 pm or on the weekend.)

Seller The seller also has many arrangements to make:

- Pack and confirm moving day and time.
- Remove any items that are not to convey.
- Put in a change of address and stop newspapers.
- Collect instruction booklets and/or warranties on appliances to give purchaser.
- Collect all keys to the property to be turned over to the buyer.
- Verify that all conditions required by inspection or other contingencies have been met.
- Arrange for a thorough cleaning of the property before the walk-through.
- Review the HUD-1, if available.

In some states, the sellers may be required to execute an **affidavit of title**. This affidavit is a sworn statement in which the sellers assure the title insurance company (and the buyer) that no other defects in the title have occurred since the date of the title examination (e.g., judgments, bankruptcies, divorces, unrecorded deeds or contracts, unpaid repairs or improvements that might lead to mechanics' liens). The affidavit gives the title insurance company a basis on which to sue the sellers should their statements in the affidavit be incorrect.

In areas where real estate sales transactions are customarily closed through an escrow, the escrow instructions usually provide for an extended coverage policy to be issued to the buyer effective the date of closing. The seller has no need to execute an affidavit of title.

IN PRACTICE Licensees often assist in preclosing arrangements as part of their service to clients. In some states, licensees are required to advise the parties of the approximate expenses involved in closing when a real estate sales contract is signed. In other states, licensees have a statutory duty to coordinate and supervise closing activities. Aside from state laws on this issue, a licensee without a specific role in the closing may still be the person with the most knowledge about the transaction. Because of this, many licensees feel it is part of their fiduciary duty to be present at a face-to-face closing.

■ SAMPLE CHECKLIST

A sample checklist of the process from offer and acceptance to the actual closing is shown in Figure 9.5. Some steps may occur simultaneously and depend on the geographic location of the property and local custom; some steps may occur in a different order than that given. Generally, the checklist provides an easy reminder of each of the steps involved. Actual dates for actions initiated or completed can be filled in for each step. Attention must be paid to specified time frames set for any action to take place. If the action is not completed within the given time frame, the contract may be voidable.

FIGURE 9.5

Contract to Closing Checklist

_____ 1. Offer to purchase including any contingencies, amendments, and/or addenda signed and initialed where necessary by both buyers and sellers. Offer becomes a sales contract.

_____ 2. Earnest money deposited by broker according to state law.

_____ 3. Copy of contract sent to closing agent to initiate title work.

_____ 4. Buyer makes formal application for financing as described in sales contract. (Buyer may have presented a preapproval letter along with original offer to purchase.)

_____ 5. Lender provides borrower with Good Faith Estimate (GFE) and truth-in-lending (TIL) statement within three days of application.

_____ 6. Lender orders credit report and appraisal.

_____ 7. Buyer orders any property inspections as required by contingency to contract.

_____ 8. Either buyer or seller orders termite (or wood-boring insects) report.

_____ 9. Copy of inspection report, along with list of requested corrections, provided to seller.

_____ 10. Final loan approval letter received from lender.

_____ 11. Seller makes arrangements for any repairs required as a result of inspection reports, or any repairs required by the lender.

_____ 12. Closing agent orders title search and survey, if required.

_____ 13. Any defects in the title are brought to the attention of the seller for resolution.

_____ 14. Closing agent obtains title insurance policies for lender and new owner.

_____ 15. Buyer arranges for homeowners insurance with copy sent to closing agent.

_____ 16. Definite closing date, time, and place are set with notice to buyer and seller.

_____ 17. Lender prepares mortgage documents and sends to closing agent.

_____ 18. Closing agent obtains payoff figures for any existing mortgages.

_____ 19. Closing agent prepares deed and Settlement Statement (HUD-1).

_____ 20. Buyer confirms closing figures on HUD-1 with closing agent.

_____ 21. Buyer arranges for utilities hook-up, confirms with movers and post office.

_____ 22. Buyer makes walk-through inspection of premises.

_____ 23. Buyer arranges for cashier's check or certified funds to bring to closing.

_____ 24. Closing takes place (seller is reminded to bring keys and garage door openers).

_____ 25. Deficiencies determined by the walk-through inspection to be resolved at the settlement table or closing rescheduled for a later date.

_____ 26. Closing agent records deed and loan documents.

_____ 27. Closing agent makes pay-off on existing loans.

_____ 28. Closing agent distributes funds to seller and brokers.

■ CONDUCTING THE CLOSING

Closing is called by many names. For example, in some areas, closing is called settlement, or settlement and transfer. In some parts of the country, the parties in the transaction sit around a table and exchange copies of documents, a process called passing papers ("We passed papers on the new house Wednesday morning"). In other regions, the buyer and the seller never meet; the paperwork is handled by an escrow agent in a process called closing escrow ("We'll close escrow on our house next week"). The main concerns are that the buyer receives marketable title and that the seller receives the purchase price.

The western states that were influenced primarily by Spanish law generally close "in escrow." In the middle and eastern parts of the country, closing (or settlement) is done by either an attorney or a title company escrow agent.

Face-to-Face Closing

In a face-to-face closing, the parties meet face to face.

Face-to-face closings may be held at the office of the title company, the lending institution, an attorney for one of the parties, the broker, the county recorder, or the escrow company. Those attending a closing may include

- the buyer;
- the seller;
- the real estate salespeople or brokers (both the buyer's and the seller's agents);
- the seller's and the buyer's attorneys;
- representatives of the lending institutions involved with the buyer's new mortgage loan, the buyer's assumption of the seller's existing loan, or the seller's payoff of an existing loan; and
- a representative of the title insurance company.

Occasionally, the sales transaction has gone poorly and the buyers and sellers are feeling very adversarial toward each other. In such a case, the two parties might be seated in separate rooms in the settlement agent's office and papers passed back and forth through an intermediary.

Closing Agent or Closing Officer   A closing agent may be a representative of the title company, the lender, the real estate broker, or the buyer's or seller's attorney. Some title companies and law firms employ paralegal assistants who conduct closings for their firms. In most cases, the role of the closing agent is to represent the terms of the contract—not the personal interests of either the buyer or the seller.

The Exchange   The **exchange** is made when the parties are satisfied that everything is in order. The seller delivers the signed deed to the buyer, who accepts it. All pertinent documents are then recorded in the correct order to ensure continuity of title. For example, if the seller pays off an existing loan and the buyer obtains a new loan, the seller's satisfaction of mortgage must be recorded before the seller's deed to the buyer. Because the buyer cannot pledge the property as security for the new loan until ownership has been transferred, the buyer's new mortgage or deed of trust is recorded after the deed. Generally, there is no distribution of funds until the documents have been recorded. In most cases, this means that the sellers do not actually receive the proceeds from the sale for a day or two; likewise, any real estate commissions due to the brokers are not paid immediately.

Closing in Escrow

In an escrow closing, a
third party coordinates the
closing activities on behalf
of the buyer and the seller.

In an **escrow closing**, a disinterested third party is authorized to act as escrow agent (escrow holder) and to coordinate the closing activities. The escrow agent may be an attorney, a title company, a trust company, an escrow company, or the escrow department of a lending institution.

Escrow Procedure   After the sales contract is signed, the buyer and the seller execute escrow instructions to the escrow agent. The selection of the escrow agent is determined by negotiation, custom, or state law. The broker turns over the earnest money to the escrow agent, who deposits it in a special trust, or escrow, account.

The buyer and the seller deposit all pertinent documents and other items with the escrow agent before the specified date of closing.

The seller usually deposits

- the deed conveying the property to the buyer,
- title evidence (abstract and attorney's opinion of title, certificate of title, title insurance, or Torrens certificate),
- existing hazard or homeowner insurance policies,
- a letter or mortgage reduction certificate from the lender stating the exact principal remaining (if the buyer is assuming the seller's loan),
- affidavits of title (if required),
- a payoff statement (if the seller's loan is to be paid off), and
- other instruments or documents necessary to clear the title or to complete the transaction.

The buyer deposits

- the balance of the cash needed to complete the purchase, usually in the form of a certified check;
- loan documents (if the buyer secures a new loan);
- proof of hazard or homeowners insurance, including (where required) flood insurance; and
- other necessary documents, such as inspection reports required by the lender.

The escrow agent has the authority to examine the title evidence. When marketable title is shown in the name of the buyer and all other conditions of the escrow agreement have been met, the agent is authorized to disburse the purchase price to the seller, minus all charges and expenses. The agent then records the deed and mortgage or deed of trust if a new loan has been obtained by the purchaser.

If the escrow agent's examination of the title discloses liens, a portion of the purchase price can be withheld from the seller. The withheld portion is used to pay the liens to clear the title.

If the seller cannot clear the title, or if for any reason the sale cannot be consummated, the escrow instructions usually provide that the parties be returned to their former status, as if no sale occurred. The escrow agent reconveys title to the seller and returns the purchase money to the buyer.

Internal Revenue Service (IRS) Reporting Requirements

Due to the Taxpayer Relief Act of 1997, it may not be necessary to file a Form 1099-S with the IRS if the capital gain is less than $250,000 for an individual or $500,000 for a couple. Any gain from the sale of a home may be excluded if the seller meets the **ownership and use tests** described in IRS Publication 523, *Selling Your Home*:

> To claim the exclusion, you must meet the ownership and use tests. This means that during the 5-year period ending on the date of the sale, you must have:
> ■ Owned the home for at least 2 years (the ownership test), and
> ■ Lived in the home as your main home for at least 2 years (the use test).

Certain real estate closings must be reported to the IRS on Form 1099-S. The affected properties include sales or exchanges of

■ land (improved or unimproved), including air space;
■ an inherently permanent structure, including any residential, commercial, or industrial building;
■ shares in a cooperative housing corporation.

Information to be reported includes the sales price, the amount of property tax reimbursement credited to the seller, and the seller's Social Security number. If the closing agent does not notify the IRS, the responsibility for filing the form falls on the mortgage lender, although the brokers or the parties to the transaction ultimately could be held liable.

Broker's Role at Closing

Depending on local practice, the licensee's role at closing can vary from simply collecting the commission to conducting the proceedings. In the states that require an attorney's participation, a licensee's responsibility is essentially finished as soon as the real estate contract is signed. Even so, most licensees continue to be involved all the way through closing because it is also in their best interest that the transactions move successfully and smoothly to a conclusion. On behalf of their clients, licensees take care of all details so that the closing can proceed smoothly. This may mean actively arranging for title evidence, surveys, appraisals, and inspections or repairs related to structural conditions, water supplies, sewerage facilities, or toxic substances.

Licensees should avoid recommending a single source for any inspection or testing services. If a buyer suffers any injury as a result of a provider's negligence, the licensee might also be named in any lawsuit. The better practice is to give clients the names of several professionals who offer high-quality services. In addition, licensees who receive any compensation or reward from a source they recommend to a client must disclose such an arrangement to the client. Licensees must never receive compensation from an attorney or a lender.

IN PRACTICE   Although real estate licensees do not often conduct closing proceedings, they usually attend. Often, the parties look to their agents for guidance, assistance, and information during what can be a stressful experience. Licensees must be thoroughly familiar with the process and the procedures involved in preparing a closing statement, which includes the expenses and prorations of costs to close the transaction.

Mortgage Disclosure Improvement Act

The Mortgage Disclosure Improvement Act (MDIA) has changed how buyers and sellers, lenders, mortgage brokers, title agents, and real estate licensees prepare for a closing. The timeliness of certain disclosures now affects the date of closings. Lenders and licensees should keep in mind the numbers 3, 7, and 3:

- 3 business days from application to provide the truth-in-lending statement (TIL) and Good Faith Estimate (GFE)
- 7 business days before the signing of loan documents, after the borrower receives the final truth-in-lending statement and good-faith estimate
- 3 business days to wait for closing if the APR has changed more than 0.125% from the original or most recent TIL and GFE

The intent of this law is to prevent consumers from receiving an enticing low rate at the initial application and then learning at settlement that the lender is charging more in fees. Licensees should encourage their buyers to discuss all loan options with their lenders before signing a contract so that lenders can provide the disclosures in a timely fashion. Borrowers should lock in interest rates with a date that is about 10 days from an anticipated settlement. Any change to the interest rate, loan amount, loan product, or lender's or escrow fees can affect the APR, which may then require a redisclosure. Redisclosures can potentially delay settlement.

Before closing, everyone involved in the real estate transaction should check and double-check that the GFE and TIL forms are consistent with the original application. No one—buyers, sellers, or real estate agents—should schedule closings that do not account for the seven-day waiting period.

■ REAL ESTATE SETTLEMENT PROCEDURES ACT (RESPA)

The **Real Estate Settlement Procedures Act (RESPA)** is a federal consumer law that requires certain disclosures about the mortgage and settlement process and prohibits certain practices, such as kickbacks and referral fees, that can increase settlement costs for homebuyers.

RESPA regulations apply to first-lien residential mortgage loans made to finance the purchases of one- to four-family homes, cooperatives, and condominiums, for either investment or occupancy, as well as second or subordinate liens for home equity loans when a purchase is financed by a federally related mortgage loan. Federally related loans can be loans made by banks, savings and loan associations, or other lenders whose deposits are insured by federal agencies; loans insured by the Federal Housing Administration (FHA) and guaranteed by the Department of Veterans Affairs (VA); loans administered by HUD; and loans intended to be sold by the lenders to Fannie Mae, Ginnie Mae, or Freddie Mac. RESPA, formerly administered by HUD, is now administered by the Consumer Financial Protection Bureau (CFPB).

RESPA does not apply to the following settlements:

- Loans on large properties (more than 25 acres)
- Loans for business or agricultural purposes
- Construction loans or other temporary financing
- Vacant land (unless a dwelling will be placed on the lot within two years)

- A transaction financed solely by a purchase-money mortgage taken back by the seller
- An installment contract (contract for deed)
- A buyer's assumption of a seller's existing loan (if the terms of the assumed loan are modified, or if the lender charges more than $50 for the assumption, the transaction is subject to RESPA regulations)

RESPA prohibits certain practices that increase the cost of settlement services:

- Section 8 prohibits kickbacks and fee-splitting for referrals of settlement services, and unearned fees for services not actually performed. Violations are subject to criminal and civil penalties, including fines up to $10,000 and/or imprisonment up to one year. Consumers may privately pursue a violator in court; the violator may be liable for an amount up to three times the amount of the charge paid for the service.
- Section 9 prohibits sellers from requiring that homebuyers buy title insurance from a particular company. Buyers may sue the seller for such a violation; violators are liable for up to three times the amount of all charges paid for the title insurance.
- Section 10 prohibits lenders from requiring excessive escrow account deposits, money set aside to pay taxes, hazard insurance, and other charges related to the property.

To make it easier for borrowers to understand costs, lenders are required to provide a standard Good Faith Estimate (GFE) that clearly discloses key loan terms and closing costs. More important, most of these disclosed costs cannot vary greatly between the time that the GFE is issued and closing.

IN PRACTICE   Although RESPA's requirements are aimed primarily at lenders, real estate licensees fall under RESPA when they refer buyers to particular lenders, title companies, attorneys, or other providers of settlement services. Licensees who offer computerized loan origination (CLO) are also subject to regulation. Remember: Buyers have the right to select their own providers of settlement services.

Disclosure Requirements

Lenders and settlement agents have the following disclosure obligations at the time of loan application and loan closing or within three business days of receiving the loan application. If the lender denies the loan within three days, then RESPA does not require that the lender provide the following documents:

- *Special information booklet.* This HUD booklet must be given at the time of application or provided within three days of loan application. It provides the borrower with general information about settlement (closing) costs and explains the various provisions of RESPA, including a line-by-line description of the HUD-1.

- *Good-faith estimate of settlement costs.* The three-page GFE must contain the exact language specified by HUD, making it easier for borrowers to compare loan conditions from one lender to another (see Figure 9.6).

F I G U R E 9.6

Good Faith Estimate (GFE)

OMB Approval No. 2502-0265

Good Faith Estimate (GFE)

Name of Originator		Borrower	
Originator Address		Property Address	
Originator Phone Number			
Originator Email		Date of GFE	

Purpose

This GFE gives you an estimate of your settlement charges and loan terms if you are approved for this loan. For more information, see HUD's *Special Information Booklet* on settlement charges, your *Truth-in-Lending Disclosures,* and other consumer information at www.hud.gov/respa. If you decide you would like to proceed with this loan, contact us.

Shopping for your loan

Only you can shop for the best loan for you. Compare this GFE with other loan offers, so you can find the best loan. Use the shopping chart on page 3 to compare all the offers you receive.

Important dates

1. The interest rate for this GFE is available through [   ]. After this time, the interest rate, some of your loan Origination Charges, and the monthly payment shown below can change until you lock your interest rate.

2. This estimate for all other settlement charges is available through [   ].

3. After you lock your interest rate, you must go to settlement within [ ] days (your rate lock period) to receive the locked interest rate.

4. You must lock the interest rate at least [ ] days before settlement.

Summary of your loan

Your initial loan amount is	$
Your loan term is	years
Your initial interest rate is	%
Your initial monthly amount owed for principal, interest, and any mortgage insurance is	$ per month
Can your interest rate rise?	☐ No ☐ Yes, it can rise to a maximum of %. The first change will be in .
Even if you make payments on time, can your loan balance rise?	☐ No ☐ Yes, it can rise to a maximum of $
Even if you make payments on time, can your monthly amount owed for principal, interest, and any mortgage insurance rise?	☐ No ☐ Yes, the first increase can be in and the monthly amount owed can rise to $. The maximum it can ever rise to is $.
Does your loan have a prepayment penalty?	☐ No ☐ Yes, your maximum prepayment penalty is $.
Does your loan have a balloon payment?	☐ No ☐ Yes, you have a balloon payment of $ due in years.

Escrow account information

Some lenders require an escrow account to hold funds for paying property taxes or other property-related charges in addition to your monthly amount owed of $ [   ].
Do we require you to have an escrow account for your loan?
☐ No, you do not have an escrow account. You must pay these charges directly when due.
☐ Yes, you have an escrow account. It may or may not cover all of these charges. Ask us.

Summary of your settlement charges

A	Your Adjusted Origination Charges *(See page 2.)*	$
B	Your Charges for All Other Settlement Services *(See page 2.)*	$
A + B	**Total Estimated Settlement Charges**	$

FIGURE 9.6

Good Faith Estimate (GFE) (Continued)

Understanding your estimated settlement charges

Some of these charges can change at settlement. See the top of page 3 for more information.

Your Adjusted Origination Charges

1. Our origination charge
This charge is for getting this loan for you.

2. Your credit or charge (points) for the specific interest rate chosen

☐ The credit or charge for the interest rate of [   ] % is included in "Our origination charge." (See item 1 above.)

☐ You receive a credit of $ [   ] for this interest rate of [   ] %. This credit **reduces** your settlement charges.

☐ You pay a charge of $ [   ] for this interest rate of [   ] %. This charge (points) **increases** your total settlement charges.

The tradeoff table on page 3 shows that you can change your total settlement charges by choosing a different interest rate for this loan.

A   Your Adjusted Origination Charges $

Your Charges for All Other Settlement Services

3. Required services that we select
These charges are for services we require to complete your settlement. We will choose the providers of these services.

Service	Charge

4. Title services and lender's title insurance
This charge includes the services of a title or settlement agent, for example, and title insurance to protect the lender, if required.

5. Owner's title insurance
You may purchase an owner's title insurance policy to protect your interest in the property.

6. Required services that you can shop for
These charges are for other services that are required to complete your settlement. We can identify providers of these services or you can shop for them yourself. Our estimates for providing these services are below.

Service	Charge

7. Government recording charges
These charges are for state and local fees to record your loan and title documents.

8. Transfer taxes
These charges are for state and local fees on mortgages and home sales.

9. Initial deposit for your escrow account
This charge is held in an escrow account to pay future recurring charges on your property and includes ☐ all property taxes, ☐ all insurance, and ☐ other [   ].

10. Daily interest charges
This charge is for the daily interest on your loan from the day of your settlement until the first day of the next month or the first day of your normal mortgage payment cycle. This amount is $ [   ] per day for [   ] days (if your settlement is [   ]).

11. Homeowner's insurance
This charge is for the insurance you must buy for the property to protect from a loss, such as fire.

Policy	Charge

B   Your Charges for All Other Settlement Services $

A + B   Total Estimated Settlement Charges $

 Good Faith Estimate (HUD-GFE) 2

FIGURE 9.6

Good Faith Estimate (GFE) (Continued)

Instructions

Understanding which charges can change at settlement

This GFE estimates your settlement charges. At your settlement, you will receive a HUD-1, a form that lists your actual costs. Compare the charges on the HUD-1 with the charges on this GFE. Charges can change if you select your own provider and do not use the companies we identify. (See below for details.)

These charges **cannot increase** at settlement:	The total of these charges **can increase up to 10%** at settlement:	These charges **can change** at settlement:
■ Our origination charge ■ Your credit or charge (points) for the specific interest rate chosen *(after you lock in your interest rate)* ■ Your adjusted origination charges *(after you lock in your interest rate)* ■ Transfer taxes	■ Required services that we select ■ Title services and lender's title insurance *(if we select them or you use companies we identify)* ■ Owner's title insurance *(if you use companies we identify)* ■ Required services that you can shop for *(if you use companies we identify)* ■ Government recording charges	■ Required services that you can shop for *(if you do not use companies we identify)* ■ Title services and lender's title insurance *(if you do not use companies we identify)* ■ Owner's title insurance *(if you do not use companies we identify)* ■ Initial deposit for your escrow account ■ Daily interest charges ■ Homeowner's insurance

Using the tradeoff table

In this GFE, we offered you this loan with a particular interest rate and estimated settlement charges. However:

■ If you want to choose this same loan with **lower settlement charges,** then you will have a **higher interest rate.**
■ If you want to choose this same loan with a **lower interest rate,** then you will have **higher settlement charges.**

If you would like to choose an available option, you must ask us for a new GFE.

Loan originators have the option to complete this table. Please ask for additional information if the table is not completed.

	The loan in this GFE	The same loan with lower settlement charges	The same loan with a lower interest rate
Your initial loan amount	$	$	$
Your initial interest rate[†]	%	%	%
Your initial monthly amount owed	$	$	$
Change in the monthly amount owed from this GFE	No change	You will pay $ **more** every month	You will pay $ **less** every month
Change in the amount you will pay at settlement with this interest rate	No change	Your settlement charges will be **reduced** by $	Your settlement charges will **increase** by $
How much your total estimated settlement charges will be	$	$	$

[†] *For an adjustable rate loan, the comparisons above are for the initial interest rate before adjustments are made.*

Using the shopping chart

Use this chart to compare GFEs from different loan originators. Fill in the information by using a different column for each GFE you receive. By comparing loan offers, you can shop for the best loan.

	This loan	Loan 2	Loan 3	Loan 4
Loan originator name				
Initial loan amount				
Loan term				
Initial interest rate				
Initial monthly amount owed				
Rate lock period				
Can interest rate rise?				
Can loan balance rise?				
Can monthly amount owed rise?				
Prepayment penalty?				
Balloon payment?				
Total Estimated Settlement Charges				

If your loan is sold in the future

Some lenders may sell your loan after settlement. Any fees lenders receive in the future cannot change the loan you receive or the charges you paid at settlement.

 Good Faith Estimate (HUD-GFE) 3

The only fees that the lender may collect before the applicant receives the GFE are for a credit report and appraisal. Once the GFE is issued, lenders are committed and may only modify the GFE in specific instances. If certain information or circumstances change after the original GFE is issued, then a new GFE must be issued. Issuing a new GFE triggers a new three-day waiting period; in this case, closing may not occur until after three days have passed.

The GFE indicates which closing costs may or may not change prior to settlement and, if they do, by how much. The fees are divided into three categories:

- *No tolerance or **zero tolerance***—fees that may not increase before closing: lender charges for taking, underwriting, and processing the loan application, including points, origination fees, and yield spread premiums
- *10% tolerance*—fees that cannot increase by more than 10% in any given category: settlement services for which the lender selects the provider or for which the borrower selects the provider from the lender's list; title services and title insurance, if the lender selects the provider; and recording fees
- *Unlimited tolerance*—fees for services that are out of the lender's control: services for which the borrower chooses the provider (such as escrow and title insurance), impounds for taxes, mortgage interest, and the cost of homeowners insurance

Mortgage Servicing Disclosure Statement This statement tells the borrower whether the lender intends to service the loan or to transfer it to another lender. It will also provide information about resolving complaints.

The last page of the GFE is a worksheet consumers can use to compare different loans and terms to aid in price shopping. The lender is responsible for the accuracy of the GFE and the actual costs that the lender charges on the HUD-1.

Settlement Statement (HUD-1) RESPA requires that the **Settlement Statement (HUD-1)** itemize all charges that are normally paid by a borrower and a seller in connection with settlement, whether required by the lender or another party, or paid by the lender or any other person (see Figure 9.4). Charges required by the lender that are paid before closing are indicated as paid outside of closing (POC). The third page of the HUD-1 form provides for a comparison of the original GFE estimates to the actual charges appearing on the HUD-1. Lenders are permitted to "correct" any violation of the tolerances by reimbursing the borrower within 30 days of settlement.

RESPA prohibits lenders from requiring borrowers to deposit amounts in escrow accounts for taxes and insurance that exceed certain limits, thus preventing the lenders from taking advantage of the borrowers. While RESPA does not require that escrow accounts be set up, certain government loan programs and some lenders require escrow accounts as a condition of the loan. RESPA places limits on the amounts that a lender may require: on a monthly basis, the lender may require only one-twelfth of the total of the disbursements for the year, plus an amount necessary to cover a shortage in the account. No more than one-sixth of the year's total disbursements may be held as a cushion (a cushion is not required). Once a year, the lender must perform an escrow account analysis and return any amount over $50 to the borrower. By law, borrowers have the right to inspect a completed HUD-1 form, to the extent that the figures are available, one business day before the closing (sellers are not entitled to this privilege). Lenders must retain these statements for two years after the closing date. In addition, state laws generally require that licensees retain all records of a transaction for a specific period.

RESPA's Consumer Protections

1. CLO regulation
2. CBA disclosure
3. Settlement cost booklet
4. Good-faith estimate of settlement costs
5. Uniform Settlement Statement
6. Prohibition of kickbacks and unearned fees

Kickbacks and Referral Fees   RESPA prohibits the payment of **kickbacks**, or unearned fees, in any real estate settlement service. It prohibits referral fees when no services are actually rendered. The payment or receipt of a fee, a kickback, or anything of value for referrals for settlement services includes activities such as mortgage loans, title searches, title insurance, attorney services, surveys, credit reports, and appraisals.

Controlled Business Arrangements

To streamline the settlement process, a real estate firm, title insurance company, mortgage broker, home inspection company, or even a moving company may agree to offer a package of services to consumers, a system called a **controlled business arrangement (CBA)**. RESPA permits a CBA as long as a consumer is clearly informed of the relationship among the service providers, that participation is not required, that other providers are available, and that the only thing of value received by one business entity from others, in addition to permitted payments for services provided, is a return on ownership interest or franchise relationship.

Fees must be reasonably related to the value of the services provided and not be fees exchanged among the affiliated companies simply for referring business to one another. This referral-fee prohibition may be a particularly important issue for licensees who offer **computerized loan origination (CLO)** services to their clients and customers.

■ PRORATIONS

Most closings involve the division of financial responsibility between the buyer and the seller for such items as loan interest, taxes, rents, fuel, and condominium or homeowners association fees. These allowances are called **prorations**. Prorations are necessary to ensure that expenses are divided fairly between the seller and the buyer. For example, the seller may owe current taxes that have not yet been billed; the buyer would want a credit from the seller at the closing. When taxes must be paid in advance, the seller is entitled to a rebate at the closing. If the buyer assumes the seller's existing mortgage or deed of trust, the seller usually owes the buyer an allowance for accrued interest through the date of closing.

The Arithmetic of Prorating

Accurate prorating involves the following four considerations:

■ Nature of the item being prorated
■ Whether the item is accrued and requires the determination of an earned amount
■ Whether the item is prepaid and requires the determination of an unearned amount (i.e., a refund to the seller)
■ What arithmetic processes must be used

The computation of a proration involves identifying a yearly charge for the item to be prorated, then dividing by 12 to determine a monthly charge for the item. Also, it is usually necessary to identify a daily charge for the item by dividing the monthly charge by the number of days in the month. These smaller portions are then multiplied by the number of months or days in the prorated period to determine the accrued or unearned amount that will be figured in the settlement.

The rules or customs governing the computation of prorations for the closing of a real estate sale vary widely from state to state. The following are some general guidelines for preparing the closing statement:

- In most states (including Texas), the seller owns the property on the day of closing, and prorations or apportionments are usually are made up to and including the day of closing. A few states specify that the buyer owns the property on the closing date. In that case, adjustments are made as of the day preceding the day on which title is closed.

- Mortgage interest, general real estate taxes, water taxes, insurance premiums, and similar expenses are usually computed by using 360 days in a year and 30 days in a month. However, the rules in some areas provide for computing prorations on the basis of the actual number of days in the calendar month of closing. The agreement of sale should specify which method will be used.

- Accrued or prepaid general real estate taxes are usually prorated at the closing. When the amount of the current real estate tax cannot be determined definitely, the proration is usually based on the last obtainable tax bill.

- Special assessments for municipal improvements such as sewers, water mains, or streets are usually paid in annual installments over several years, with annual interest charged on the outstanding balance of future payments. The seller normally makes the current payments, and the buyer assumes all future payments. The special assessment installment generally is not prorated at the closing. A buyer may insist that the seller allow the buyer a credit for the seller's share of the interest to the closing date. The agreement of sale may address the manner in which special assessments will be handled at closing.

- Rents are usually adjusted on the basis of the actual number of days in the month of closing. The seller customarily receives the rents for the day of closing and pays all expenses for that day. If any rents for the current month are uncollected when the sale is closed, the buyer often agrees by a separate letter to collect the rents, if possible, and remit the prorated rata share to the seller.

- Security deposits made by tenants to cover the last month's rent of the lease or to cover the cost of repairing damage caused by the tenant are generally transferred by the seller to the buyer.

Real Estate Taxes   Proration of real estate taxes varies widely depending on how the taxes are paid in the area where the real estate is located. In some states, real estate taxes are paid in advance—that is, if the tax year runs from January 1 to December 31, taxes for the coming year are due on January 1. In this case, the seller, who has prepaid a year's taxes, should be reimbursed for the portion of the year remaining after the buyer takes ownership of the property. In other areas, taxes are paid in arrears, on December 31 for the year just ended. In this case, the buyer should be credited by the seller for the time the seller occupied the property.

Sometimes, taxes are due during the tax year, partly in arrears and partly in advance; sometimes they are payable in installments. Tax payments can even be more complicated if city, state, school, and other property taxes start their tax years in different months.

Mortgage Loan Interest   On almost every mortgage loan, the interest is paid in arrears. The buyer and the seller must understand that a mortgage payment due on June 1, for example, includes interest due for May. Thus, the buyer who assumes a mortgage on May 31 and makes the June payment pays for the time the seller occupied the property and should be credited with a month's interest. On the other hand, the buyer who places a new mortgage loan on May 31 may be pleasantly surprised to learn that the first mortgage payment is not due for another month.

■ SUMMARY

The transaction process from contract to closing involves many steps. Major categories are as follows:

- Loan approval:
  — Application
  — Credit report and score
- Appraisal
- Inspection:
  — Report
  — Resolution
- Title work:
  — Chain of title
  — Abstract of title
  — Cloud on the title
- Preparation for closing:
  — Closing agent
  — Buyer
  — Seller

Closing (settlement and transfer) is the point at which ownership of a property is transferred in exchange for the selling price.

To complete the transaction, the buyer requires the following:

- Title evidence—a current abstract of title with opinion of title from the buyer's attorney or title commitment from the title insurance company
- Seller's deed
- Affidavit of title by the seller and documents showing the removal of prior encumbrances
- Mortgage reduction certificate from the lender, if the buyer is assuming the loan
- Survey and the results of required inspections
- Leases, if tenants reside on the premises
- Successful final property inspection (walk-through)
- Closing statement showing the amount and distribution of funds

To complete the transaction, the seller requires the following:

- Payoff statement from the seller's lender noting the amount owed
- Evidence that the buyer has the necessary funds
- Closing statement showing the distribution of funds

Depending on state law and local custom, closing may be conducted through a

- licensed escrow company, in which case the parties may execute documents separately and never meet, or
- a face-to-face meeting of the parties at the escrow company, title company, lender's office, or attorney's office.

An escrow holder (escrow agent) is a disinterested third party authorized to coordinate the closing activities.

The Internal Revenue Service (IRS) may require completion and submission of the Form 1099-S statement of income to the seller showing the seller's Social Security number. The seller may be exempt from paying capital gains tax under the Taxpayer Relief Act of 1997.

The Real Estate Settlement Procedures Act (RESPA) is a federal law enacted to protect consumers in the settlement process as follows:

- Requires accurate and timely information about the actual costs of a transaction
- Eliminates kickbacks and other referral fees
- Prohibits lenders from requiring excessive escrow account deposits

RESPA does not apply to a transaction financed solely by a purchase-money mortgage taken back by a seller, installment contracts (contract for deed), or a buyer's assumption of a seller's existing loan.

RESPA requires that lenders and settlement agents provide a

- special information booklet produced by HUD to every person from whom they receive or for whom they prepare a loan application (except for refinancing),
- good-faith estimate of settlement costs to the borrower no later than three business days after receiving a loan application, and
- Settlement Statement (HUD-1) to the borrower and the seller that itemizes all charges to be paid in connection with closing.

A closing (settlement) statement involves an accounting of the amounts paid by or received by the parties, as follows:

- Debit (give) is a charge that must be paid by the buyer or the seller at closing.
- Credit (receive) is the amount entered in favor of the buyer or the seller.
- In most instances, a debit to one party is a credit to the other party.
- Certain charges are prorated, divided between the buyer and the seller, in one of two ways:
  - Yearly charge is divided by a 360-day year (banking year), or 12 months of 30 days each.
  - Yearly charge is divided by a 365-day year (366 days in leap year) to determine the daily charge and the actual number of days in the proration period, and then the number of days is multiplied by the daily charge.
- In most states, the charges are prorated as of the date of closing, with the seller being responsible for the date of closing.

CHAPTER 9 REVIEW QUESTIONS

1. Which statement is *TRUE* of real estate closings in most states?
   a. Closings are generally conducted by real estate salespersons.
   b. The buyer usually receives the rents for the day of closing.
   c. The buyer must reimburse the seller for any title evidence provided by the seller.
   d. The seller usually pays the expenses for the day of closing.

2. All of the following are responsibilities of the closing agent *EXCEPT*
   a. ordering the title search and the survey.
   b. arranging for homeowners insurance.
   c. obtaining title insurance policy for the lender.
   d. preparing the deed and the HUD-1.

3. All encumbrances and liens shown on the report of title, other than those waived or agreed to by the purchaser and listed in the contract, must be removed so that the title can be delivered free and clear. The removal of such encumbrances is typically the duty of the
   a. buyer.
   b. seller.
   c. broker.
   d. title company.

4. The appraisal method most likely used on a specialty-use building, like a church, is the
   a. cost approach.
   b. income method based on the collections only.
   c. comparative method based on the sale of other churches in the city.
   d. church income and collection method.

5. The Uniform Residential Loan Application requires the borrower(s) to complete the form with all of the following information *EXCEPT*
   a. the value of a paid-for boat.
   b. funds for the down payment and closing costs.
   c. credit score.
   d. a legal description of the property being purchased.

6. According to the Taxpayer's Relief Act of 1997, which of the following is *TRUE* of a couple that is selling their home where they have lived for the last 11 years?
   a. They will only pay capital gains tax at the lowest rate.
   b. They will avoid capital gains tax if they purchase another home within six months.
   c. They may avoid capital gains tax if one or both of them is 62 years old.
   d. They may avoid capital gains tax up to $450,000.

7. A mortgage reduction certificate is executed by
   a. an abstract company.
   b. an attorney.
   c. a lending institution.
   d. a grantor.

8. Which charge noted on the Good Faith Estimate (GFE) must be the same or less than the charge noted on the HUD-1?
   a. Cost of settlement services when the lender selects the provider
   b. Lender charges for taking and underwriting the loan
   c. Cost of settlement services when the borrower selects the provider from the list provided by the lender
   d. Cost of homeowners insurance

9. All of the following are tasks to be done by the buyer in preparation for closing *EXCEPT*
   a. arrange for homeowners insurance.
   b. contact utilities to start service.
   c. schedule repairs needed as result of home inspection.
   d. obtain cashier's check for funds needed at closing.

10. The document that provides borrowers with general information about settlement costs, RESPA provisions, and the Settlement Statement is the
    a. HUD-1 form.
    b. special information booklet.
    c. good-faith estimate of settlement costs.
    d. closing statement.

CHAPTER 10

Common Contract Mistakes

■ **LEARNING OBJECTIVES** *When you have completed this chapter, you will be able to*

- ■ **describe** issues with the identification of the parties and the property in a sales contract;
- ■ **describe** issues in the sales contract regarding checkboxes, signatures, effective dates, and addenda;
- ■ **discuss** the proper and improper use of the Special Provisions paragraph of the sales contract;
- ■ **explain** what makes property real or personal and the need to address these issues in the sales contract; and
- ■ **describe** the terms *marketable title* and *cloud on the title*.

■ INTRODUCTION

Although TREC forms were created to prevent contract mistakes, fulfill regulatory requirements, protect the rights of buyers and sellers, and protect licensees from taking part in the unauthorized practice of law, the system is not infallible. Regardless of their education, experience, or hours of preparation, new and experienced licensees alike commonly make mistakes when filling out sales contracts, contingencies, amendments, and addenda. Anyone with several years of experience in real estate can probably add many more examples to the list. For the listing broker who will be receiving the original offers, this chapter can identify red flags to look for on behalf of the seller.

Verbal Offers

Some agents believe that it is not correct to present verbal offers. While the statute of frauds says that a contract must be in writing in order to be enforceable, a verbal offer isn't yet a contract. Remember that all offers are to be presented, whether verbal or written. A seller will accept a good offer, regardless of whether it is verbal or written.

■ CONTRACT EXAMPLES

Different sections of a TREC-promulgated contract—including the mistakes—are featured here, followed by recommendations for improvement.

Naming the Parties

1. **PARTIES:** The parties to this contract are __Mrs. Portner__
(Seller) and __Kristina Kay Wright and Benjamin Charles Wright__ (Buyer).
Seller agrees to sell and convey to Buyer and Buyer agrees to buy from Seller the Property defined below.

Mistake #1: The seller's legal name is not Mrs. Porter. Include the seller's full legal name. The name used here should reflect the name on the property's title (if the name was listed correctly when the seller took title to the property). In addition, because Texas is a community property state, the licensee will need to furnish marital status. To be accurate, the seller should be listed as "Carol Anne Porter, a single person."

Mistake #2: The buyers' marital status is also missing. The buyers should be listed as "Kristina Kay Wright and husband Benjamin Charles Wright."

Naming the Property

2. **PROPERTY:** The land, improvements and accessories are collectively referred to as the "Property".
A. LAND: Lot __128__ Block __17__ , __Section of Shady Hills__
Addition, City of __Lakeview__ , County of __Smith__ ,
Texas, known as __12690 Pinehall Court 76544__
(address/zip code), or as described on attached exhibit.

Mistake: Legal description is incomplete because the section number is not provided. Agents frequently fail to include the section number with the subdivision name. To be accurate, the subdivision should be listed as "Section 4 of Shady Hills." Remember, a street address is never a sufficient legal description.

Checkboxes within Paragraphs

☐(1) Within __5__ days after the effective date of this contract, Seller shall furnish to Buyer and Title Company Seller's existing survey of the Property and a Residential Real Property Affidavit promulgated by the Texas Department of Insurance (T-47 Affidavit). **If Seller fails to furnish the existing survey or affidavit within the time prescribed, Buyer shall obtain a new survey at Seller's expense no later than 3 days prior to Closing Date.** If the existing survey or affidavit is not acceptable to Title Company or Buyer's lender(s), Buyer shall obtain a new survey at ☐Seller's ☐Buyer's expense no later than 3 days prior to Closing Date.

Mistake: In the event that the existing survey provided by the seller within five days of the effective date of the contract is not acceptable to the title company or the buyer's lenders, it is unclear which party (buyer or seller) is responsible for paying for the new survey. The paragraphs of the TREC-promulgated contracts contain checkboxes that can easily be overlooked; however, overlooking these items can cause delays in the transactions and contention between the parties, not to mention make the licensee look incompetent.

Licensees should become familiar with all the checkbox options in the TREC-promulgated forms, including in the Possession paragraph, where the licensee needs to indicate whether possession will be granted "upon closing and funding" or "according to a temporary residential lease form." In addition, if possession does not happen "upon closing and funding," the licensee will need to use the appropriate TREC temporary lease and indicate that in paragraph 22 of the contract.

Special Provisions

11. SPECIAL PROVISIONS: (Insert only factual statements and business details applicable to the sale. TREC rules prohibit licensees from adding factual statements or business details for which a contract addendum, lease or other form has been promulgated by TREC for mandatory use.)

    A. This contract is subject to appraisal
    B. Seller is to stay in the house 48 hours after closing and funding
    C. Buyer has the right to terminate this contract if the property has termites

Mistake #1: Remove A, as licensees should not structure "subject to" or "contingent upon" provisions. This falls outside of "factual statements."

Mistake #2: Remove B, as TREC promulgates a form for this purpose.

Mistake #3: Remove C, as it is addressed in paragraph 23 of the contract.

When the parties need to add factual statements or business details to their agreement, they may use paragraph 11. When the parties want to define legal rights and remedies, they should seek competent legal advice. Licensees are prohibited from including legal rights or remedies in paragraph 11, but buyers and sellers and their attorneys are not. A factual statement states what someone will or will not do. A legal right or remedy states what will happen if someone does or does not do a particular act. An allowable statement under this paragraph might say, "Seller to leave swing set in backyard."

Default

The following is typical of the Default paragraph in most contracts. The only time this paragraph gets really looked at is when the contract is falling out and everyone wants to point the finger of guilt at everyone else. When either party is threatening to walk out on the contract, a careful reading of the default section may make them more inclined to try to work out the problem.

15. DEFAULT: If Buyer fails to comply with this contract, Buyer will be in default, and Seller may (a) enforce specific performance, seek such other relief as may be provided by law, or both, or (b) terminate this contract and receive the earnest money as liquidated damages, thereby releasing both parties from this contract. If Seller fails to comply with this contract, Seller will be in default and Buyer may (a) enforce specific performance, seek such other relief as may be provided by law, or both, or (b) terminate this contract and receive the earnest money, thereby releasing both parties from this contract.

Signatures and Effective Date

All sales contracts have space at the end for the signatures of all parties and a space for the effective date, to be filled out by the broker. All too often, effective dates are not entered or signatures or initials are missing on the sales contract or one or more of the addenda. Point to remember: a soon-to-be ex-spouse is still required to sign the sales contract to avoid any possible future title claims. This is why it is so important to get that signature on the listing agreement as soon as it is taken in order to avoid a confrontation at the time an offer is received.

The Electronic Signatures in Global and National Commerce Act (ESIGN) and the Uniform Electronic Transactions Act (UETA) provide that "signatures" made via electronic means are just as binding as hand-written ones. To use electronic signatures in a real estate transaction in Texas, both parties must agree to it in an electronic consent form.

Addenda

Any addenda that are to be a part of the contract must be identified in paragraph 22 of the TREC-promulgated contracts (see Chapter 6). Do not indicate in paragraph 22 that an addendum is being used and then not attach one, and do not attach an addendum without indicating in paragraph 22 that one is being used.

Using the TREC-Promulgated Contract Form for a 1031 Exchange

It is sometimes tempting to use a One to Four Family Residential Contract to purchase the up-leg property when someone is intending to perform a 1031 exchange. While 1031 exchanges are increasing in popularity now that the capital gains taxes have increased, care must still be given to the form of the exchange. One of the key words in the IRS Code is intent to exchange, which presupposes that it is manifested in the original paperwork. If the One to Four Family Residential Contract must be used due to time or other considerations, then paragraph 11 (Special Provisions) will be used to accomplish the objective. The seller or a lawyer must prepare language similar to the following:

> *The labeled buyer in this contract wishes to effect an IRS Section 1031 exchange and, therefore, this contract is not to be considered a contract to purchase, but rather a binder on terms and conditions that the exchanger (buyer) will agree to in a subsequent exchange agreement. The exchanger warrants to the seller that there will be no additional expense or delay as a result of the exchange.*

The two parts should be very clear in their purpose.

1. The buyer now has the intent developed initially, and this will be consistent throughout the transaction.
2. The seller understands that there will be no additional expense or delay.

Note that many residential agents and some sellers may hesitate at being involved in something they have never done before. The procuring agent should take great care to provide context to the contract with the listing agent prior to submission of the offer.

Some real estate practitioners will want to follow strict deeding practices, while others will consider "pool" deeding acceptable. If formal procedures are to be followed, the seller should be informed that they will, in fact, come into title to accomplish the exchange. Now is the time for the seller's agent to recommend that the seller get an attorney.

■ COMMON AREAS OF CONCERN

Real or Personal

There is probably more frustration, argument, and litigation over the matter of real versus personal property and whether or not something conveys with the property than over any other area of selling real estate. For the peace of mind of everyone involved, the listing agent needs to take special care in listing items that do convey and those that do not convey. On the other hand, the selling agent should carefully list all items that the purchaser wants to have included in the sale, regardless of whether it is real property or not. Technically, the dining room chandelier is a fixture—but when it was great-grandma's passed down through generations, it becomes very personal.

Usually the problem does not become evident until the final walk-through shortly before the closing. Get a group of listing agents together, and they can go on for hours with stories about missing items they have replaced (often at their own cost) in order to keep the settlement on track. Here are some examples:

- *In the yard.* The six prize rose bushes the seller couldn't bear to part with, the budding magnolia tree planted two years ago in memory of the owner's mother, and freshly planted tomato plants in the garden are all real property.
- *In the kitchen.* The listing showed that a refrigerator conveyed. When the purchaser first visited the house, a large side-by-side refrigerator/freezer was solidly in place. However, at walk-through, the big fancy appliance was gone and had been replaced with a small, 15-year-old refrigerator that had been in the garage. The listing only said "refrigerator" and refrigerators are technically personal property (can be moved) so, after that experience, the buyer agent started listing serial numbers for all appliances expected to be left in the house.
- *In the dining room.* Corner cupboards in the dining room looked to be permanent attachments, but when the buyers returned to their new home after settlement, the cupboards were gone. Neither the listing nor the contract addressed the cupboards in any way. Buyers assumed they were part of the real property; sellers assumed they were movable personal property. Agents are shopping for replacements.

Title Questions

Most contracts clearly state that the seller is responsible for providing marketable title to the property. As mentioned before, the term *marketable* means a title that has no defects that could carry over as a problem for the new owners at whatever time they decide to sell.

Sometimes the cloud on the title is minor: a misspelling of a grantor's name, an incorrect date, or a slight error in the legal description. In more serious cases, such as a missing name of the grantor or a gap in the chain of title, it may be necessary to file a suit for quiet title. This is not necessarily a huge problem, but court action always takes time. Occasionally, the cloud is more like a thunderstorm, as was the case described below.

■ **FOR EXAMPLE** Buyers and sellers had finalized a sales contract, and the transaction was in process. A routine title search discovered that the county had an easement across one side of the property to provide access to the sewer line. Normally, this would not be an issue, but unfortunately, that easement went right under one side of the in-ground swimming pool. Despite the fact that county engineers said that they would never have any need to make use of the easement—that, in fact, they had a totally different way of handling sewer backup problems without digging up the area—the county legal department was not willing to sign off on it. The title company was actually willing to "insure over" the defect, but that might have left the buyers with a potential problem in the future.

The buyers produced an estimate from a landscaping company for what it would cost to dig out the pool and replace all the landscaping: close to $50,000. They asked the sellers to reduce the sales price of the house by that much. At first, the sellers were ready to let the contract go into default, but eventually they came to an agreement with the buyers to reduce the sales price by $25,000 and the sale did go to settlement.

Ironically, when the sellers purchased the property from the original owners, the problem of the easement never came up, although it certainly would have been in place at that time. Was the survey faulty? Or not done? Did the original title company neglect to check for easements? Should title insurance have covered this issue? If the sellers refused to cooperate with the buyers request for a reduction in price, could the buyers have sued them for specific performance? Could the buyers be forced to accept title insurance that had insured over the defect? There are many questions and no easy answers.

Possession

Paragraph 10 of the One to Four Family Residential Contract can be challenging when possession is upon closing and funding. Occasionally, closing does not occur in a timely manner, and sometimes the closing doesn't occur at all. Examples of potential closing delays which have occurred one day prior to closing include the following:

- Late appraisal that did not make contract price
- Specified repairs were not made, and the final walk-through was a disappointment
- Buyer became unemployed
- Underwriter rejected the loan at the last minute

A delayed or cancelled closing can affect buyers, sellers, movers, and agents. If timing is critical to one of the parties, then the risk must be balanced, which means the downside for one party is balanced with risk (financial loss) on the other side.

■ SUMMARY

Even when preprinted forms are used for sales contracts, there are many opportunities for mistakes to be made. Some of the most common are

- not using complete legal names of the parties,
- not providing an adequate legal description,
- not checking all applicable boxes in the contract,
- inserting factual statements in the Special Provisions paragraph, and
- including addenda without indicating that in paragraph 22, or indicating the use of addenda in paragraph 22 without including the addenda.

Default remedies need to be explained to both buyer and seller.

Signatures, initials, and an effective date are required on the contract, and signatures and initials are required on all addenda and amendments.

Other common areas of concern are

- handling real and personal property, and
- problems with clear title.

CHAPTER 10 REVIEW QUESTIONS

1. Which is the *BEST* way to list the seller's name on the contract?
    a. Will Jones
    b. Billy Jones
    c. William J. Jones
    d. W. J. Jones

2. A husband and wife are selling their home. They are separated, and she actually lives in another town. It is still important to have her signature on
    a. the listing agreement.
    b. the sales contract.
    c. both the listing agreement and the sales contract.
    d. neither the listing agreement nor the sales contract.

3. All of the following are acceptable for a legal description of the property *EXCEPT*
    a. an exhibit attached to the contract.
    b. 4092 Terrace Ct., Dallas, TX 75211.
    c. Lot 140 Block 3, Section 2 of Wedgewood Terrace Addition, City of Lakeview, County of Smith, Texas, known as 12690 Pinehall Court 76544.
    d. Lot 64 Block 83, Section 2 of Friendly Hills Addition, City of Austin, County of Travis, Texas, known as 2365 Veterans Boulevard 78711.

4. Any addenda to be attached to the contract
    a. should be listed in the Special Provisions paragraph.
    b. do not need to be signed if the contract has already been fully executed.
    c. should be signed electronically.
    d. should be signed by the parties and listed in paragraph 22 of the contract.

5. All of the following are real property *EXCEPT*
    a. chandelier.
    b. built-in dishwasher.
    c. storm door.
    d. free-standing workbench.

6. All of the following are personal property *EXCEPT*
    a. oriental rug in dining room.
    b. wall-to-wall carpet in bedroom.
    c. refrigerator in the kitchen.
    d. bookcase in the living room.

7. A careful review of the default section of a sales contract can
    a. support a buyer in deciding to walk away from the contract.
    b. encourage a seller to refuse to remedy a defect in the title.
    c. help either buyer or seller understand the financial impact of default.
    d. help place the blame on the other party.

8. What does it mean when a property has marketable title?
    a. The property is worth more than $250,000.
    b. The property has been properly insured during the seller's ownership of the property.
    c. The property title is free of defects.
    d. The property will likely sell within four to six weeks.

9. Which of the following is an example of a cloud on the title?
    a. An error in the property's legal description
    b. A dispute of the property's legal ownership
    c. A misspelling of a grantor's name
    d. All of these

10. The Uniform Electronic Transactions Act (UETA) provides that
    a. sales contracts must be signed electronically after December 31, 2012.
    b. handwritten signatures are no longer valid.
    c. signatures by electronic means are as binding as handwritten ones.
    d. electronic signatures only apply to fax copies.

Glossary

abstract of title A provision in a deed of trust that the lender may declare all sums due and payable upon any monetary or non-monetary default.

acceleration clause The clause in a mortgage or deed of trust that can be enforced to make the entire debt due immediately if the borrower defaults on an installment payment or other covenant.

acceptance An expression of intent to be bound by the terms and conditions of an offer. To bind the agreement, the acceptance must be communicated to the person making the offer. An offer pertaining to real estate must be made in writing and accepted in writing.

accretion The increase or addition of land by the deposit of sand or soil washed up naturally from a river, lake, or sea.

acknowledgment Formal declaration by the person signing the document that he/she is free to act before a Notary Public or other authorized to do so.

actual notice Express information or fact; that which is known; direct knowledge.

ad valorem tax A tax levied according to value, generally used to refer to real estate tax; also called the general tax.

addendum Material added to a contract that is part of the contract; must be signed by all parties.

adjustable-rate mortgage (ARM) A loan consisting of an index (variable) plus a margin (fixed) which determines the interest rate. The most popular indices are COFI, LIBOR, and one-year CMT.

adverse possession The actual, open, notorious, hostile, and continuous possession of another's land under a claim of title. Possession for a statutory period may be a means of acquiring title.

affidavit of title A written statement, made under oath by a seller or grantor of real property and acknowledged by a notary public, in which grantors (1) identify themselves and indicate marital status, (2) certify that since the examination of the title, no defects have occurred, and (3) certify that they are in possession of the property.

air rights The right to use the open space above a property, usually allowing the surface to be used for another purpose.

alienation clause A provision in a deed of trust which allows the lender to exercise the acceleration clause upon the transfer of title by the borrower to another.

amendment A change to the existing content of a contract (i.e., if words or provisions are added to or deleted from the body of the contract); must be initialed by all parties.

amortized loan A loan in which the principal, as well as the interest, is payable in monthly or other periodic installments over the term of the loan.

annexation Process of converting personal property into real property.

annual percentage rate (APR) The true cost of borrowing when non-exempt fees are calculated as prepaid interest. The APR is a required disclosure under the Truth in Lending Act (TILA).

appraisal An estimate of the quantity, quality, or value of something. The process through which conclusions of property value are obtained; also refers to the report that sets forth the process of estimation and conclusion of value.

appurtenance A right, privilege, or improvement belonging to, and passing with, the land; "runs with the land."

area preference People's desire for one area over another, based on a number of factors such as history, reputation, convenience, scenic beauty, and location.

asbestos A mineral once used in insulation and other materials that can cause respiratory diseases.

assessment The imposition of a tax, charge, or levy, usually according to established rates.

assets Used alongside liabilities to determine an applicant's net worth.

assignment The transfer of ownership in any negotiable instrument, especially real estate notes.

assume A buyer is personally obligated for the payment of the entire debt of a seller; that is, the buyer assumes the debt. The original seller is not liable for the debt if the property is foreclosed on.

attorney's opinion of title An abstract of title that an attorney has examined and has certified to be, in the attorney's opinion, an accurate statement of the facts concerning the property's ownership.

avulsion The sudden tearing away of land, as by earthquake, flood, volcanic action, or the sudden change in the course of a stream.

balloon payment A payment in which the final payment is greater than two times any regularly scheduled payment.

bargain and sale deed A deed that carries with it no warranties against liens or other encumbrances but that does imply that the grantor has the right to convey title. Grantors may add warranties to a deed at their discretion.

base line The main imaginary line running east and west and crossing a principal meridian at a definite point; used by surveyors for reference in locating and describing land under the rectangular (government) survey system of legal description.

beneficiary (1) The person for whom a trust operates or in whose behalf the income from a trust estate is drawn. (2) A lender in a deed of trust loan transaction.

bilateral contract A contract in which all parties to the instrument are legally bound to act as prescribed; also called a contract of sale.

breach of contract Violation of any terms or conditions in a contract without legal excuse; for example, failure to make a payment when it is due.

bring down A search of the public record made after closing and before new documents are filed for liens.

Broker-Lawyer Committee The Broker-Lawyer Committee drafts and revises contract forms for use by real estate licensees, expedites real estate transactions, and reduces controversies while protecting the interests of the parties involved.

bundle of legal rights The concept of land ownership that includes ownership of all legal rights to the land—possession, control within the law, enjoyment, exclusion, and disposition.

buydown An upfront fee paid to a lender to reduce the interest rate.

buyer agency agreement An employment contract in which the broker is employed as the buyer's agent—the buyer, rather than the seller, is the principal or client.

carbon monoxide (CO) A colorless, odorless gas that occurs as a by-product of fuel combustion that may result in death in poorly ventilated areas.

certificate of occupancy Permission by the municipal inspector to occupy a completed building structure after being inspected and having complied with building codes.

certificate of eligibility Sets forth the maximum guarantee to which the veteran is entitled when applying for a VA loan.

certificate of reasonable value (CRV) A form indicating the appraised value of a property being financed with a VA loan.

certificate of title A statement of opinion on the status of the title to a parcel of real property based on an examination of specified public records.

chain of title The succession of conveyances, from some accepted starting point, whereby the present holder of real property derives title.

closing An event where promises made in a sales contract are fulfilled and mortgage loan funds (if any) are distributed to the buyer.

closing agent Completes settlement statements, disburses funds, and files documents to be recorded and sent to the IRS.

cloud on title Any document, claim, unreleased lien, or encumbrance that may impair the title to real property or make the title doubtful; usually revealed by a title search and removed by either a quitclaim deed or suit to quiet title.

codicil A supplement or an addition to a will, executed with the same formalities as a will, which normally does not revoke the entire will.

commingling The illegal act by a real estate broker of placing client or customer funds with personal funds. By law, brokers are required to maintain a separate trust or escrow account for other parties' funds held temporarily by the broker.

common elements Parts of a property that are necessary or convenient to the existence, maintenance, and safety of a condominium or are normally in common use by all the condominium residents. Each condominium owner has an undivided ownership interest in the common elements.

community property A system of property ownership based on the theory that each spouse has an equal interest in the property acquired by the efforts of either spouse during marriage.

computerized loan origination (CLO) An electronic network for handling loan applications through remote computer terminals linked to various lenders' computers.

condemnation A judicial or administrative proceeding to exercise the power of eminent domain, through which a government agency takes private property for public use and compensates the owner.

condominium The absolute ownership of a unit in a multiunit building based on a legal description of the airspace the unit actually occupies, plus an undivided interest in the common elements.

conforming loan A loan that meets the underwriting guidelines of Fannie Mae and Freddie Mac.

consent   Expressing or implying permission, approval, or agreement of an action or decision.

consideration   Anything of value, usually money, that encourages another to enter into a contract.

construction loan   A short-term loan usually made during the construction phase of a building project; often called interim financing.

constructive notice   Notice given to the world by recorded documents. All people are charged with knowledge of such documents and their contents, whether or not they have actually examined them. Possession of property is also considered constructive notice that the person in possession has an interest in the property.

contingency   A provision in a contract that requires a certain act to be done or a certain event to occur before the contract becomes binding.

contract   A legally enforceable promise or set of promises that must be performed, and for which the law provides a remedy if a breach of the promise occurs. A contract may be either unilateral, by which only one party is bound to act, or bilateral, by which all parties to the instrument are legally bound to act as prescribed; also called a contract of sale.

contract of sale   A contract that is accepted and signed by the seller.

controlled business arrangement (CBA)   An arrangement whereby a package of services (real estate firm, title insurance company, mortgage broker, home inspection company) is offered to consumers.

conventional loan   A loan initiated by a depository institution or a qualified intermediary. Private financing and government-sponsored loan products are not conventional.

cooperative   A residential multiunit building whose title is held by a trust or corporation that is owned by and operated for the benefit of people living within the building who are the beneficial owners of the trust or shareholders of the corporation, each possessing a proprietary lease.

co-ownership   Title ownership held by two or more persons.

corporation   An entity or organization, created by operation of law, whose rights of doing business are essentially the same as those of an individual. The entity has continuous existence until it is dissolved according to legal procedures.

cost approach   The process of estimating the value of a property by adding to the estimated land value the appraiser's estimate of the reproduction or replacement cost of the building, less depreciation.

counteroffer   A rejection of an offer that may not later be accepted, and a new offer specifying what terms the party is willing to accept.

covenants, conditions, and restrictions (CC&Rs)   Private agreements that affect the land use. They may be enforced by an owner of real estate and included in the seller's deed to the buyer; specifically used in condominium projects.

credit   On a closing statement, an amount entered in a person's favor—either an amount the party has paid or an amount for which the party must be reimbursed.

credit report   Documents a person's creditworthiness and outlines negative elements affecting that person's credit score.

credit score   A rating of a borrower's creditworthiness based on history of payment, amount owed, length of credit history, new credit, and other factors.

cross-hatch   A mark drawn on an offer, allowing the buyer and/or seller to initial to accept changes to the offer.

debit   On a closing statement, an amount charged; that is, an amount that the debited party must pay.

Deceptive Trade Practices Act (DTPA)   A consumer protection act which protects the public from any false, misleading, or deceptive act, and from a licensee taking advantage of the consumer's lack of knowledge, ability, experience, or capacity to a grossly unfair degree (i.e., an unconscionable act).

deed   A written instrument conveying an interest in property. There are various types of deeds, including grant, quitclaim, warranty, special warranty, and sheriff's.

deed in lieu of foreclosure   An alternative to foreclosure in which the lender agrees to accept a deed to the property instead of taking the time and expending the cost of foreclosure.

deed of trust   A three-party instrument used to create a security interest in a property, as evidenced by a note. The lender is the beneficiary, the borrower is the trustor, and the trustee benefits both the trustor (when the loan is paid) and beneficiary (in case of foreclosure).

deed restrictions   A provision in the deed which prohibits the grantee from unrestricted use of the property. Such restrictions include size of improvements, percentage of masonry, and distance from something. Any restriction that violates any law is unenforceable; however, the deed remains valid.

deficiency judgment   A personal judgment levied against the borrower when a foreclosure sale does not produce sufficient funds to pay the mortgage debt in full.

depreciation (1) In appraisal, a loss of value in property due to any cause, including physical deterioration, functional obsolescence, and external obsolescence. (2) In real estate investment, an expense deduction for tax purposes taken over the period of ownership of income property.

devise A gift of real property by will. The donor is the devisor, and the recipient is the devisee.

disclosure Relevant information or facts that are known or should have been known.

discount point A unit of measurement used for various loan charges; one point equals 1% of the amount of the loan.

draws Under a construction loan, payments that the lender disburses during construction.

earnest money Money deposited by a buyer under the terms of a contract, to be forfeited if the buyer defaults, but to be applied to the purchase price if the sale is closed.

easement A right to use the land of another for a specific purpose, such as for a right-of-way or utilities; an incorporeal interest in land.

easement appurtenant An easement that "runs with the land."

easement by necessity An easement allowed by law as necessary for the right of ingress and egress over a grantor's land.

easement by prescription An easement acquired by continuous, open, and hostile use of the property for the period of time prescribed by state law.

easement in gross Generally used by utility companies to create "utility easements" over other properties, often when the land is developed and recorded prior to building.

eminent domain The right of a government or municipal quasi-public body to acquire property for public use through a court action called condemnation, in which the court decides that the use is a public use and determines the compensation to be paid to the owner.

encroachment A structure or extension of a structure which extends over a boundary line. The line may be a building line (setback) or property line.

encumbrance Anything such as a mortgage, tax, or judgment lien; an easement; or a restriction on the use of the land.

equitable right of redemption The ability of a borrower to redeem the property after foreclosure. Under Texas law, lenders that use the deed of trust form do not give a redemption period. Instead, there is a right of redemption for a tax sale, which gives homeowners two years for owner-occupied properties and six months for non-owner-occupied properties to pay all taxes, fees, and costs.

equitable title The interest held by a vendee under a contract for deed or an installment contract; the equitable right to obtain absolute ownership to property when legal title is held in another's name.

erosion The gradual and imperceptible wearing away of the land by natural forces, such as wind, rain, and flowing water.

escheat The reversion of property to the state or county, as provided by state law, in cases where a decedent dies intestate without heirs capable of inheriting, or when the property is abandoned.

escrow closing A disinterested third party is authorized to act as escrow agent (escrow holder) and to coordinate the closing activities on behalf of the buyer and the seller.

escrow or impound account Collects property taxes and insurance.

estate at sufferance The tenancy of a lessee who lawfully comes into possession of a landlord's real estate but who continues to occupy the premises improperly after his or her lease rights have expired.

estate at will An estate that gives the lessee the right to possession until the estate is terminated by either party; the term of this estate is indefinite.

estate for years An interest for a certain, exact period of time in property leased for a specified consideration.

estate from period to period An interest in leased property that continues from period to period—week to week, month to month, or year to year.

estate in land The degree, quantity, nature, and extent of interest a person has in real property.

exchange The seller delivers the signed deed to the buyer, who accepts it. All pertinent documents are then recorded in the correct order to ensure continuity of title.

exclusive-agency listing A listing contract under which the owner appoints a real estate broker as his or her exclusive agent for a designated period of time to sell the property, on the owner's stated terms, for a commission. The owner reserves the right to sell without paying anyone a commission if the sale is to a prospect who has not been introduced or claimed by the broker.

exclusive-right-to-sell listing A listing contract under which the owner appoints a real estate broker as his or her exclusive agent for a designated period of time to sell the property on the owner's stated terms and agrees to pay the broker a commission when the property is sold, whether by the broker, the owner, or another broker.

executed contract A contract in which all parties have fulfilled their promises and thus performed the contract.

executory contract A contract under which something remains to be done by one or more of the parties.

express contract   A contract in which the parties state the terms and show their intentions in words, either oral or written.

face-to-face closing   The buyer and seller meet together for closing; may be held at the office of the title company, the lending institution, an attorney for one of the parties, the broker, the county recorder, or the escrow company.

Fannie Mae   A government-sponsored enterprise established to purchase any type of mortgage loans in the secondary mortgage market from the primary lenders.

Farmer Mac   A government-sponsored enterprise that works like Fannie Mae and Freddie Mac, but for agricultural real estate loans.

Federal Home Loan Bank (FHLB)   A source, for member institutions, of low cost funds when needed for liquidity to meet reserve requirement or have funds to lend. These borrowings are called "advances" and are secured by pledged loans already in their portfolio.

Federal Reserve System (the Fed)   The country's central banking system, which is responsible for the nation's monetary policy by regulating the supply of money and interest rates.

fee simple   The highest interest in real estate recognized by the law; the holder is entitled to all rights to the property; the maximum possible estate or right of ownership of real property, continuing forever; also called fee simple absolute.

fee simple defeasible   An estate in which the holder has a fee simple title that may be divested upon the occurrence or nonoccurrence of a specified event.

fee simple determinable   A fee simple estate qualified by a special limitation. Language used to describe limitation includes the words so long as, while, or during.

fee simple subject to a condition subsequent   If an estate is no longer used for the purpose conveyed, it reverts to the original grantor by the right of reentry.

first mortgage or deed of trust   A mortgage that has priority over all other mortgages.

fixture   An item of personal property that has been converted to real property by being permanently affixed to the realty.

flood insurance   Required for any property within Federal Emergency Management Agency (FEMA) declared flood zones.

foreclosure   A remedy for lenders in the event of a default, which is done under "the power of sale" provision in the deed of trust. This provision allows the lender to proceed without a judicial process; in other words, this is a non-judicial foreclosure.

Freddie Mac   A government-sponsored enterprise established to purchase primarily conventional mortgage loans in the secondary mortgage market; under supervision of FHFA.

freehold estate   An estate in land in which ownership is for an indeterminate length of time, in contrast to a leasehold estate.

future interest   A person's present right to an interest in real property that will not result in possession or enjoyment until sometime in the future, such as a reversion or right of re-entry.

general partnership   A typical form of joint venture in which each general partner shares in the administration, profits, and losses of the operation.

general warranty deed   A deed in which the grantor fully warrants good, clear title to the premises. Used in most real estate deed transfers, a general warranty deed offers the greatest protection of any deed.

Ginnie Mae   A government agency that plays an important role in the secondary mortgage market. It guarantees mortgage-backed securities using FHA and VA loans as collateral.

Good Faith Estimate (GFE)   An estimate of all closing fees that must be provided to a borrower within three days of the loan application as required by the Real Estate Settlement Procedures Act (RESPA).

grantee   A person who receives a transfer of real property from a grantor.

granting clause   Words in a deed of conveyance that state the grantor's intention to convey the property at the present time. This clause is generally worded as "convey and warrant," "grant," "grant, bargain, and sell," or the like.

grantor   The owner transferring title to or an interest in real property to a grantee.

gross lease   A lease of property according to which a landlord pays all property charges regularly incurred through ownership, such as repairs, taxes, insurance, and operating expenses. Most residential leases are gross leases.

ground lease   A lease of land only, on which the tenant usually owns a building or is required to build as specified in the lease. Such leases are usually long-term net leases; the tenant's rights and obligations continue until the lease expires or is terminated through default.

growing-equity mortgage   A loan in which the monthly payments increase annually, with the increased amount being used to directly reduce the principal balance outstanding and, thus, shorten the overall term of the loan.

habendum clause   That part of a deed beginning with the words "to have and to hold," following the granting clause and defining the extent of ownership the grantor is conveying.

heir One who might inherit or succeed to an interest in land under the state law of descent when the owner dies without leaving a valid will.

holographic will A will that is written, dated, and signed in the testator's handwriting.

home equity line of credit (HELOC) A home equity loan in which the lender extends a line of credit that the borrower can use at will.

home equity loan Any borrowing using the equity in the home as collateral. The maximum loan or combined loans may not exceed 80% LTV.

home inspection Professional inspection of property to ascertain conditions of all systems and appliances; may note minor structural, roof, or moisture problems.

homestead The personal residence of a family or single person which is protected from creditor seizure except real estate loans and mechanics' liens.

hypothecation To pledge property as security for an obligation or loan without giving up possession of it.

implied contract A contract in which the agreement of the parties is demonstrated by their acts and conduct.

impound or escrow account An account that most mortgage lenders require borrowers to have for funds to pay future real estate taxes and insurance premiums; also called escrow account.

improvement Any structure erected on a site to enhance the value of the property.

in arrears Payments made at the end of a payment period.

income approach The process of estimating the value of an income-producing property through capitalization of the annual net income expected to be produced by the property during its remaining useful life.

index An objective economic indicator to which the interest rate for an adjustable-rate mortgage is tied.

interest A charge made by a lender for the use of money.

interest-only mortgage A loan in which only interest is paid at required intervals (monthly, quarterly, etc.) and the entire principal is payable at maturity.

intestate Without a will. If there are heirs, then intestate succession will occur: the estate will be apportioned depending on the surviving relatives. If there are no heirs, then the estate will go to the state by the process of escheat.

involuntary alienation The act of involuntarily transferring property to another, such as through eminent domain or adverse possession.

joint tenancy Ownership of real estate between two or more parties who have been named in one conveyance as joint tenants. Upon the death of a joint tenant, the decedent's interest passes to the surviving joint tenant or tenants by the right of survivorship.

kickback Any payment received for a referral when no service is rendered.

kick-out clause Allows the seller to keep the property on the market with full disclosure in the multiple listing service that there is a contract in place, but other offers are welcome. If a new offer is made, there is a specified time (usually no more than 24 to 72 hours) for the original buyers to remove the home sale contingency and proceed with the contract.

land The earth's surface, extending downward to the center of the earth and upward infinitely into space, including things permanently attached by nature, such as trees and water.

land contract A sales agreement between seller and buyer; no mortgage or deed of trust involved; title to the property not received by buyer until full payment is made.

lease A written or oral contract between a landlord (the lessor) and a tenant (the lessee) that transfers the right to exclusive possession and use of the landlord's real property to the lessee for a specified period of time and for a stated consideration (rent). By state law, leases for longer than a certain period (generally one year) must be in writing to be enforceable.

lease purchase The purchase of real property, the consummation of which is preceded by a lease that is typically done for tax or financing purposes.

leasehold estate A tenant's right to occupy real estate during the term of a lease, generally considered a personal property interest.

legal description Use of one of the three accepted methods of identifying a specific property: government survey, lot and block, or metes and bounds.

legally competent People who are recognized by law as being able to contract with others; those of legal age and sound mind.

lessee A tenant.

lessor A landlord.

letter of intent (LOI) Used to outline the basic terms that a buyer may agree to prior to a complex sales agreement. Non-binding language is usually inserted so as to not create a contract. Used primarily in commercial transactions.

liabilities Used alongside assets to determine an applicant's net worth.

license (1) A privilege or right granted to a person by a state to operate as a real estate broker or salesperson. (2) The revocable permission for a temporary use of land—a personal right that cannot be sold.

lien An encumbrance that is usually a monetary charge against property that provides security for a debt.

lien theory Supposes that the borrower (real estate) holds legal title to the property while the lender has a lien on the title.

life estate An interest in real or personal property that is limited in duration to the lifetime of its owner or some other designated person or persons.

limited liability company (LLC) A form of business organization that combines the most attractive features of limited partnerships and corporations.

limited partnership A business arrangement whereby the operation is administered by one or more general partners and funded, by and large, by limited or silent partners, who are by law responsible for losses only to the extent of their investments.

liquidated damages An amount predetermined by the parties to a contract as the total compensation to an injured party should the other party breach the contract.

lis pendens A recorded legal document giving constructive notice that an action affecting a particular property has been filed in either a state or a federal court.

littoral rights (1) A landowner's claim to use water in large navigable lakes and oceans adjacent to his or her property. (2) The ownership rights to land bordering these bodies of water up to the high-water mark.

loan origination fee A charge (usually 1% of the loan amount) for initiating the loan process consisting of completing the loan application, pulling the credit report, sending verification of deposits and employment, and preparing everything needed by the underwriter.

loan-to-value ratio (LTV) The amount borrowed as a percentage of the value or purchase price.

lot and block A method of describing real property that identifies a parcel of land by reference to lot and block numbers within a subdivision, as specified on a recorded subdivision plat.

manufactured housing Dwellings that are built off-site and trucked to a building lot where they are installed or assembled.

margin The fixed amount, as a percentage, which is added to an index (variable) to make an adjustable rate mortgage (ARM).

market value The most probable price property would bring in an arm's-length transaction under normal conditions on the open market.

marketable title A title that is free from encumbrances, defensible, and salable.

mechanic's lien A statutory lien created in favor of contractors, laborers, and materialmen who have performed work or furnished materials in the erection or repair of a building.

metes and bounds A legal description of a parcel of land that begins at a well-marked point and follows the boundaries, using directions and distances around the tract, back to the place of beginning.

mold A form of fungus that can be found almost anywhere and can grow on almost any organic substance, so long as moisture, oxygen, and an organic food source are present. Mold growth can gradually destroy what it is growing on, as well as cause serious health problems.

month-to-month tenancy A periodic tenancy under which the tenant rents for one month at a time. In the absence of a rental agreement (oral or written), a tenancy is generally considered to be month to month.

monument A fixed natural or artificial object used to establish real estate boundaries for a metes-and-bounds description.

mortgage A real estate loan. Texas does not use the mortgage form, which is a two-party instrument (the mortgagor and the mortgagee).

mortgage insurance premium (MIP) The FHA insurance that is a percentage of the loan amount that the borrower is charged as a premium. Also called mutual mortgage insurance (MMI).

mortgage lien A voluntary lien given to a lender by a borrower as security for a real estate loan.

multiple listing service (MLS) A marketing organization composed of member brokers who agree to share their listing agreements with one another in the hope of procuring ready, willing, and able buyers for their properties more quickly than they could on their own. Most multiple listing services accept exclusive right-to-sell or exclusive-agency listings from their member brokers.

negotiable instrument A written promise or order to pay a specific sum of money that may be transferred by endorsement or delivery. The transferee then has the original payee's right to payment.

net lease A lease requiring the tenant to pay not only rent but also costs incurred in maintaining the property, including taxes, insurance, utilities, and repairs.

net listing A listing based on the net price the seller will receive if the property is sold. Under a net listing, the broker can offer the property for sale at the highest price obtainable to increase the commission. This type of listing is illegal in many states.

net worth   Calculated by determining the borrower's assets and liabilities.

nonconforming loan   Any loan that does not meet Fannie Mae or Freddie Mac standards.

nonhomogeneity   A lack of uniformity; dissimilarity. Because no two parcels of land are exactly alike, real estate is said to be nonhomogeneous.

novation   Substituting a new obligation for an old one or substituting new parties to an existing obligation.

nuncupative will   An oral will declared by the testator in his or her final illness, made before witnesses and afterward reduced to writing.

offer   A promise made by one party, requesting something in exchange for that promise.

offer to purchase   First action taken by one wishing to purchase a property; sometimes called a contract, but it is not in fact a contract until all parties have signed.

offeree   The person to whom the offer is made.

offeror   The person who makes the offer.

oil and gas lease   An agreement by which a landowner allows for the exploration and production of oil and gas on the landowner's property in return for payment.

open listing   A listing contract under which the broker's commission is contingent on the broker's producing a ready, willing, and able buyer before the property is sold by the seller or another broker.

option   An agreement to keep open for a set period an offer to sell or purchase property.

ownership and use tests   Tests that determine whether capital gain from the sale of a home may be excluded.

package loan   A loan that uses the real estate and the personal property as collateral.

partition   The division of co-tenants' interests in real property when the parties do not all voluntarily agree to terminate the co-ownership; takes place through court procedures.

partnership   An association of two or more individuals who carry on a continuing business for profit as co-owners. Under the law, a partnership is regarded as a group of individuals rather than as a single entity.

payment cap   The limit on the amount the monthly payment can be increased on an adjustable-rate mortgage when the interest rate is adjusted.

percentage lease   A lease, commonly used for commercial property, whose rental is based on the tenant's gross sales at the premises; it usually stipulates a base monthly rental plus a percentage of any gross sales above a certain amount.

personal property   Items, called chattels, that do not fit into the definition of real property; movable objects.

plat map   A map of a town, section, or subdivision indicating the location and boundaries of individual properties.

point of beginning (POB)   In a metes-and-bounds legal description, the beginning point of the survey, which is also the point of ending.

police power   The government's right to impose laws, statutes, and ordinances, including zoning ordinances and building codes, to protect the public health, safety, and welfare.

power of attorney   A written instrument authorizing a person, the attorney-in-fact, to act as agent for another person to the extent indicated in the instrument.

preapproval letter   The lender has taken information from the borrower and determined that, if everything the borrower said is true, then the borrower is likely to get the loan.

prepayment penalty   A fee for the early payment of a loan balance. VA, FHA, Fannie Mae, and Freddie Mac loans do not have prepayment penalties.

primary mortgage market   The market in which loans are originated by mortgage bankers, brokers, banks, thrifts, private investors, and credit unions.

principal meridian   The main imaginary line running north and south and crossing a base line at a definite point; used by surveyors for reference in locating and describing land under the rectangular (government) survey system of legal description.

prior appropriation   A concept of water ownership in which the landowner's right to use available water is based on a government-administered permit system.

priority   The order of position or time. The priority of liens is generally determined by the chronological order in which the lien documents are recorded; tax liens, however, have priority even over previously recorded liens.

private mortgage insurance (PMI)   Insurance provided by private carrier that protects a lender against a loss in the event of default and foreclosure.

probate   A legal process by which a court determines who will inherit a decedent's property and what the estate's assets are.

promissory note   A financing instrument that states the terms of the underlying obligation, is signed by its maker, and is negotiable (transferable to a third party).

promulgate   To publish and make available for use.

proprietary lease   A lease given by the corporation that owns a cooperative apartment building to the shareholder for the shareholder's right as a tenant to an individual apartment.

prorations   Expenses, either prepaid or paid in arrears, that are divided or distributed between the buyer and the seller at the closing.

pur autre vie   "For the life of another." A life estate pur autre vie is a life estate that is measured by the life of a person other than the grantee.

purchase-money mortgage (PMM)   Funds borrowed to purchase the property, as distinguished from any type of refinance. Purchase money is also called soft money, while other borrowings are called hard money. Some real estate practitioners refer to expensive money as hard money, but it is a misnomer.

quitclaim deed   A conveyance by which grantors transfer whatever interest they have in the real estate, without warranties or obligations.

radon   A naturally occurring gas from the decay of radioactive materials.

range   A strip of land six miles wide, extending north and south and numbered east and west according to its distance from the principal meridian in the rectangular (government) survey system of legal description.

rate cap   The limit on the amount the interest rate can be increased at each adjustment period in an adjustable rate loan. The cap may also set the maximum interest rate that can be charged during the life of the loan.

real estate   Land; a portion of the earth's surface extending downward to the center of the earth and upward infinitely into space, including all things permanently attached to it, whether naturally or artificially.

Real Estate Settlement Procedures Act (RESPA)   The federal law that requires certain disclosures to consumers about mortgage loan settlements. The law also prohibits the payment or receipt of kickbacks and certain kinds of referral fees.

real property   The interests, benefits, and rights inherent in real estate ownership.

reconveyance deed   A deed used by a trustee under a deed of trust to return title to the trustor.

recording   The act of entering or recording documents affecting or conveying interests in real estate in the recorder's office established in each county. Until it is recorded, a deed or mortgage ordinarily is not effective against subsequent purchasers or mortgagees.

rectangular survey system   A system established in 1785 by the federal government, providing for surveying and describing land by reference to principal meridians and base lines.

Regulation Z   Implements the Truth in Lending Act, requiring credit institutions to inform borrowers of the true cost of obtaining credit.

release deed   A document, also called a deed of reconveyance, that transfers all rights given a trustee under a deed of trust loan back to the grantor after the loan has been fully repaid.

remainder interest   The remnant of an estate that has been conveyed to take effect and be enjoyed after the termination of a prior estate, such as when an owner conveys a life estate to one party and the remainder to another.

rescission   The practice of one party canceling or terminating a contract, which has the effect of returning the parties to their original positions before the contract was made.

reverse mortgage   A loan under which the homeowner receives monthly payments, a lump sum, or a line of credit based on his or her accumulated equity. The loan must be repaid at a prearranged date, upon the death or moving of the owner, or upon the sale of the property.

reversionary interest   The remnant of an estate that the grantor holds after granting a life estate to another person.

reversionary right   The return of the rights of possession and quiet enjoyment to the lessor at the expiration of a lease.

revocation   Cancelling or annulling licensed privileges or rights.

right of first refusal   A clause allowing the tenant the opportunity to buy the property before the owner accepts an offer from another party.

right of survivorship   The right, upon the death of a joint tenant, that the decedent's interest passes to the surviving joint tenant or tenants.

riparian rights   An owner's rights in land that borders on or includes a stream, river, or lake. These rights include access to and use of the water.

sales comparison approach   The process of estimating the value of a property by examining and comparing actual sales of comparable properties.

satisfaction   Release or discharge of when a note has been fully paid. This document returns to the borrower all interest in the real estate originally conveyed to the lender. Entering this release in the public record shows that the debt has been removed from the property.

school section   Section 16 of a township square.

second mortgage or deed of trust   A lien junior to the first mortgage or deed of trust.

secondary mortgage market   A market for the purchase and sale of existing mortgages, designed to provide greater liquidity for mortgages; mortgages are first originated in the primary mortgage market.

section   A portion of a township under the rectangular (government) survey system. A township is divided into 36 sections, numbered 1 through 36. A section is a square with mile-long sides and an area of one square mile, or 640 acres.

security deposit   A payment by a tenant, held by the landlord during the lease term, and kept (wholly or partially) on default, or on destruction of the premises by the tenant.

separate property   Under community property law, property owned solely by either spouse before the marriage, acquired by gift or inheritance after the marriage, or purchased with separate funds after the marriage.

Settlement Statement (HUD-1)   A special HUD form that itemizes all charges to be paid by a borrower and a seller in connection with the settlement.

severalty   Ownership of real property by one person only; also called sole ownership.

severance   Changing an item of real estate to personal property by detaching it from the land (e.g., cutting down a tree).

short sale   When a lender agrees to accept less than the amount due on the mortgage note.

situs   The personal preference of people for one area over another, not necessarily based on objective facts and knowledge.

special warranty deed   A deed in which the grantor warrants, or guarantees, the title only against defects arising during the period of his or her tenure and ownership of the property, and not against defects existing before that time.

statute of frauds   That part of a state law that requires certain instruments, such as deeds, real estate sales contracts, and certain leases, to be in writing to be legally enforceable.

straight loan   A loan in which only interest is paid during the term of the loan, with the entire principal amount due with the final interest payment.

subdivision plat   A map of a subdivision indicating the location and boundaries of individual properties.

"subject to"   Buyer takes title of property and makes payments on the existing loan but is not personally obligated to pay the debt in full. Original seller might continue to be liable for debt.

sublease   The leasing of premises by a lessee to a third party for part of the lessee's remaining term. *See also* assignment.

subsurface rights   Ownership rights in a parcel of real estate to the water, minerals, gas, oil, and so forth that lie beneath the surface of the property.

suit for specific performance   If the seller breaches a real estate sales contract, the buyer may sue, asking the court to force the seller to go through with the sale and convey the property as previously agreed.

suit to quiet title   A court action intended to establish or settle the title to a particular property, especially when there is a cloud on the title.

surface rights   Ownership rights in a parcel of real estate that are limited to the surface of the property and do not include the air above it (air rights) or the minerals below the surface (subsurface rights).

survey   The process by which boundaries are measured and land areas are determined; the on-site measurement of lot lines, dimensions, and position of a house on a lot, including the determination of any existing encroachments or easements.

synthetic stucco   Exterior insulation finish systems (EIFS), which do not allow moisture to escape, possibly leading to moisture problems and mold.

tacking   Combining successive periods of continuous occupation by different parties to reach the required total number of years necessary to establish a claim for a prescriptive easement.

taxation   The process by which a government or municipal quasi-public body raises monies to fund its operation.

tenancy in common   A form of co-ownership by which each owner holds an undivided interest in real property. Each individual owner has the right to partition. Unlike joint tenants, tenants in common have right of inheritance.

testate   Having made and left a valid will.

testator   A person who has made a valid will.

Texas Real Estate Commission (TREC)   Texas regulatory agency created to administer the Texas Real Estate License Act. It has rule-making authority, and its rules have the full force and effect of law.

Texas Real Estate License Act (TRELA)   Protects the public through regulation of licensed real estate brokerage practitioners, real estate inspectors, residential service companies, and entities offering timeshare interests.

thrifts   A generic term for a savings association.

time is of the essence   A phrase in a contract that requires the performance of a certain act within a stated period of time.

time-share   A form of ownership interest that may include an estate interest in property and that allows use of the property for a fixed or variable time period.

time-share estate   An estate in which the owner's occupancy and use of the property are limited to the contractual period purchased.

time-share use The right to occupy and use the facilities for a certain number of years, after which the owner's rights in the property terminate.

title (1) The right to ownership or the ownership of land. (2) The evidence of ownership of land.

title insurance A policy insuring the owner or mortgagee against loss by reason of defects in the title to a parcel of real estate, other than encumbrances, defects, and matters specifically excluded by the policy.

title search The examination of public records relating to real estate to determine the current state of the ownership.

tort An act that damages another individual and gives rise to legal action.

township The principal unit of the rectangular (government) survey system. A township is a square with 6-mile sides and an area of 36 square miles.

township line All the lines in a rectangular survey system that run east and west, parallel to the base line six miles apart.

township tier Township lines that form strips of land and are designated by consecutive numbers north or south of the base line.

trade fixture An article installed by a tenant under the terms of a lease and removable by the tenant before the lease expires.

transfer tax Tax stamps required to be affixed to a deed by state and/or local law.

trigger terms Specific credit terms, such as down payment, monthly payment, and amount of finance charge or term of loan.

tri-merge credit report A credit report that contains credit information and credit scores from all three major credit reporting agencies.

trust A fiduciary arrangement whereby property is conveyed to a person or institution, called a trustee, to be held and administered on behalf of another person, called a beneficiary. The one who conveys the trust is called the trustor.

trustee One to whom something is entrusted and who holds legal title to property and administers the property for the benefit of a beneficiary; or a member of a board entrusted with the administration of an institution or organization, such as a cooperative.

trustee's deed A deed executed by a trustee conveying land held in a trust.

trustor A borrower in a deed of trust loan transaction; one who places property in a trust; also called a grantor or settler.

Truth in Lending Act (TILA) Federal government regulates the lending practices of mortgage lenders through this act.

underground storage tank (UST) Commonly found on sites where petroleum products are used or where gas stations and auto repair shops are located. In residential areas, tanks are used to store heating oil. Over time, neglected tanks may leak hazardous substances into the environment.

underwriter Approves, rejects, or returns the loan package to processing with contingency requirements that must be met before resubmission for approval.

unenforceable contract A contract that has all the elements of a valid contract, yet neither party can sue the other to force performance of it. For example, an unsigned contract is generally unenforceable.

Uniform Probate Code (UPC) An act created in an effort to streamline the probate process.

unilateral contract A contract in which only one party is bound to act.

usury Charging interest at a higher rate than the maximum rate established by state law.

valid contract A contract that complies with all the essentials of a contract and is binding and enforceable on all parties to it.

void contract A contract that has no legal force or effect because it does not meet the essential elements of a contract.

voidable contract A contract that seems to be valid on the surface but may be rejected or disaffirmed by one or both of the parties.

voluntary alienation The act of voluntarily transferring property to another, such as by gift or sale.

walk-through A final inspection in which the buyer verifies that all necessary repairs have been made, that the property has been well maintained, and that all systems and fixtures are in substantially the same condition that they were in at the time the contract was finalized.

walk-through items Items that must be brought into normal working condition before settlement.

water rights Common law rights held by owners of land adjacent to rivers, lakes, or oceans; includes restrictions on those rights and land ownership.

will A written document, properly witnessed, providing for the transfer of title to property owned by the deceased, called the testator.

zero tolerance Items on final Good Faith Estimate that may not differ from the original.

ANSWER KEY

CHAPTER 1 REVIEW QUESTIONS

1. **c.** The TREC administers the act.
2. **d.** The DTPA protects the public from false, misleading, deceptive, and unconscionable acts.
3. **c.** Licensees cannot advise a person regarding the validity or legal sufficiency of an instrument or the validity of title to real property.
4. **c.** In addition, licensees don't have to use the promulgated forms when acting as a principal, when an agency of the United States government requires a different form, or when no standard contract form promulgated by the TREC exists.
5. **d.** The licensee could also use a form prepared by an attorney.
6. **a.** The DTPA offers treble damages and a mental anguish award.
7. **a.** One spouse does not need to provide a seller's disclosure to the other spouse in a divorce proceeding.
8. **a.** There are exceptions to the disclosure requirement. TREC Form OP-H includes the language required by the Texas Property Code, but the form itself is not required by the property code.
9. **c.** TREC does not supply a promulgated form for the sale of five-unit residential buildings.
10. **b.** If a contract is entered without the seller providing the notice required by this section, the purchaser may terminate the contract for any reason within seven days after receiving the notice.

CHAPTER 2 REVIEW QUESTIONS

1. **c.** Annual crops, also known as emblements, are considered personal property.
2. **d.** The right of disposition allows property to be sold, willed, transferred, or otherwise disposed of.
3. **b.** The cost of the item has no bearing on the decision of whether it is real or personal property.
4. **c.** The mineral rights would be subsurface rights because the minerals are located in land below the surface.

5. **b.** The lumber is still personal property when delivered; becomes real property after it has been built into the structure.
6. **b.** In a condominium, the owner has a fee simple interest in the unit, along with a percentage interest in the common elements.
7. **d.** Community property considers a married couple as equal partners rather than as one entity; all property acquired during the marriage is equally divided unless received by gift or inheritance.
8. **d.** In a cooperative, the owner has a proprietary right to occupy a unit and own shares in the corporation.
9. **d.** In states that allow for tenancy by the entirety, the couple is considered to be one unit and have rights of survivorship if one party dies.
10. **b.** Although the word seems somewhat contradictory, in severalty means a single owner (severed from others.)

CHAPTER 3 REVIEW QUESTIONS

1. **a.** The TREC does not promulgate a form for the sale of 10-unit apartment buildings.
2. **d.** Bilateral means that each of the parties agrees to give something; i.e., buyer and seller, seller and listing broker, landlord and tenant.
3. **a.** A property disclosure agreement is not needed for a duplex.
4. **b.** A contract for deed for a period of two years is an executory contract.
5. **c.** A contract for sale must include the elements of offer and acceptance, consideration, legally competent parties, and consent and legal purpose, and must be in writing to be enforceable. If any element is missing, the contract is void.
6. **b.** An option is a unilateral contract (only a promise by one party) that gives a potential buyer an opportunity to purchase a property at a given amount within a stated time-frame. In most cases, a fee is paid for the option.
7. **a.** An exclusive-agency listing authorizes one broker to represent the principal; however, the seller retains the right to sell the property without paying a commission to the broker.

8. **b.** There are many clauses that may be included in a listing agreement, but the one that is required by most states is a definite date for termination of the contract. In fact, in some states, the lack of a definite termination date could cause a suspension or revocation of the broker's license.

9. **c.** A tenancy for years has specific starting and ending dates. No notice is required because the agreement is automatically terminated on the ending date specified in the lease.

10. **d.** A tenancy by sufferance is created when a tenant who lawfully occupied the property continues to stay on after the expiration date of the lease without the permission of the landlord. If the lease does not have a "hold-over" clause that governs the rights of both landlord and tenant, state law will govern.

CHAPTER 4 REVIEW QUESTIONS

1. **a.** A fee simple interest provides an owner with total ownership and control over a property with the exception of certain governmental powers.

2. **c.** A fee simple determinable has a special limitation or what can, or cannot, be done with the property. If the limitation is violated, the property may revert back to the original owner.

3. **a.** Governmental powers are those of police power, escheat, eminent domain and taxation.

4. **c.** Homestead is a legal life estate that protects some amount of real and personal property from creditors; the homestead is not protected from real estate taxes or a mortgage.

5. **b.** When an owner conveys property but retains a life estate, the party to whom the property will go upon the death of the owner has a remainder interest.

6. **c.** Protection from creditors is called homestead rights and varies from state to state.

7. **a.** An easement in gross gives an individual or a company the rights to an easement across a number of properties; a commercial easement in gross may be assigned, conveyed, or inherited. A personal easement in gross usually terminates on the death of the easement owner.

8. **a.** An easement by necessity is not for convenience; it provides ingress and egress from land which must not be landlocked.

9. **a.** A fee simple absolute interest is the highest interest a person may have in real estate.

10. **c.** A Phase I assessment is generally associated with a commercial real estate purchase.

CHAPTER 5 REVIEW QUESTIONS

1. **d.** Any change in the contract first requires the initials of the party making the change. The contract is not actually ratified until the other party has also initialed the change. The cross-hatch with initials could be dated to ensure no future controversy.

2. **d.** State license law has strict regulations about the disposition of earnest money funds; they absolutely cannot be used by the broker for any business or personal purpose.

3. **c.** The title company will research the chain of title to be sure there are no other claims on the property, but this is not a detail included in a sales contract.

4. **b.** In today's electronic world, there may be a question as to when acceptance, rejection, or counteroffer has been made and accepted. A standard contract may state that electronic transmissions are valid.

5. **b.** Even though some, or all, of the earnest money deposit may eventually become the property of the broker, it must initially be placed in a special account as specified by state law.

6. **b.** Metes-and-bounds is the oldest of the methods used for legal description; it describes a property using linear measurements, natural and specific landmarks, and directions from a point-of-beginning (POB) around to a return to the POB.

7. **b.** Historically, the school was usually located in Section 16 of the rectangular (government) survey system. Section 16 is still called the "school section" although the actual school may be elsewhere.

8. **c.** The street address is adequate for some business transactions but never as a legal description. Municipalities often change street names or numbering systems as communities grow.

9. **b.** A *lis pendens* (lien pending) is merely serving legal notice that a suit may be coming. The three remedies available to a seller if a buyer defaults are rescission of the contract, suit for specific performance, or a suit for damages.

10. **d.** In many states, the buyer assumes the risk of any damage to the property during the time between contract and closing; other states have determined that the risk should remain with the seller and have incorporated portions of the Uniform Vendor and Purchaser Risk to protect the buyer.

CHAPTER 6 REVIEW QUESTIONS

1. **d.** If the sale of home contingency is allowed to continue up to the date of settlement, the seller has no protection. On the projected settlement date, the contract could become void. At the least, the seller should retain the right to continue marketing the property with a kick-out clause to the buyer.

2. **b.** A disclosure of lead-based paint hazard is required for all properties built before 1978. Because lead-based paint has proven to be hazardous to children, a family with young children may want to have the property inspected.

3. **c.** Any contingency must be satisfactorily accomplished before a contract can proceed to closing. If the contingency is not resolved, the contract becomes void; in the meantime, it is voidable.

4. **b.** An appraisal indicating a value that is less than the agreed upon sales price might make it impossible for the buyer to obtain the financing as described, due to the lender's loan-to-value ratio. One solution is for the seller to reduce the sales price to an amount that will allow the financing needed.

5. **c.** A home inspector has general knowledge about the various systems in a house: plumbing, electric, heating, and cooling, along with major appliances. The inspector may also point out problems with drainage, termite destruction, or roof damage. The inspector is not an expert in any one field and will recommend a specialist if it seems necessary.

6. **a.** The use of an amendment form and an addendum form are often confused. An amendment is a change to what it is in the original contract; an addendum is new material being added to the contract. In either case, the other party must sign off on the change or addition for the contract to remain in full force.

7. **a.** Home and pest inspections are the two most common types of inspections for homebuyers.

8. **c.** A short sale may be an option if the property's final selling price will be less than is the amount owed on the loan (i.e., the loan is "underwater").

9. **d.** The period between the inspection and the end of the option period should be used to negotiate any necessary repairs identified by the inspection.

10. **b.** While all of these contingencies are intended to protect the buyer, the loan contingency is used most often.

CHAPTER 7 REVIEW QUESTIONS

1. **a.** The term *mortgagor* is often confused with *mortgagee*. The mortgagor is the borrower (similar ending). The lender is the mortgagee.

2. **d.** The acceleration clause in a mortgage contract makes the entire loan amount due when a borrower defaults. Without an acceleration clause, the lender would have to sue each time a payment was missed.

3. **c.** A credit union makes mortgage loans to its members and is part of the primary mortgage market. Fannie Mae and Freddie Mac purchase packages of loans on the secondary market, and Ginnie Mae guarantees mortgage-backed securities created in the secondary market.

4. **b.** The primary market lenders for single-family residences are generally commercial or mutual savings banks, savings associations, or credit unions. Life insurance companies and pension funds usually invest in larger projects.

5. **b.** Freddie Mac was originally created to purchase conventional loans and package them for sale as securities on the secondary market. Today Freddie Mac occasionally purchases government loans as well.

6. **a.** The rate of interest charged on a fixed-rate loan does not change. The actual monthly payment may change slightly on an annual basis due to fluctuations in the real estate taxes and homeowner insurance premiums.

7. **c.** Although it is called an FHA loan, the funds are actually received from an FHA-approved lender. FHA insures the loan in case of default by the borrower.

8. **b.** With a fully-amortized loan, each monthly payment is the same, but in the beginning, the portion allowed for interest is larger than that allowed toward the principal. Over the years, the principal amount increases and the amount of interest decreases.

9. **d.** The Equal Credit Opportunity Act does not allow a lender to discriminate on the basis of race, color, religion, national origin, sex, age, marital status, or source of income. Insufficient amount of income would cause a loan to be denied.

10. **d.** The Truth in Lending Act requires disclosure of all costs of credit to a consumer. Regulation Z of that act specifies that if any one of the terms of financing are advertised, all of the terms must be disclosed, including the annual percentage rate (APR).

CHAPTER 8 REVIEW QUESTIONS

1. **b.** A general warranty deed provides the covenants of seisin, against encumbrances, quiet enjoyment, further assurance, and warranty forever. The grantor even defends the title on behalf of everyone who has held title in the past. (In most cases, a purchaser will still choose to have further protection by purchasing a title insurance policy.)

2. **d.** The covenant of quiet enjoyment has nothing to do with noisy neighbors; the seller is ensuring that there will be no future claims against the title to the property.

3. **b.** A bargain and sale deed contains no express warranties, but it does imply that the grantor holds title to the property. The purchaser has limited legal recourse if defects in the title come up later.

4. **d.** Eminent domain and escheat are both cases of involuntary alienation of property. The owner does not choose to have the state take over the property either for public use (eminent domain) or when there are no heirs (escheat).

5. **c.** An individual who dies "testate" has a will indicating how property is to be distributed; to die "intestate" means to die without a will, which passes real and personal property to the decedent's heirs according to state law.

6. **c.** The purpose of probate is to determine that a will is processed correctly. Probate proceedings take place in the county or city where the decedent resided and also in the county or city where real property is located. Probate procedures are governed by state law.

7. **d.** The chain of title is the record of ownership going back at least 60 years in the public records. Any gap in the chain of title will be addressed as a "cloud on the title."

8. **a.** Properly recorded documents provide constructive notice to the world of one person's rights to a property. Purchaser C should have made a title search prior to purchasing A's property.

9. **b.** In addition to what is found in the public records, a standard title insurance policy insures against forged documents, conveyances by incompetent grantors, incorrect marital statements, and improperly delivered deeds.

10. **c.** A lender requires a borrower to obtain a title insurance policy in an amount that will cover the amount of the mortgage loan. If the purchaser wants additional coverage, an owner's policy may be added.

CHAPTER 9 REVIEW QUESTIONS

1. **d.** In the majority of states, the seller is responsible for all expenses, including the day of closing; in others, the buyer becomes responsible on the day of closing.

2. **b.** The closing agent has many responsibilities leading up to the day of closing, but obtaining homeowners insurance is the responsibility of the purchaser. Most likely, this will need to be done fairly early in the transaction as part of information submitted to the lender.

3. **b.** The seller must be able to show proof that any existing loan or other liens have been paid in full. The closing agent obtains a pay-off figure from the existing lender and may bring an existing lien to the seller's attention, but the seller is ultimately responsible.

4. **a.** Capitalization will not work because there is no rent paid, and market data will not work because there is insufficient data and the variances are too great to correlate.

5. **c.** The borrower's credit score is not needed to complete the Uniform Residential Loan Application.

6. **d.** The sellers must have occupied the home as a principal home for two of the last five years to avoid capital gains tax.

7. **c.** When a buyer assumes the seller's existing mortgage loan, the lender is usually required to furnish a mortgage reduction certificate that certifies the amount due on the loan, the interest rate, and the date and amount of the last payment.

8. **b.** The lender charges for taking, underwriting, and processing the loan application may not increase prior to closing. If they do increase, the lender must issue a new Good Faith Estimate, which triggers a three-day waiting period before the loan can close.

9. **c.** The buyer makes the requests for repairs for defects discovered in a home inspection; the seller is the one who must schedule the appointments and is responsible for seeing that the work is done.

10. **b.** Within three days after loan application, the lender must provide the borrower with a special information booklet that explains the various costs of closing, RESPA provisions and regulations, and the requirement for use of the Settlement Statement (HUD-1).

CHAPTER 10 REVIEW QUESTIONS

1. **c.** It is best to use an individual's full first name (no nicknames) and middle initial.

2. **c.** Even though a couple is separated, the absent spouse may still have dower or curtesy rights to the property (depending on state law). The absent spouse will have to sign an eventual sales contract, and having the signature on the listing agreement provides better insurance that this will happen.

3. **b.** Street addresses do not qualify as legal descriptions.

4. **d.** Because the addendum becomes part of the contract, it must be signed by all parties. Paragraph 22 lists all addenda included as part of the contract.

5. **d.** Any item that is permanently attached becomes part of the real property. A freestanding item that can be moved is considered personal property. A buyer could make a contract contingent on the seller leaving the workbench, but the seller would have to agree.

6. **b.** Wall-to-wall carpeting is installed and becomes real property. If the buyer has any concerns about what items will convey, they should be listed in the original offer to purchase.

7. **c.** When either the seller or buyer is considering defaulting on the contract, a careful reading of the default remedy clause can show the monetary consequences of such a decision.

8. **c.** A property title that is not free of defects is said to have a "cloud on the title."

9. **d.** A cloud on the title does not have to be a serious problem and may include issues like the misspelling of a grantor's name, an incorrect date, or a slight error in the legal description.

10. **c.** The UETA does not require electronic signatures. To use electronic signatures in a real estate transaction in Texas, both parties must agree to it in an electronic consent form.

Index